The Fiction of Emyr Humphreys

Writing Wales in English

CREW

CREW series of Critical and Scholarly Studies
General Editor: Professor M. Wynn Thomas (CREW, Swansea
University)

This *CREW* series is dedicated to Emyr Humphreys, a major figure in the literary culture of modern Wales, a founding patron of the *Centre for Research into the English Literature and Language of Wales*, and, along with Gillian Clarke and Seamus Heaney, one of *CREW*'s Honorary Associates. Grateful thanks are extended to Richard Dynevor for making this series possible.

Other titles in the series
Stephen Knight, *A Hundred Years of Fiction* (978-0-7083-1846-1)
Barbara Prys-Williams, *Twentieth-Century Autobiography* (978-0-7083-1891-1)
Kirsti Bohata, *Postcolonialism Revisited* (978-0-7083-1892-8)
Chris Wigginton, *Modernism from the Margins* (978-0-7083-1927-7)
Linden Peach, *Contemporary Irish and Welsh Women's Fiction* (978-0-7083-1998-7)
Sarah Prescott, *Eighteenth-Century Writing from Wales: Bards and Britons* (978-0-7083-2053-2)
Hywel Dix, *After Raymond Williams: Cultural Materialism and the Break-Up of Britain* (978-0-7083-2153-9)
Matthew Jarvis, *Welsh Environments in Contemporary Welsh Poetry* (978-0-7083-2152-2)
Harri Garrod Roberts, *Embodying Identity: Representations of the Body in Welsh Literature* (978-0-7083-2169-0)
Diane Green, *Emyr Humphreys: A Postcolonial Novelist?* (978-0-7083-2217-8)
M.Wynn Thomas, *In the Shadow of the Pulpit: Literature and Nonconformist Wales* (978-0-7083-2225-3)

The Fiction of Emyr Humphreys

Contemporary Critical Perspectives

Writing Wales in English

LINDEN PEACH

UNIVERSITY OF WALES PRESS
CARDIFF
2011

Reprinted 2011

www.uwp.ac.uk

British Library Cataloguing-in-Publication Data
A catalogue record for this book is available form the British Library.

ISBN 978-0-7083-2216-1
e-ISBN 978-0-7083-2404-2

Printed in Wales by Dinefwr Press, Llandybïe

For Angela

CONTENTS

GENERAL EDITOR'S PREFACE

The aim of this series is to produce a body of scholarly and critical work that reflects the richness and variety of the English-language literature of modern Wales. Drawing upon the expertise both of established specialists and of younger scholars, it will seek to take advantage of the concepts, models and discourses current in the best contemporary studies to promote a better understanding of the literature's significance, viewed not only as an expression of Welsh culture but also as an instance of modern literatures in English worldwide. In addition, it will seek to make available the scholarly materials (such as bibliographies) necessary for this kind of advanced, informed study.

M. Wynn Thomas
CREW (*Centre for Research into the English Literature and Language of Wales*)
Swansea University

PREFACE

It almost goes without saying that Emyr Humphreys, a prolific writer for over half a century, has made an outstanding contribution to the literature and culture of Wales. The diversity of this contribution – as novelist, short-story writer, poet, dramatist, television producer – makes it difficult to assess. But, undoubtedly, Humphreys's greatest achievement has been his fiction, especially his novels. Although he has worked in both the Welsh and English languages, it is the novels in English on which his future reputation will probably depend. Humphreys began writing when the literary, critical and scholarly environment was very different from what it is now and, indeed, Wales then was very different from post-Assembly Wales.

Humphreys initially thought of himself as a 'Protestant' novelist, but this term, which he has now rejected, does not do him justice. In discussing the kind of writer Humphreys is, this book explores more appropriate descriptions of his work, such as 'dramatic', 'dissident' and 'dilemma' fiction, which include some of the qualities which he associated with the 'Protestant' novel, but which more fully encapsulate his unique contribution to Welsh literature and culture.

In some respects, the English and Welsh binary is more misleading when applied to Humphreys than to other Welsh writers who work in English. Although he has written more fiction in English than Welsh, having learned Welsh as an adult, he has been immersed in Welsh-language literature and culture and in his native north Wales where, with the exception of the Second World War and a few years afterwards, he has lived all his life. Although outside the scope of this particular study, his Welsh-language work, especially his drama and contribution to Welsh television and radio, are important. The English–Welsh binary is complicated in his case, too, by his interest in, and passion for, European literature and drama which has also had a profound influence on his work.

The subjects of this study are the extent to which his work is illuminated by late twentieth- and early twenty-first-century critical approaches and the relevance of his work to the twenty-first-century reader. The book is divided into two parts. Part one provides the reader with different frameworks and contexts within which Humphreys's fiction may be read. It suggests that at the heart of his work is an interest in the history of modern Wales but a history that has never been fully present. This dimension of his work is examined through ideas and concepts provided by the European linguistic philosopher Jacques Derrida. If this Derridean reading provides new insights into Emyr Humphreys's work, the same is argued for psychoanalytic approaches through which aspects of his work, such as sexuality, violence and father–daughter relationships, are more fully revealed. Equally important is his experimentation with narrative perspectives which is discussed in part one in regard to the modernist writers, such as Bertolt Brecht, Kate Roberts, Virginia Woolf and William Faulkner, whom he admired, and demonstrated more fully in the select readings of some of his novels in part two. This book also explores how Humphreys's fiction makes a significant contribution to understanding feminism, and what is contentiously referred to as 'post-feminism', in twentieth-century Wales, through characters whose lives are aligned with movements addressing the social and civic injustices suffered by women and others who have been brought up in an environment where feminism has been taken for granted.

Part two provides readings of key texts from a range of critical perspectives including 'performative' concepts of gender identity; contested masculinities; different concepts of time; the influence of Brecht; the 'stranger' as a psychoanalytic as well as a social concept; the daughter as a figure located simultaneously in socio-symbolic and psycho-symbolic fields of understanding, and debates around war, pacifism and cultural discourse. It does not seek to provide definitive or exhaustive readings of Humphreys's work, even if that were a desirable objective. Through an examination of some of Humphreys's key works of fiction, frameworks and contexts are discussed in which Humphreys's unique contribution to Welsh literature and culture may be better understood.

ACKNOWLEDGEMENTS

I am especially grateful to Edge Hill University which has provided me with research grants to consult the Emyr Humphreys's archive at the National Library of Wales, Aberystwyth, and two periods of sabbatical leave without which this book could not have been written. I am indebted to colleagues at the university and, especially the dean of the Faculty of Arts and Sciences, Dr Nigel Simons, for his support. I would like, also, to express my gratitude to staff at the National Library of Wales, Aberystwyth, for their cheerful assistance and guidance. I am indebted once again to Professor M. Wynn Thomas, Emyr Humphreys Professor of Welsh Writing in English in the Centre for Research into the English Language and Literature of Wales, Swansea University, for his advice, encouragement and support.

Note on Editions of Works
by Emyr Humphreys

Unless indicated in the endnotes, references to the primary works of fiction are to the following editions:

Emyr Humphreys, *The Little Kingdom* (London: Eyre & Spottiswoode, 1946); *A Man's Estate* (1955; rpt. London and Melbourne: J. M. Dent & Sons Ltd, 1988); *A Toy Epic* (1958; rpt. Bridgend: Seren, 1989); *Outside the House of Baal* (1965; rpt. London and Melbourne: J. M. Dent & Sons Ltd, 1988); *Natives* (London: Secker & Warburg, 1968); *National Winner* (1971; rpt. Cardiff: University of Wales Press, 2000); *The Best of Friends* (1978; rpt. London: Sphere, 1996); *The Anchor Tree* (London: Hodder and Stoughton, 1980); *Salt of the Earth* (1985; rpt. London: Sphere, 1996); *An Absolute Hero* (1986; rpt. London: Sphere, 1988); *Open Secrets* (1988; rpt. Cardiff: University of Wales Press, 2000); *Bonds of Attachment* (1991; rpt. Cardiff: University of Wales Press, 2001); *Unconditional Surrender* (1996; rpt. Bridgend: Seren, 1997); *The Gift of a Daughter* (Bridgend: Seren, 1998); *Ghosts and Strangers* (Bridgend: Seren, 2001); *Old People are a Problem* (2003; rpt. Bridgend: Seren, 2004); *The Shop* (Bridgend: Seren, 2005); *The Woman at the Window* (Bridgend: Seren, 2009).

Part One

Frames and Contexts

1

Humphreys's Life and Works

Since this introduction to Emyr Humphreys's fiction is intended for readers, from outside as well as within Wales, who are new to his work as well as those who would like to explore his writings in more depth, it seems appropriate to begin by fleshing out some of the important facts and contexts of his life. This is especially necessary since the writing of his fiction has spanned more than half a century and has included a crossover from one century to another.

SELECT BIOGRAPHICAL CONTEXTS

Emyr (Owen) Humphreys's life and work have been shaped by interests and commitments that have proved important to Welsh literature in English and, more generally, Welsh culture and media. Stephen Knight has described him as 'part of the new generation who were university educated and committed to Wales'.[1] He goes on to argue: 'He must, in terms of productivity, seriousness and versatility rank as the major Welsh novelist writing in English, the only one whose effort, quality and dedication to writing about his country could place him in the Nobel-winning class.'[2]

Humphreys was born on 15 April 1919, less than a year after the conclusion of the First World War, in Prestatyn in north Wales and brought up in the nearby village of Trelawnyd (then called Newmarket). It was an English-speaking and Anglican environment and, although the Anglican Church was disestablished in Wales in 1920, Humphreys

did consider for a while becoming an Anglican priest. His parents
were not particularly pious people and neither came from Anglican
families: his mother came from a Calvinistic Methodist background
(the Welsh Calvinistic Methodists separated from the Church of
England to establish an indigenous Nonconformist denomination in
1811) and his father from a Congregationalist family.[3]

In Trelawnyd might be said to have begun the first of his lifelong
commitments: to north Wales. He has lived there virtually all his life;
he now lives in Llanfairpwll, Ynys Môn (Anglesey). Although some of
his novels, including one of his most recent works, *The Shop*, are partly
or wholly set in Europe, north Wales has always been the preferred
location for his fiction.[4]

Reflecting on his north Wales childhood, Humphreys has recalled:
'When I was a child Rhyl was a recognisable centre of the universe.
All roads led to Rhyl.'[5] Many readers from other parts of Wales, and
certainly those from outside Wales, may underestimate the significance
of Rhyl and the north Wales coastline in Welsh and Welsh anglophone culture. It was, as we shall see in a discussion of specific novels
in chapters 3 and 7, a long-established resort where Welsh-language,
Welsh-anglophone and English cultures (especially from across the
Wirral where the power and influence of England was omnipresent)
met, interacted and, in some respects, became confused. When
Humphreys grew up, it presented an alternative to inland Welsh-
language, Nonconformist and conservative Wales, provided an escape
from rural Wales, offered young people from north Wales and beyond
new freedoms and provided access to more contemporary, even
Anglo-American, lifestyle choices. More worryingly, from a Welsh
perspective, it defined north-east Wales in ways which in many respects
were to prove detrimental.

Humphreys was educated at Rhyl County School where the influence of one of his teachers and the protest burning of the bombing
school at Penyberth, which occurred when he was in the sixth form,
as we shall see in a moment, not only converted him to nationalism
but helped him better understand the contradictory environment in
which he was brought up in Trelawnyd. From Rhyl County School, he
went on to read history, which became a lifelong interest, at what was
then the University College of Wales, Aberystwyth. Opened in 1872, it
provided the setting for his third novel, *A Change of Heart: A Comedy*
(1951).[6] It was here that he learned to speak Welsh and became further
committed to the Welsh language and to Welsh culture.

Although Humphreys has published several works in Welsh, he has remained haunted to some extent by the fact that he has felt best able to do justice to his considerable creative powers through what was his first language:

> It is a *Kulturkampf*, between the imperial language and the defeated native language, and what I've been doing in both poetry and in fiction in English, whether I like it or not, is using the language of cultural supremacy to try to express something that comes directly from the suppressed native culture.[7]

It is in this regard that Humphreys can be seen as a 'translator' of communities which, because they are largely Welsh-language communities, have a specific cultural centre. In a recent interview, he has described how

> A number of things collided: the protest burning of the bombing school at Penyberth by three Welsh nationalists who were leading intellectual and artistic figures in Welsh-language culture,[8] and the connection with Mr Moses Jones, the schoolmaster who introduced me to Welsh history and politics, all happened before I began to learn the language. So ... I first began to acquire a sense of national identity by being provided with the historical and political understanding that allowed me to review the landscape, and only after that did I begin to acquire the language.[9]

Of particular significance was the influence of Saunders Lewis, one of the arsonists and a leading writer and cultural figure in Welsh-speaking Wales, and his now famous speech from the dock at the court in Caernarfon where he was first brought to trial. M. Wynn Thomas shrewdly summarizes the change which Lewis helped to bring about in Humphreys's thinking:

> From then on his native place was to be, for him, intimately and insepa-rably connected to his new mental geography, because Saunders Lewis had finally enabled him to understand the silences, inconsistencies and incongruities that he had looked on uncomprehendingly in his early social background.[10]

Humphreys's conversion to nationalism around the time of the arson attack on the RAF bombing school is paralleled in the life of one of the key protagonists in his novel *Outside the House of Baal* (1965). The Reverend Joe Miles insists:

> I'm against that bombing school in Caernarvonshire and I'm against the draining away of our young people to London and the Midlands and Luton too. And I'm against a lot of other things too. And I'd do

something about it. Before it's too late. I wouldn't want to go on being in
the middle of a dying country.[11]

At the outbreak of the Second World War, after only two years at
university, Humphreys bravely registered as a conscientious objector.
The experience informs what must be one of the most vivid fictional
accounts of wartime pacifism, in *Outside the House of Baal*, and is
explored more extensively as a dimension of Welsh culture and nationalism in the later novel, *Open Secrets* (1988).[12] It is also a subject to which
Humphreys returns in his most recent fiction. In *The Shop*, Pentregwyn
General Stores is shunned during the Second World War because its
owner declares himself a conscientious objector. Doing so could not
have been an easy decision for Humphreys himself, as these fictional
events clearly demonstrate. The tribunals that were set up, when Neville
Chamberlain announced the introduction of conscription in April 1939,
to hear claims for exemption on grounds of conscience had no military
members and were able to grant absolute exemption. However, as the
prospect of a German invasion became more real, public opinion turned
against conscientious objectors. Some were dismissed from employment
and some employees refused to work alongside them.

Humphreys's father was wounded in the First World War and he
has recalled how he 'never knew him as anything except an invalid', a
fact which no doubt fuelled his pacifism.[13] As a conscientious objector,
Humphreys was sent to work on the land in Pembrokeshire and in
other parts of Wales (on which he drew in a number of his novels
including *Outside the House of Baal* and, nearly half a century later,
Unconditional Surrender).[14] During this period, which lasted until
1944, he began work on *A Toy Epic*.[15] Thereafter, in the closing years
of the war, he became a relief worker in the Middle East, worked
with the United Nations and, in 1946, worked with the Save the
Children Fund. The latter provided him with material for *The Voice
of a Stranger* (1949),[16] concerned with three relief workers in post-
war Italy, one a Welshman who, like Humphreys, is from north Wales
and a conscientious objector, and *The Italian Wife* (1957). In fact,
Humphreys's experiences in Italy contributed to a lifelong interest in
Europe, to which we will return in chapter 3.

Humphreys's marriage to Elinor Jones, the daughter of a
Congregational minister, in 1946, saw the beginning of two further
lifelong commitments: to his wife, by whom he has had four children,
and to Nonconformity to which, as an Anglican churchman who had

thought at one time of becoming a priest, he converted. In becoming an Annibynnwr (Welsh Independent), Humphreys found a spiritual home in the 'progressive' wing of Nonconformity where his pacifism and his Christianity came together. Pacifism had been an aspect of chapel ideology in twentieth-century Wales since the establishing of the pacifist journal *Y Deyrnas* (The Kingdom), which, although it closed in 1919, left an enduring legacy. Robert Pope has pointed out that *Y Deyrnas* had

> supported the claims of the individual conscience, the primary need for real peace in a war-torn Europe and a recognition that higher principles of justice and fairness needed to be built into the social fabric nationally and internationally in order to end the possibility of future conflict.[17]

In truth, however, pacifists in the Nonconformist movement, as is made clear in *Outside the House of Baal*, frequently encountered support for war among traditional Nonconformist denominations.

Despite having learned the Welsh language and become a Welsh nationalist and a Welsh Independent, Humphreys did not return to live and work in Wales immediately on conclusion of the war. Demobilized, he became a teacher at Wimbledon Technical College in London for three years. But in 1951, because he and his wife made the decision that they wanted their children to be brought up 'in Welsh',[18] he returned to north Wales, as a teacher at Pwllheli Grammar School (in whose exercise books many of the drafts of his early novels were written).[19]

Post-war Wales had a tripartite school system that had been established by the 1944 Education Act, based on selection by examination at eleven years of age. In this pre-comprehensive school system – the first comprehensive school was opened in Ynys Môn in 1954 – academically gifted children attended grammar schools, a few of which had existed for hundreds of years, such as the one in which Humphreys taught, while those who were perceived as less academic went to either a secondary modern or a technical school. The 1960s and 1970s ushered in another and very different sea change with the expansion of comprehensive education in Britain from 1965 onwards that created the system in which many twenty-first-century students in their late teens and early twenties reading this book would have been educated. Humphreys himself was educated in a different system in which Church schools played a strong part. The Welsh Intermediate Education Act of 1889 established a national system of intermediate secondary schools in which children gained a place through an entry examination. Church schools were integrated into the state system following the Balfour Act of 1902. As is made clear in *A Toy Epic* (1958), discussed in chapter 7, the Church schools discouraged the use of the Welsh language. Their absorption into the state system, which for a time they then dominated, was opposed by the non-denominational schools.

Humphreys's period as a schoolteacher in north Wales was short lived. He worked as a producer for BBC Radio from 1955 until 1958, when he became a drama producer for BBC television. Subsequently, as Gerwyn Wiliams has pointed out, 'In collaboration with his son Siôn, an independent television producer, Emyr Humphreys has been amongst the most prolific and significant dramatists to have made their mark on S4C.'[20] For three years, from 1962 until 1965, he was a freelance writer and director, but thereafter took up a post as a lecturer in drama at the then University College of North Wales, Bangor. In 1972, he made what might appear to have been another brave decision when, having won two major literary prizes for *Hear and Forgive* (1952) and *A Toy Epic* (1958), his fourth and seventh novels in order of publication respectively, he resigned his university post to devote himself to his writing.[21]

Humphreys, who is a fellow of the Royal Society of Literature, has won numerous national awards: *Hear and Forgive* won the Somerset Maugham Award, 1953; *A Toy Epic* won the Hawthornden Prize, 1958; *Bonds of Attachment* won the Arts Council of Wales Book of the Year Award, 1992; and *The Gift of a Daughter* won the Arts Council of Wales Book of the Year Award, 1998. *Old People are a Problem* was shortlisted for the Arts Council of Wales Book of the Year in 2004. Humphreys received the Siân Phillips Award in 2004 and, in 1987, he was made an honorary fellow of the University of Wales. In 1988, he was awarded an honorary professorship of the University Wales, Bangor; and, in 1990, he was awarded a D.Litt. from the University of Wales, Cardiff. He has also been made an honorary fellow by Swansea University, where a Chair of Welsh writing in English has been created in his honour.

KEY WORKS

Humphreys's first novel, *The Little Kingdom* (1946), which may be regarded as Wales's first significant postcolonial novel, was published in the year in which he married.[22] Set in north Wales, and featuring Owen Richards, the Welsh nationalist son of a lecturer in history at Aberystwyth, where Humphreys himself read history, it concerns the rising tide of nationalism in the country which is contrasted with earlier attitudes of assimilation and adjustment to English culture. The novel's plot hinges around the not entirely attractive Owen's opposition to his property entrepreneur uncle's plans to sell land to the ministry of war for a new airfield. Making reference to Shakespeare's *Julius Caesar*, the novel unveils the personal and political conflicts of the time in ways which bring Shakespeare's later history plays to mind.

When *The Little Kingdom* was published, Dylan Thomas was still alive and had not yet published *Under Milk Wood*.[23] George Orwell's political fable, *Animal Farm*, had been published the previous year, but his most famous novel, *Nineteen Eighty Four*, was not to be published for another three years.[24] The key figures in literary criticism were not the Anglo-American and European theorists with which early twenty-first-century students of literature may be familiar, such as Mikhail Bakhtin, Roland Barthes, Judith Butler, Hélène Cixous, Jacques Derrida, Terry Eagleton and Julia Kristeva. The emphasis in literary study was upon close reading of texts, as opposed to the more historical literary approach of the first part of the twentieth century and the more theoretical approaches of the late twentieth century.

The close analysis of literary texts, which became known as 'practical criticism', was encouraged by critics such as I. A. Richards and William Empson. Empson's groundbreaking and influential *Seven Types of Ambiguity* was published in 1930, and the influence of his analysis of the relationship between meaning and the deployment of ambiguity can be seen throughout Humphreys's work.[25] The Cambridge University critic F. R. Leavis, who made his mark with *Revaluation, Tradition and Development in English Poetry* (1936), published his *The Great Tradition* (1948) two years after Humphreys published his first novel and his *The Common Pursuit* (1952) only four years later.[26] At one level, there is a strong alignment between Empson's close reading of ambiguity and Leavis's advocacy of close reading of the literary text. It is important to remember that this is one of the contexts in which Humphreys emerged as a writer because it reminds us that his texts repay the kind of close analytical reading which became the staple of literary criticism in the mid-twentieth-century and later. Indeed, even allowing for the profound influence of European linguistics on late twentieth-century criticism, close reading has remained one of the core activities of literary study.

In the 1950s, Humphreys was a prolific writer and *The Little Kingdom* was soon followed by *The Voice of a Stranger* (1949), *A Change of Heart* (1951), *Hear and Forgive* (1952), *A Man's Estate* (1955), of which he published a Welsh translation, *Etifedd y Glyn* (1981), *The Italian Wife* (1957) and *A Toy Epic* (1958).[27] As will be discussed in the next chapter, two of these novels, *A Man's Estate* and *A Toy Epic*, demonstrate Humphreys's interest in modernism and experimental narrative. In this regard, several modernist writers had a profound influence upon his work, including the American novelist William Faulkner, who won the Nobel Prize for Literature in 1950, Virginia Woolf and the north Welsh modernist writer Kate Roberts about whom Humphreys made a television documentary.[28]

To put Humphreys's prolific activity within a wider British context, especially as he was published by London publishers, it is worth noting that the years 1946–65 have not been generally associated with an invigorated literary culture. It was not a time when the novel flourished in Britain and, as Jago Morrison points out, from the most 'influential critics', such as Bernard Bergonzi, David Lodge and Malcom Bradbury, 'there is little sense of vibrancy or fresh development'.[29] Morrison argues:

> For several decades after the end of the Second World War, the novel appeared to be dead. As a vehicle for literary experimentation, on the one hand, it had been taken to the limits by modernists like Joyce, Woolf and Beckett. And, on the other hand, beset by the mass media of film, television and computers, book fiction could not hope to survive as a form of entertainment. For many commentators in the 1960s, fiction's fate seemed sealed.[30]

Morrison aligns the 'death' of the novel with the influence of the Second World War:

> In an important way, the 'death of the novel' thesis of the 1950s, 1960s and 1970s reflects an anxiety in that period about the possibility of adequately addressing contemporary historical concerns in fiction. The scale of violence in the Second World War, the Nazi genocide, the atom bombing of Japan and, after them, the paranoiac politics of the Cold War – with a nuclear conflagration held in suspense only by the promise of 'mutually assured destruction' – all of this seemed to have rendered fiction too flimsy a medium for history.[31]

The fortunes of literary fiction were soon to recover after the immediate post-war inertia to which Morrison refers and Humphreys, in many respects, can be seen to be ahead of his time. When he published *The Little Kingdom* (1946), the Second World War had only just finished, demobilization was not yet complete and rationing was not to end until 1954. Nevertheless, there is a confidence in Humphreys's early work which belies the general creative inertia that some critics argue characterized the contemporary British novel at that time. Although Wales, as part of the United Kingdom, was a participant in the colonial project, Humphreys's creative energy may have been a product of the way in which the gradual decolonization of many parts of the world chimed with the reinvigorated nationalist spirit in Wales, and especially in north Wales where Humphreys lived. Morrison reminds us:

> As if the historic legacies of the Second World War did not provide enough of a challenge for writers, the period that followed has been one of repeated sea change across the Anglophone world. Amongst the most important of these has been the wholesale repulsion of European colonialism, beginning with India/Pakistan in the immediate post-war years, and spreading across the entire globe over the next three decades.[32]

The Little Kingdom was published ten years after the arson on the RAF bombing school and thirty years after the Welsh Nationalist Party, Plaid Genedlaethol Cymru, was founded at the Pwllheli Eisteddfod in 1925, both historical events that, as we have seen, were important to Humphreys's own conversion to nationalism.

In 1958, Humphreys published his first major Welsh-language work, *Y Tri Llais: Nofel.*[33] Further work in the Welsh language followed: *Dinas: Drama Gyfoes*, with W. S. Jones (1970),[34] *Bwrdd Datblygu Teledu Cymraeg* (1979),[35] *Darn O Dir* (1986),[36] a translation of *A Man's Estate*, and *Dal Pen Rheswm*, a series of conversations edited by R. Arwel Jones (1999).[37] At the end of the 1960s, he published the first of his volumes of poetry, *Ancestor Worship: A Cycle of Eighteen Poems* (1970),[38] to be followed by *Landscapes: A Sequence of Songs* (1979),[39] *The Kingdom of Brân* (1979)[40] and *Pwyll a Rhiannon* (1980).[41] His poetry was also published in *Penguin Modern Poets* (1979, with two key English-language Welsh poets of the time, John Ormond and John Tripp)[42] and *Miscellany Two* (1981);[43] his *Collected Poems* was published in 1999.[44] His indebtedness to Saunders Lewis was openly acknowledged in *Theatr Saunders Lewis* (1979).[45]

Notwithstanding Humphreys's capacity to work across genres and in the two principal languages of Wales, his ambitions as a writer continued to manifest themselves most prolifically in the

English-language Welsh novel. In the 1960s, Humphreys published two of his most important novels, *The Gift* (1963) and *Outside the House of Baal*, together with a collection of short fiction, *Natives* (1968).[46] Of these works, *Outside the House of Baal* was his most ambitious narrative to date. Written in an episodic structure, which will be discussed in chapter 8, which brings to mind the European novella and what the Russian critic Mikhail Bakhtin termed the 'chronotope', to which we will return in chapter 2, it is a modernist novel which interleaves the lives of two elderly people, the Reverend J. T. Miles and his sister-in-law Kate, who share a house. As the narrative moves backwards in time through key events in their lives and in twentieth-century Wales, the novel alternates past and present in a comprehensive and complex examination of what is meant by 'time' and 'being'.

When Humphreys's *Outside the House of Baal*, undoubtedly one of the major English-language Welsh novels of the twentieth century, was published, the Wales of the 1960s, and Britain generally, could not have been more different from the late 1940s. Rationing had come to an end in 1954 and the 'Swinging Sixties', as they came to be called, captured a sense of social and cultural change, especially as far as social expression, freedom of speech and sexuality were concerned. In 1960, D. H. Lawrence's *Lady Chatterley's Lover*, written in 1928, was published in Britain and the publishers were prosecuted under the Obscene Publications Act 1959.[47] A number of writers and academics spoke for the novel at the trial, including E. M. Forster, Helen Gardner, Richard Hoggart and the Welsh cultural critic, and soon to be a novelist himself, Raymond Williams.

The 1960s saw the beginning of the politicized feminism, to which we will return in chapter 5, configured around campaigns for equality in employment and public life and also focusing on the behaviour of men towards women and what women had a right to expect. One aspect of this feminism, highlighting how feminism as a cultural movement had developed, was captured in Germaine Greer's *The Female Eunuch* (1970) which argued that women were cut off from their sexuality and faculty of desire and denied their capacity for action.[48] The way in which female sexuality was constructed, Greer argued, was demeaning and confining to women who should know and celebrate their own bodies. Societal rules, prejudices and preconceptions about women, this second-wave feminism stressed, subjugated and isolated them.

During this decade, another important English-language Welsh novelist emerged: Raymond Williams's *Border Country* was published

in 1960.[49] It was to become the first part of a trilogy, which undoubtedly influenced the concept of Humphreys's Land of the Living
sequence, tracing social and cultural change in Wales over several
generations of the same family. The second part of this trilogy,
Second Generation, was published a year before *Outside the House of
Baal*.[50] Katie Gramich points out that there is a paradox in Williams's
Border Country: 'it is very much a novel of the new "personal" type
which Williams takes pains to decry in *The Long Revolution* ... [but]
in its historical span and detailed social description, a realist text'.[51]
Humphreys's and Williams's work share this ostensible paradox, but
it is far less of a contradiction when we recognize that both novelists
are concerned not so much with writing realist fiction, which Gramich,
quoting Engels, describes as 'typical characters in typical situations',[52]
as 'dilemma fiction', a genre discussed in chapter 2.

In the 1970s, Humphreys published three novels, *National Winner*
(1971),[53] *Flesh and Blood* (1974)[54] and *The Best of Friends* (1978),[55]
which, together with four novels written within about six years of
each other in the second half of the 1980s, *Salt of the Earth* (1985),[56]
An Absolute Hero (1986),[57] *Open Secrets* and *Bonds of Attachment*
(1991),[58] were eventually constituted as the septet Land of the Living
(which for a time in the late 1980s Humphreys was going to call Bonds
of Attachment). The representation of radical, independently minded
women has always been a trope in Humphreys's fiction. The first texts,
within the chronology of Land of the Living rather than by date of
publication, focus on two independent women, Amy Parry and Enid
Prydderch, who become students together at Aberystwyth. But the
principal protagonist is Amy who 'progresses' from being an orphan,
brought up in relative poverty, to being the lady of the manor. She
marries twice, her first husband being the poet Cilydd Moore, the
widower of her best friend Enid, and she becomes the mother and
stepmother to three children.

The final Land of the Living novel, *Bonds of Attachment*, is an
ambitious modernist narrative which marks a return to the more
experimental work of the 1950s and 1960s, *A Man's Estate*, *A Toy Epic*
and *Outside the House of Baal*. It alternates the first-person narrative
of one of Amy's sons, Peredur, with that of his dead father through
Cilydd's archive of notebooks.

In addition to the Land of the Living saga, Humphreys published
four other novels in the 1980s and 1990s, which were prolific decades for
him: *The Anchor Tree* (1980),[59] *Jones: A Novel* (1984),[60] *Unconditional*

Surrender and *The Gift of a Daughter* (1998).[61] *The Anchor Tree* is Humphreys's only novel set in America. It is a first-person narrative by a visiting professor of history who is also a descendant of a Welsh visionary who founded a Christian community in Pennsylvania in the eighteenth century which is now overgrown and forgotten. *Unconditional Surrender* and *The Gift of a Daughter* are discussed in chapter 10. The former impressively reflects Humphreys's reinvigorated interest in modernist narrative evident in *Bonds of Attachment*.

Like *Bonds of Attachment*, although in a different way, *Unconditional Surrender* switches between stories told by two narrators covering events that unfold at a local and world level between May and August 1945. It focuses on a rector in a north Wales parish who is concerned about his daughter, Megan. She is involved with a local boy who is a conscientious objector and is threatened, in her father's view, by the arrival of a young German prisoner of war. The Reverend Edwin Pritchard's anxieties are shared by the second narrator, Countess Cecilia von Leiten, who, like the clergyman, is the product of an oppressive past, in her case the European aristocracy.

The second 'modernist' novel from this period, *The Gift of a Daughter*, again reflects Humphreys's interest in independently minded women. In this novel, Aled Morgan, a former Welsh-language activist, is faced with an increasingly strong-minded daughter who falls in love with a young Englishman whom he despises. The novel combines references to ancient Welsh and European, specifically Etruscan, history. However, there is a sense throughout the text of a type of nationalism which retreats into an ancient past and which fails to confront successfully a modernizing repackaging of history. Aled and his family live in an old farmhouse which they have modernized, and which symbolically has a prehistoric stone on the property. What comes to the fore in this novel is a critique of Wales as a bourgeois nationalist country in which tradition is supplanted by a modernizing present.

In the twenty-first century, Humphreys, whose writing shows no signs of waning, has produced what is undoubtedly some of his most interesting work. This includes two collections of linked stories or novellas: *Ghosts and Strangers* (2001), which, as discussed in chapter 11, explores the extent to which we are strangers even to ourselves and how the present is always haunted by the past, and *Old People are a Problem* (2003), which is as much concerned with the problems of young people as with those of elderly people.[62] One of the most important themes in this collection of stories is protest, which is also pursued in *The Shop*. Like *The Gift of a Daughter*, this novel constantly moves between a Welsh and European frame of reference and, like *Ghosts and Strangers*, it locates Wales within a wider European and global economy. Although *The Shop* is a first-person narrative told by a male narrator, its main focus is his female friend, an ambitious young photographer, Bethan Mair Nichols, whose own voice enters into the novel through her writing to him.

The Shop is a development of the critique of bourgeois, nationalist Wales in *The Gift of a Daughter* and of the celebration of progress, which, in Humphreys's view, characterizes the modern, in the Land of the Living novels. In returning to Wales, to take over Pentregwyn General Stores, which has been left by her great-aunt Selwen, Bethan finds herself caught between different versions of the future of the stores. These different ambitions reflect alternative versions of social commitment in twentieth- and twenty-first-century Wales. Bethan's great-aunt saw the stores as a community centre, as an organic cafe and as providing a book-barter service. Bethan, on the other hand, envisages the stores as a film studio and a centre for experimental documentaries. As a documentary film-maker and a photographer, she serves as a vehicle for further examination of a theme which occurs in a number of earlier works, including 'A Man in the Mist' in *Old People are a Problem*: the extent to which the media can contribute to establishing Welsh identity in the twenty-first century and the relationship of media research to more traditional academic scholarship. *The Shop* also shares with some of the stories in *Old People are a Problem* an interest in relationships between women of different generations and the way in which these relationships bring together significantly different periods of history.

In 2005, Humphreys also published *The Rigours of Inspection: Poems and Stories* (2005).[63] His works of the last ten years are especially interesting because they involve an exploration of the mythical and ideological imperatives of both tradition and modernity in relation to the nation, the family and the community.

FICTION AND HALF A CENTURY OF CHANGE

Wynn Thomas points out that Humphreys's *Outside the House of Baal*, 'his most impressive attempt not only to describe but also to calibrate the changes that had drastically refashioned Welsh society during

the first sixty or so years of this century', was inspired by a remark
which Humphreys's elderly mother made to him that had caused him
to realize that her 'picture of life had been significantly different from
his own'.[64] For many readers, the 'picture of life' in Humphreys's early
novels and in many of the Land of the Living novels will be equally
different from their own.

We have spoken of the importance of the Welsh language to
Humphreys and of the significance of Welsh-language media in his
working life. The Wales in which Humphreys began writing was one
which did not have a capital city; Cardiff was not to be proclaimed the
capital of Wales until 1955. Although Undeb Cymru Fydd (The New
Wales Union) was established in 1941 to safeguard Welsh interests and
the Welsh Courts Act 1942 permitted limited use of the Welsh language
in law courts for the first time since the Act of Union 1536, the Welsh
language did not yet enjoy equal status with English in the legal or
public sector. The former was to come with the Welsh Language Act
1967 and the latter with the Welsh Language Act 1993. Throughout
the 1970s, the establishment of Welsh-language television was one
of the main aims of the campaigns of Cymdeithas yr Iaith Gymraeg
(The Welsh Language Society), established in 1962 following Saunders
Lewis's sombre broadcast, *Tynged yr Iaith* (The Fate of the Language).
It is easy to forget, now that we are used to Welsh-language radio, television and film, that, although the BBC Welsh region was established
in Cardiff in 1937 and BBC Radio Wales did broadcast programmes
in Welsh, including work by Humphreys, Radio Cymru did not begin
broadcasting until January 1977 and Sianel Pedwar Cymru (Channel
Four Wales) began broadcasting only on 1 November 1982.

As we have also seen, and shall discuss further in the course of this
book, the picture of life with which Humphreys presents us is focused
on north Wales. This emphasis is significant for Welsh literary history
since it is with industrial south Wales that the Welsh novel, especially
in English, is most often associated. Stephen Knight has pointed out
that the 'Welsh situation' has been defined in the industrial novel as
being about 'declining heavy industry and rapidly changing politics'.[65]
He argues: 'Of about twenty major landmarks in the international
working-class novel, that is the novels that define the possibilities and
test the limits of the form, the Welsh writers have produced about a
quarter.'[66] In 1955, one of the most famous slate quarries in north
Wales, at Blaenau Ffestiniog, closed, sending shock waves throughout
the country. In one respect, the impact of the loss of industry in north

Wales was different from in south Wales. Of course, in both parts of Wales, indeed in Wales generally, the economic impact was keenly felt. But the closure of the slate quarries in north Wales amounted to more than the loss of employment. It also involved the loss of a culture because the slate industry in Wales was a Welsh-speaking industry. Unlike the south Wales coalfields, the north Wales slate quarries drew workers largely from the local area. They provided workers with a forum for serious discussions in Welsh, in the quarry cabins, albeit at the expense of the exclusion of women. The local quarries made important contributions to regional eisteddfodau (the International Eisteddfod was established at Llangollen in 1947) and the larger quarries had their own bands. Ten years before Humphreys's first published novel, a fellow north Wales writer, Kate Roberts, who was to exercise an important influence on Humphreys's work, as discussed in chapter 2, published *Traed Mewn Cyffion* (1936), about the struggle of a quarry family in the last decades of the nineteenth century and in the twentieth century up to the beginning of the First World War.[67]

In surveying Humphrey's fifty-year literary career, it is important to realize that his work spans one of the most important centuries in the history of modern Wales in regard to socio-economic change and the recognition of Welsh identity. His writings are rooted in a diverse range of different personal, social and cultural contexts. Humphreys is unique in being an author to whom critics who examine the second flowering of Welsh writing in English in the mid-twentieth century, who explore the English-language Welsh novel in the 1980s and 1990s, or assess the condition of Welsh writing at the beginning of the new millennium, have to make reference. His work crosses from a past milieu from which few of his then literary contemporaries within and outside Wales are still alive to a contemporary milieu in which his work is reviewed alongside that of important new twenty-first-century voices. Moreover, his work warrants consideration whether the critical focus is the novel, short fiction, drama or poetry, or whether the subject of study is Welsh writing or the history of the media in Wales.

2

What Kind of Fiction?

'Dissident', 'dramatic', 'dilemma', 'Protestant', 'modernist'. Each of these terms may be used to describe Humphreys's fiction and he has used three of them to describe himself.

'DISSIDENT' V 'PROTESTANT' WRITER

In a conversation with Wynn Thomas, Emyr Humphreys says that he no longer considers his description of himself, nearly fifty years earlier, as a 'Protestant novelist' appropriate.[1] At that time, he thought of a 'Protestant novelist' as one whose work was based on 'the idea of Christian progress', itself founded on 'faith, hope and love'.[2] This earlier definition of himself aligns his work with a category of literature, the Christian novel, which is more recognized in the United States, even in twenty-first-century American bookstores, than in Britain. However, in his discussion with Thomas, he argues that the concern with 'Christian' ideas is not the most fully developed dimension of his work:

> At that time there was much talk of the Catholic novelists, such as Evelyn Waugh and Graham Greene, and there was also a great post-war awareness of the French novelist Mauriac. So I was using the word 'Protestant' in contradistinction to them. I wouldn't want that religious connotation any more because such Catholic writers as Saunders Lewis and David Jones have possibly been more of an influence than any other writers on me.[3]

Looking back to the European writers Tolstoy and Dostoevsky, Humphreys suggests that a recurring feature of his work over the past fifty years is a concern with protagonists who 'are the product of some kind of progress that was both individual and social', arising from their involvement 'in situations in which they are forced to act, to make a choice, to consider right and wrong, human destiny, their own destiny and salvation'.[4] This emphasis suggests that religious conflict is only one element in what might be described as 'dilemma' novels.

In conversation with Thomas, Humphreys maintains that he now thinks of himself as a 'protesting' or, preferably, 'dissident' novelist.[5] In rethinking the kind of work he has written in this way, he aligns himself with the modernist writers of the first half of the twentieth century: 'You can't think of a great writer of that period that wasn't dissident, or an outsider – Brecht, Ezra Pound, even Eliot was an exile from St. Louis living in London.'[6] In notes towards an article, 'The writer and the new media', which appear to date from the mid-1960s, he states boldly: 'The natural state of the modern writer [:] exile.' This is contextualized with reference to 'breaking up the old order – language – society' and the impact which the First World War had upon art in the early twentieth century.[7]

As some of the radical aspects described in chapter 1 suggest, 'dissident' is a word which might describe Humphreys's life: his conversion to Welsh nationalism in the 1930s, his wartime pacifism and his rejection of Anglicanism. Indeed, there are links between the radicalism in Humphreys's life and the subject matter of his fiction, particularly in the way in which many of his characters face personal and testing dilemmas as Humphreys must have done himself. An alternative term to 'Protestant novelist' which he used in relation to his work in the early 1950s was 'dramatic novelist'. In a draft essay in his archive, Humphreys explains:

> Critics often encourage and exhort novelists to get inside their characters, and quite rightly so. But that is not all and certainly not enough. The dramatic novelist must get inside, absorb and somehow manipulate the course of events which he must transform by sweat and alchemy into a work of art, he must work upon the situation with the bellows of his theme ...[8]

Throughout his career as a novelist, Humphreys has set 'drama' and 'fiction' in opposition to each other in terms of their responses to modernity. At times, he has thought of the novel as 'dead'. In the set

of notes on the novel and modernism referred to earlier, which appear
to have been written in the 1960s, he declared that 'by 1914, the novel
[was] dead' and, thinking of the influence of European writing after
the First World War, he ponders 'is *Eng Lit* out of date'.[9] By contrast,
he associated drama, particularly European drama, with a 'heroic way
of life' and thought in terms of the 'epic & dramatic', to which we will
return in a discussion of Land of the Living.[10]

Thinking of his work as contributions to dissident, dilemma fiction,
changes the critical focus of Humphreys's work considerably. Thus,
the way in which his early work is divided into distinct groups in the
New Companion to the Literature of Wales becomes problematic. Its
argument that there is one group of novels 'concerned with the vulner-
ability of idealism' (*The Little Kingdom*, *The Voice of a Stranger*, *A Toy
Epic* and *The Anchor Tree*) and another constituting 'The "Protestant
novel" proper' (*A Change of Heart*, *Hear and Forgive*, *A Man's Estate*
and *The Italian Wife*) misrepresents the totality of the project upon
which Humphreys embarked in the 1950s and 1960s which is better
reflected in the terms 'dissident' and 'dramatic'. At different levels and
in different ways, each of the novels represents, sometimes experimen-
tally, an engagement with a form of writing that is concerned with
'some kind of progress that was both individual and social' and with
situations giving rise to social, cultural and moral dilemmas.[11]

The notion of 'progress' was itself topical and problematic in the
post-war years for the reasons which appeared to make the 'British'
novel a redundant form, referred to in chapter 1. The Nazi genocide, the atom bombing of Japan and the prospect of nuclear war
undermined, and rendered futile, the automatic linking of history
with human, societal and moral 'progress'. Thus, the dilemma which
Humphreys tackles in his fiction is the dilemma in which the British
novel after the war was embroiled, as Morrison indicates:

> For many writers and thinkers . . . it is not the memory of Dresden but
> that of Auschwitz which must stand as the most potent symbol of depar-
> ture from modernity's optimistic faith in time as a benign force . . . the
> idea of history as something positive and transcendent that can give
> meaning to each individual's life seems a pointless mockery in the face of
> that genocide.[12]

In many post-war novels, this led to what Morrison describes as a
'sense of disorientation and loss of faith in time as something progressive, coherent and meaningful'.[13] Although this loss of faith can also be

found in earlier twentieth-century writers, such as Conrad and Joyce, for many post-war writers it was much more pronounced.

While Humphreys does not reject the notions of progress, history and time to the extent of some post-war novelists, especially American writers such as Kurt Vonnegut, this does not mean that these subjects are not treated as problematic in Humphrey's work. In fact, it is in the tension between different perspectives on history and progress in post-war Britain that his principal dilemma as a novelist is located, from *The Little Kingdom* to *Unconditional Surrender*.

During the early 1950s, Humphreys seems to have been wrestling with some of the technical problems which the dissident, dilemma novel posed for the author, not the least of which is authorial intervention. Ironically, he found that the dilemma novel, as he conceived it, placed him in a wider dilemma as a writer than he might have initially envisaged. If he were to be true to his writer's conscience, then he would have to reject the literary norm of the time:

> The intellectual climate in which Joyce and Virginia Woolf flourished believed it was a sign of weakness ... to possess any set of beliefs ... If an author indulged himself in comment – apart from the 'technical weakness' of not allowing the characters and the scenes to speak for themselves – he was bound to reveal a system of prejudices that would annoy and distract the cultivated reader.[14]

Under the influence of European linguistic theory, the emphasis in literary interpretation in the twentieth century shifted from the author to the reader who was perceived as 'creating' the text. It largely aligned itself with the emphasis of the early twentieth-century modernists upon what contemporary theory labels 'writerly' texts which make demands on the reader to engage in 'writing' the texts in their own minds. Although Humphreys is himself a product of 'modernism', as suggested earlier, he did regard this aspect of modernism, the assumption that writers 'were not in any way personally concerned with the events they describe', as a sleight of hand:

> During the past half century some of the ablest English novelists deliberately abandoned an important convention ... the right of the author to comment on the action, the characters, the situations and scenes, the plots and the themes, of the story which he is telling.[15]

His novels of the late 1940s and 1950s explore an aesthetically acceptable line between allowing 'the characters and scenes to speak for themselves' and authorial intervention 'arising from the passionate interest of the author in what goes on in his book'.[16] In practice, this dilemma is worked out through experimentation with first-person and third-person narrative. Humphreys maintained: 'the way you combine these two ways of proceeding determines the kind of fiction you produce'.[17]

However, the issue of authorial intervention in the narrative was not the only, and perhaps not even the major, dilemma to which the dissident novel gave rise. A further issue was the tension between the three principal elements in the dramatic novel as Humphreys conceived it: the idea of individual progress; the presentation of personal, social and cultural situations which create the context(s) for some kind of progress; and the ways in which love and hope bring about a resolution of the dilemmas explored. This kind of novel required a delicate balance between the emphasis upon progress and the depiction of social and moral dilemmas.

In fact, the difficulty of achieving a balance among the different elements of the dramatic novel bedevilled Humphreys's early work, as is evident in *A Change of Heart* (1951). Initially, *A Change of Heart* is focused upon the psychological and moral problems of a university professor of English, Howell Morris. His difficulties have their roots, on the one hand, in his mother's psychological problems and her influence over him and, on the other, in the wider Nonconformist community. Morris, who is an alcoholic and is sexually impotent, marries an ex-student who dies following a backstreet operation after she is made pregnant by a jealous colleague who is committed to undermining him. However, the centre of the novel shifts from its initial focus upon Morris and his potential progress to the social and cultural contexts of his dilemmas. Ioan Williams points out that this would have been a more successful novel if Humphreys had maintained the focus throughout on Morris's moral problems.[18] In this respect, Humphreys's more successful early novels are those in which he employs a first-person narrative, such as *Hear and Forgive* (1952), which focuses upon the key protagonist's psychological and moral dilemmas arising from his relationships with his mistress and his friends, and his modernist texts, *A Man's Estate* (1955) and *A Toy Epic* (1958), which will be discussed in chapters 6 and 7, which are narrated from a number of first-person perspectives.

THE 'DRAMATIC' NOVELIST

Dissident dilemma fiction, which in the 1950s Emyr Humphreys referred to as 'dramatic' writing, is not entirely compatible with realist fiction. In this respect, attempts to label Humphreys a realist novelist are misleading. *The New Companion* maintains that: 'Emyr Humphreys has remained true to the realist novel which so many have deserted';[19] and in his conversation with Humphreys, Thomas suggested that both Kate Roberts and Emyr Humphreys were 'realists'. However, as early as 1951, Humphreys was seeing his 'dramatic' novels as dissenting from the realist tradition:

> It would be useful here to discern … a difference in the source of char-
> acters as displayed in the realistic novel and in the dramatic novel. All
> characters in realistic novels are or should be, in part or whole, observed
> from life … In the dramatic novel this cannot always be so, because the
> theme, the motive and the situation come first …[20]

Defined in this way, Humphreys clearly chose the term 'dramatic novelist' to refer to his fiction's concern with motivation, situation and dilemma. However, it also aligns his novels with theatre. In this regard, Humphreys is indebted to Shakespeare and his complex 'political' plots; to developments in the mid-twentieth-century theatre, particularly the work of Samuel Beckett and Bertolt Brecht; and to early twentieth-century Irish theatre.

The title of *A Toy Epic* (1958) suggests, as Ioan Williams has said, that it 'tackles an epic theme on a minor scale'.[21] Indeed, a number of Humphreys's early novels, like *A Toy Epic*, are redolent of Shakespearean drama in their emphasis upon a group of principal protagonists who, between them, encompass love linked to idealism, corruption and betrayal. Moreover, further reflecting Elizabethan drama, the characters in these novels are embroiled in events which seem manipulated towards some kind of individual and social progress in which love restores a sense of hope. The narratives of many of Humphreys's novels, like those in Shakespearean drama, are intricately constructed around plotting and the key themes are pursued through a main and a subplot.

In Humphreys's first novel, *The Little Kingdom* (1946), to which I referred in chapter 1, Owen Richards, a young, ruthless, ambitious nationalist politician, is reminiscent in some respects of Shakespeare's Julius Caesar. He is betrayed by his close friend Geraint Vaughan, as

Caesar was betrayed by Brutus, who, in Shakespearean or even biblical terms, condemns himself morally for his treason. The first edition of the novel has an epigraph from Shakespeare's play on the title page:

> ... the state of man
> Like to a little kingdom suffers ...
> The nature of an insurrection.
> *Julius Caesar*, Act II, Sc.1.

As in a Shakespearean drama, the key protagonist is surrounded not only by enemies and friends but also by foils. In this regard, Owen's ambitions are mirrored and mimicked in the character of Jim Catrin, whom Ioan Williams describes as a 'melodramatic simpleton ... absurd in his delusions of grandeur and his conviction that he is responsible for Owen'.[22]

The recurring motif in Shakespeare's history plays whereby 'political', the affairs of state or government, merges with 'politic', unscrupulous and cunning, enters a number of Humphreys's early novels, not least *The Voice of a Stranger* (1949) which is set in a post-war, provincial town in Italy controlled by a corrupt politician. The potential tragic love plot in the earlier novel – Owen might have been saved morally and spiritually if he had recognized the love that the daughter of one of the nationalists, Rhiannon, had for him – is developed here and brought to the fore in the love between Marcella, the daughter of the town's deputy commander, and a communist partisan committed to bringing about an end to the social and political corruption. In this novel, it seems that moving the location, as it were, from the north Wales of *The Little Kingdom* to Italy allowed Humphreys to shift the focus from the possibility of individual or social progress to a deeper-rooted sense of corruption, stagnation and hopelessness.

The influence of complex Shakespearean plots, involving love, jealousy and betrayal, on Humphreys's early work is even more pronounced in *The Voice of a Stranger* than in *The Little Kingdom*. Just as Owen in *The Little Kingdom* is betrayed by his friend Geraint Vaughan, Marcella and her husband Guido Bordoni in *The Voice of a Stranger* are betrayed by his friend and lieutenant Riccardo Forli. While Marcella's husband is away from home, Forli tries to seduce and then rape her. Although she is rescued by an American relief worker, Warner, Forli has him executed. In telling Marcella's husband that she has been unfaithful to him, Forli is responsible for Marcella's murder, too.

When Guido discovers how he has been duped, a fate redolent of Elizabethan tragic heroes, he kills both himself and his former friend. Shakespeare's influence is present in this novel in the way in which the key protagonist, who has a potential to become a 'product of some kind of progress that was both individual and social', becomes embroiled in a moral dilemma, made to believe that his wife has betrayed him, which brings about his own moral disintegration. The influence of Shakespeare is also evident in the emphasis upon the corrupt body politic as much as upon an individual heroic protagonist.

Moreover, in this novel, as in Shakespearean drama, the subplot provides a commentary upon the main plot. The idealistic love in the main plot is grotesquely inverted in the subplot in the relationship between the young Spanish woman Rosaura and Marcella's aged father who becomes her keeper. But there is a further commentary upon the selfless love of Rhiannon in *The Little Kingdom* and Marcella in *The Voice of a Stranger* found in the subplot involving the character Suori Crispi, who devotes herself to freeing her husband and son from prisoner-of-war camps. The key dimension of the dramatic novel as conceived by Humphreys – the individual's potential for progress arrested by a moral dilemma – is anchored in the subplot by Suori as it is in the main plot by Guido. Whereas the emphasis in the main plot is upon the moral dilemma which destroys Guido, in the subplot it is upon how Suori, through her ruthless dedication to her cause, survives the moral dilemmas in which she becomes embroiled through having to become the corrupt Prefect's ally and a somewhat corrupt Red Cross matron.

In some respects, *The Voice of a Stranger* is redolent of Shakespeare's *Hamlet*, similarly set in a state which is rotten to the core. The idealistic love between Hamlet and Ophelia falls victim to state-wide corruption and at the end of the play all the key protagonists are dead. Moreover, at the end of both texts, hope lies in a fairly minor character. In the case of Humphreys's novel, the future lies in the hands of the Welshman Williams, who is able to return to Wales.

However, as mentioned earlier, Shakespeare was not the only dramatist to have been an important influence on Humphreys's fiction. The way in which Humphreys thought of Beckett's work, evident in a draft of his eventually published lecture on Beckett in his archive at the National Library of Wales, highlights an important aspect of his novels. In this lecture, he conceives of Beckett's characters as caught up in dilemmas which are universal rather than personal. This view

of Beckett's work provides a gloss on the struggles explored in his
own works: 'In the theatre of Samuel Beckett, life goes on under the
most limiting conditions. Out of the darkness and the stair well and
the silence, voices cry and figures try to move. This is the basic human
condition.'[23] As such, this aspect of Beckett's work, as Humphreys saw
it, does not stand in contradistinction to his interest in Shakespeare
whose protagonists are also caught in dilemmas that are as much
universal as personal. However, in his lecture, Humphreys highlights
a further aspect of Beckett's work which, potentially, does contradict
his concept of dilemma fiction. For Humphreys, the voices in Beckett's
work 'explore the mysteries of being and the self to the anguished
limit' and are concerned with illuminating dark places.[24] Humphreys's
lecture on Beckett raises some crucial questions. What exactly does
Humphreys mean by 'the mysteries of being and the self'? The lecture
appears to have been influenced not simply by Beckett's work but by
a wider twentieth-century psychoanalytic framework. In order to
understand what Humphreys means by Beckett's writing examining
mysterious, dark spaces and how this may be embodied in Humphreys's
work, we might turn to a contemporaneous review of the work of
another modernist author who influenced Humphreys. A reviewer
of the work of the modernist writer Virginia Woolf, whose influence
on Humphreys is apparent in *A Toy Epic*, to which I shall return in a
moment, astutely argued that her work probes 'things which have long
been latent in the dark places of consciousness' and should be read
through what we might describe today as a psychoanalytic lens. The
reviewer finds in Woolf's fiction what are described as 'substitution-
symbols' in which there is a 'tendency to see "everything as something
else"'.[25] Although Humphreys's work appears more realist than much
of Woolf's, the idea of details acting as symbols for the 'dark places
of consciousness' has some relevance to the Welsh writer's fiction also.

This important, and critically neglected, quality which the works
of Beckett, Woolf and Humphreys share complicates a view of
Humphreys as a 'realist' writer in the traditional sense because it highlights a concern in Humphreys's fiction with both the conscious and the
unconscious. His interest in Beckett and Woolf suggests that his fiction
may be read on a number of levels. The notion that Woolf's fiction is
based on 'substitution-symbols' is applicable also to Beckett and, as I
shall discuss in chapter 4, to Humphreys's fiction. But the suggestion
that Humphreys's fiction can be read on a number of levels, including
the psychoanalytic, raises issues for dilemma fiction. His concerns

with progress, dilemma and resolution, as I shall discuss in chapter 4, require his protagonists to make intellectual and moral choices which might seem at odds with assumptions from psychoanalysis that not all our behaviour is conscious and can be easily understood.

However, as mentioned earlier, Humphreys's indebtedness to the Irish stage extended beyond Beckett to the work of J. M. Synge. Although Synge is not normally thought of as a modernist, his most famous, and at the time most notorious, work, *The Playboy of the Western World* (1908), achieved a directness of voice and a tightness of form that were commensurate with the modernist movement in Ireland and anticipated the direction in which W. B. Yeats's poetry was to develop. In his lecture on Beckett, Humphreys noted that the 'language of Synge is not available except for plays set among that same people'.[26] In his novels, as I hope to show in the course of this book, Humphreys develops voices which illuminate dark places and a language which is available only to fiction set among the people of particular parts of north Wales at specific times. Synge and Humphreys share a concern to explore the line between finding this kind of language and what might be termed 'realism'. Indeed, what Humphreys has said more recently about the location of his own work is applicable to Synge's writing at the beginning of the century: 'It's like a parallel existence. Fiction is a possibility – it could be, but it isn't. The world of fiction always floats a few feet above the actual ground, and enjoys a climate and atmosphere all of its own.'[27]

Humphreys's labelling of himself as a 'dramatic', and more recently, a 'dissident', as opposed to a 'Protestant', writer represents important self-evaluations of his work. The latter, especially, may be an important shift in how he sees himself as a writer. However, the terms 'dramatic', 'dissident' and 'dilemma' are more accurate reflection of his life and his fiction than 'Protestant'. Moreover, these terms, including 'Protestant', have helped him over the years to clarify the role of the artist in modern Wales and the relationship of the writer to the social and cultural changes that occurred in Wales throughout the twentieth century:

> It has become a permanent condition. I look at the world, and see that the alienation and isolation of the artist is no less than it was in my youth. If anything, it's worse because the globalization of technology and mass communications drives the individual vision to a permanent state of dissent.[28]

MODERNISM

If Humphreys was looking for a Welsh writer who embraced some of the qualities of the praise poet and the epic, then he found her in Kate Roberts. Roberts's work, in his view, demonstrates 'a note of intensity, a quality of song, that echoes the timeless celebration of tribal and social qualities characteristic of epic poets from Homer to the Hengerdd'.[29] For Humphreys, she had a complex relationship to one of the key literary movements of the first half of the twentieth century. Confusing 'modernism' and 'modernity', he has argued, 'We cannot claim for her experimental originality and in most respects her work stands outside the main stream of that modernity which generally characterises the art of this century.' Yet, in his view, she handles her material 'in a manner which secures for it the most enduring attributes of modernity'.[30]

Modernism is a radical and experimental Euro-American movement in literature and the arts which is generally associated with the first quarter of the twentieth century and with writers such as Elizabeth Bowen, T. S. Eliot, James Joyce, Ezra Pound, Jean Rhys, Dorothy Richardson, W. B. Yeats and Virginia Woolf. Although many modernist authors are particularly linked to radical ideas and practices in the wake of post-impressionism in painting or the social, cultural and technological upheaval which followed the First World War, many of them were born and brought up when Victorianism was in its last throes. Richard Sheppard points out that there were many modernists who belonged to a 'generation which had grown up amid the triumphant achievements of increasingly confident nineteenth-century science, technology and economics' but who, in the twentieth century, 'now felt that these systems were becoming dysfunctional and potentially totalitarian'.[31] He argues that 'modernism ceases to be merely the artistic manifestation of a conflict between conservative, humanist sensibilities and a modernizing, non-humanist world, and becomes the manifestation of a more or less shocked realization that modernization required more than the development of a new, appropriate sensibility'.[32] Not surprisingly, modernism had a profound influence on literature throughout the twentieth century, as is evident from the work of a number of writers who came to prominence in the mid- or late twentieth century. These include not only Emyr Humphreys himself but Samuel Beckett, Bertholt Brecht, William Faulkner, Wallace Stevens, Toni Morrison, the first African American woman novelist to win the Nobel Prize for Literature, and, in Wales, Kate Roberts.

Kate Roberts was an important influence on Humphreys's fiction as he made clear in a radio interview with M. Wynn Thomas on Radio Cymru's arts programme, *Ffresgo*, preceding the publication of *Open Secrets*, the fifth book in the Land of the Living sequence. As Gerwyn Wiliams points out, he acknowledged 'her minimal style which he himself has increasingly adopted'.[33] Land of the Living appears to be influenced by what Humphreys calls Kate Roberts's epic duo of novels (*Traed Mewn Cyffion* and *Tegwch y Bore*) in which she charts the history of a north Wales community from 1890 to 1918, and the leading female protagonist, Amy Parry, recalls Roberts's partly autobiographical female characters.[34] It might also be said that Amy Parry partly reflects how Humphreys saw Kate Roberts herself, embodying 'a range of qualities from heroic independence to colourful eccentricities'.[35]

Draft proposals among Emyr Humphreys's papers, compiled between 1986 and 1988 for a television programme entitled 'The Hidden Spring', on the life and works of four significant mid-twentieth-century writers – Kate Roberts, Saunders Lewis, Gwenallt and D. J. Williams – suggest that Roberts might have had an even more profound effect on Land of the Living than Wiliams maintains. He argues that the influence of Roberts's female characters is apparent in the independently minded Amy Parry who, like Roberts, is also for a while a teacher. However, Amy's relationship with, largely male, political thinkers and activists in Land of the Living also reflects 'The Hidden Spring'. The life stories of Kate Roberts in 'The Hidden Spring' and Amy Parry in Land of the Living, as Humphreys says of Roberts in his proposal, 'provide the most stimulating narrative link and still do justice to the parts the other authors played in the drama'.[36] The way in which Amy Parry is placed at the centre of relationships with political thinkers and activists between the wars, as Humphreys conceived of Kate Roberts in her own life, is fundamental to the narrative structure of Land of the Living. Indeed, it is this feature that separates the novels in this series from Humphreys's earlier work.

There are further important elements which the life stories of Roberts and Amy share which are highlighted in the proposal for 'The Hidden Spring': 'the brave new world of school and college'; the way they throw themselves into political battles; their involvement with a post-war world that 'inevitably moves towards politics'; and 'the dangerous romance of marriage with an adventurous extremist'.[37] Moreover, there are parallels between the world from which the core of *Outside the House of Baal* and the Land of the Living novels that are located in the first part of the narrative chronology emerged and the framework within which Humphreys conceived Roberts's early life: 'A monoglot Welsh world devoted to work (slate quarrying, smallholdings), to chapel, to education, to eisteddfodic culture.'[38] Another of the papers relating to Humphreys's proposal for 'The Hidden Spring' emphasizes, too, the way in which Kate Roberts and her fellow writers, like many of the political thinkers and writers within Amy Parry's network and within Reverend J.T.'s network in *Outside the House of Baal*, 'were offspring of Welsh nonconformity at its social and economic zenith'.[39]

It is possible to trace from *A Toy Epic* and *Outside the House of Baal* to Land of the Living, notwithstanding the experimentation in some of the novels comprising the latter, the shift in focus which Humphreys finds in the work of Kate Roberts, Saunders Lewis, Gwenallt and D. J. Williams from 'literary experiment to political protest'.[40] But there are further parallels between the Nonconformist culture in which Humphreys locates Roberts's work and *Outside the House of Baal*: 'In 19th century Wales the chapels with their old testament [*sic*] names were civic as well as religious centres and biblical conflicts between prophets and priests were the stuff of popular gossip and press coverage.'[41]

Notwithstanding Kate Roberts's influence on Humphreys, his early novels appeared at the time when the narrative sophistication and complex time structures of Faulkner's fiction were attracting extensive critical attention after he won the Nobel Prize in 1950. In a recently published interview with Wynn Thomas, Humphreys acknowledges his indebtedness to Faulkner's early novels:

> Once you get beyond thirty, you aren't influenced very much by outside factors, and I'd say that the last [writer] to have a major influence on me was Faulkner, and he was a generation older than I was.
>
> ... I had realised that he was an important writer in the immediate post-war period, but when I went to Salzburg [with his family for a year as a kind of writing fellow in 1952–3] Edmund Wilson was there [on a similar bursary], and he used to talk a lot about his friend Faulkner. There was another man there too – Lawrence Thompson – who was a Faulkner scholar, and who could discuss his work very well. This was the period when I was wrestling with *A Man's Estate* and had decided to use four voices – such techniques were very much in the air at that time.
>
> .... I particularly remember *The Sound and the Fury*, *As I Lay Dying* and *Light in August* – I remember those three novels particularly well. I haven't read them since that time, but in that period I thought they were

superb, and that Faulkner and his world corresponded, in some odd way, to the situation in Wales to some degree, in the sense that the southern states had been defeated and also that the Bible, and religion was central to the culture. It's true that there's no mention of black people in Wales, but there is the class war that corresponds to that in a way.[42]

Humphreys's most Faulknerian novel is *A Man's Estate* (1955), which will be discussed in chapter 6, and which, like Faulkner's *The Sound and the Fury* and *As I Lay Dying*, is told through a number of narrative voices, the shift in narrator being flagged by the character's name at the start of the section or chapter. There is an even wider context for Faulkner's influence on Humphreys and that is the parallels which Humphreys draws between Wales and the southern states of America. In a draft essay, 'The Welsh condition', Humphreys develops the analogy:

a defeated nation, deeply aware of defeat as part of the human condition; a conservative society more anxious to keep than to take or change; a society deeply aware of religion and haunted by guilt and failure; a society from which the scientific man is naturally inclined to escape. Add to the recipe several centuries; but take away a furiously romantic liberalism, a very ancient cult of amiability, and an anarchic nonconformity: this resembles the Welsh condition.[43]

A young Welsh person might today wonder what Wales Humphreys is thinking of. This Wales seems very different from that of his late twentieth-century and twenty-first-century work, as the American South here might not be recognizable to a contemporary young Southerner. It brings to mind the debate to which David Barnes draws attention between the optimistic conclusion of John Davies's *History of Wales* (1990) and Dai Smith's less confident ending of *A Question of History* (a revised version of his *Wales! Wales?*).[44] Indeed, Humphreys's stress on conservatism and guilt does not square easily with his own memories of the Rhyl in which he was brought up – 'It was unquestionably the place to be. Sodom and Gomorrah had somehow been sanitised …'[45] – nor with the interest in science and technology, critical where the latter is linked to war, in many of his novels from *A Toy Epic* and *Outside the House of Baal* to *The Shop*.

  A Man's Estate was not Humphreys's first modernist experiment. Although it was not published in its final form until 1958, his first experimental modernist text was *A Toy Epic*.[46] Humphreys began writing this novel in 1941 when he was working as a conscientious objector on a farm in Pembrokeshire, west Wales. The initial text, in which three boys alternately gave accounts of their childhood, was quite short and on the advice of publishers Eyre & Spottiswoode, he added part two, which was published separately in 1947, and drew up a plan for four parts. The revised text was submitted to Eyre & Spottiswoode in 1943 but, in the summer, Graham Greene, who felt it was not well written or sufficiently integrated, rejected it, suggesting that the original text could have been published in a collection of short stories. On the advice of readers' reports, T. S. Eliot at Faber also rejected it in September and again the criticism was that the text was insufficiently coherent and that the voices were not sufficiently distinguished. It appears that the text was put in the bottom drawer until Humphreys became head of radio drama for the BBC in Cardiff. As Wynn Thomas points out, Humphreys was encouraged to broadcast his own work in Welsh and he returned to a translation of some of the text which had been started by a friend in Pembrokeshire. This led him to revise and expand the text which was eventually broadcast in 1958 as *Y Tri Llais* (The Three Voices).[47]

The Welsh-language title of the work may have been influenced by Dylan Thomas's subtitle for *Under Milk Wood*: *A Play for Voices*. The Welsh-language version opens and concludes with a dream sequence, which Wynn Thomas points out may have been suggested by the eighteenth-century Welsh-language prose work, *Gweledigaetheu y Bardd Cwsc* (The Visions of the Sleeping Poet). However, it may also have been suggested by the opening sequence of *Under Milk Wood*. And, as a modernist text, *A Toy Epic* appears to have been influenced by Virginia Woolf rather than Faulkner's fiction. The different voices are introduced in exactly the same way as the voices in Woolf's *The Waves* (1931), repetitively using the construction '…, said …' as in: 'The first day I went to school, said Albie, I was escorted by my mother' (p. 23). There are a number of further significant parallels between the two novels, which will be discussed in chapter 7.

In the 1990s, Humphreys returned to writing dilemma novels which were distinctly modernist, as mentioned in chapter 1. The first of these was the final novel in the Land of the Living sequence, *Bonds of Attachment*, discussed further in chapter 9, in which one of the sons of Amy Parry, the principal female protagonist in the sequence, seeks to reconcile himself with his mother, who is now elderly, and with his deceased father, the poet Cilydd More. In this text, Humphreys returns to his modernist experiments with narrative voice already seen in *A*

Man's Estate and *A Toy Epic*, combining Peredur's first-person narrative with his father's notebooks and letters. His voice is haunted by the past but also by the fear of a future in which he is unable to understand his father and reconcile himself with his, by then deceased, mother. The novel itself, in which Peredur, through his own investigations and through his father's writings, retraces the history which the earlier novels recorded as they moved forward in time, is haunted by the other novels in the sequence.

The second modernist dilemma text of the 1990s is *Unconditional Surrender*, which will be discussed in chapter 10, in which the story is told through two first-person narratives that alternate with each other during the closing months of the Second World War after hostilities have ceased in Europe: the narrative of Reverend Edwin Pritchard, the rector of a rural parish in north Wales, and that of a former countess, Cecilia von Leiden. The text focuses on the relationships between Pritchard's daughter, Meg, a local boy who works on the land as a conscientious objector and a German prisoner of war who is in a camp in the area. Through the different perspectives of the two voices, the novel explores the way in which Pritchard's wife and daughter are becoming increasingly independently minded, inhabiting the changes in the concept of being female which the Second World War brought about, and the different ways in which Pritchard thinks about his daughter, some of which he is not fully aware. The latter introduces the theme of father-and-daughter relationships which is explored in the subsequent, more traditional novel, *The Gift of a Daughter*, in the short-story collection *Old People are a Problem* and the novel *The Shop*.

Humphreys's dramatic or dilemma narratives and his more modernist work share a concern with what the European cultural critic Louis Althusser called the 'problématique'.[48] Althusser's concept places Humphreys's interest in dilemma within a wider European perspective. Whereas we might think of Althusser's term and the contemporary, Euro-American term 'problematic' as synonymous, the former, as Robert Sheppard points out, developed at a time when 'European culture was experiencing the subversion of the most fundamental assumptions and conceptual models on which the liberal humanist epoch had been based'.[49]

As I hope to show in the discussion of selected texts in part two of this book, at the heart of the 'problématique' in Humphreys's work is, indeed, 'the subversion of ... fundamental assumptions and conceptual models on which the liberal humanist epoch has been based'. These vary from the concern with politically motivated murder in *The Little Kingdom*, murder within a family and sexploitation in *A Man's Estate*, the rise of fascism and the monstrous inhumanity on which it is based in *A Toy Epic*, to secret desires in *Outside the House of Baal* and in the Land of the Living septet, to the concern with the father-and-son relationship in *Bonds of Attachment* and the father-and-daughter relationship in *Unconditional Surrender*.

MODERNISM, DRAMA AND FILM

At the time when Humphreys began to think seriously about the impact of modernism and the arts upon his own practice as a writer, he was pondering the significance of film. Nevertheless, his understanding of film history, however compelling (for example, his argument that television revived film),[50] is less relevant to the themes of this book than the way in which his thinking about film influenced his understanding of writing. His notes towards an article on 'The writer and the new media' reveal his strong interest in silent film which was influenced by some of the principal European cultural and linguistic theorists, such as the Frankfurt School and more particularly Adorno and Marcuse. Thus, he talks about silent film, clearly with the writer in mind, in terms of language: 'History of the Silent Film – new form of communication (language understood by all then came sound & spoilt it – awful).'[51] Interestingly in terms of Humphreys's own practice as a writer of fiction, he conceives film as 'coming out of symbols'.[52] In his Welsh-language notes towards the article, he breaks the response to film, which he thinks of in his English-language notes as consisting of 'sound and vision', into two sensory responses – 'clywed' (hearing) and 'gweld' (seeing) – which are in turn linked to 'teimlo' (feeling) and 'deall' (understanding). The way in which Humphreys thought of himself as an 'intellectual novelist', focused more on the 'gweld' and 'deall' paradigm than the 'clywed' and 'teimlo' axes, is clear in some of the statements he makes in these notes. Evidently, what were important to him were the trends that emerged in art and literature after the First World War: 'truth before beauty'; 'social commitment'; 'decline of the ego, – this is me. This is my bleeding heart'; and 'The Discipline of Art'. In response to the question, 'The Writer. Who is he?', Humphreys declares: 'serves TRUTH'.[53]

In preparing his notes for 'The writer and the new media', Humphreys appears to have developed his thesis that film is 'a language understood by all' into an interest in the type of writing which is produced by the poet working in the theatre and the writer working in television and film. In notes towards an article entitled 'Drama and the common people', Humphreys begins by stating that there has been 'no real connection [between the two] since the Middle Ages'. The two in his view do meet in the Welsh chapels, music hall, in silent film and in television. It is clear from his notes that Humphreys has in mind the concept of 'the poet of the people' and believes that 'one way back [is] via the Theatre' and 'the deeper levels of meaning & feeling available only to poets'.[54] However, his Welsh-language notes on the subject, which stress 'syniadau a theimladau' [ideas and feelings], suggest that his concern with the concept of 'drama and the people' and with 'the poet of the people' were part of a wider exploration of how the writer driven by ideas could, through the development of feeling in his writing, become accessible to the people as a whole.

The link between the writer and the new media is one which is made in Humphreys's notes on many levels. First, he seeks to establish, as noted, ideological affinities between the writer as intellectual in exile and the social commitment of the new medium. Secondly, he highlights the shared potential in television/film and drama to link 'understanding' and 'feeling' in communicating with the 'common people'. Thirdly, he explores the link between the language of film and language more generally, thinking in terms of a 'grammar of film', in which the shot corresponds with the sentence and the constituent parts of the shot (cut, pan, tilt, elevate, etc.) function like the words of the sentence. Thinking about film in terms of its grammar and methods and in terms of a camera and microphone inspires Humphreys's thinking about writing in terms of 'pen and voice' and in terms of ideas and feeling.[55]

3

History, Space and Progress

Despite the importance of north-east Wales to Welsh history (it is the birthplace of Owain Glyndŵr), it has not enjoyed the kind of economic and cultural renaissance experienced by the south-east which is the site of the capital, the National Assembly, the Millennium Stadium, prestigious arts venues, national television and print journalism and large retail centres dominated by English and global chain stores. In much of his fiction, Humphreys writes of Wales from a north Wales perspective, reclaiming, like younger Welsh-language writers and musicians from north Wales, such as Meinir Gwilym, the vibrancy of the north.

I do not mean that Humphreys, who despite becoming a fluent Welsh speaker writes more in English than Welsh, has simply sought to bring the Welsh-language communities of north Wales to a non-Welsh-speaking readership or audience, although he has done this. Indeed, as regards the latter, Gerwyn Wiliams refers to the Welsh quotations in Humphreys's work, 'embedded here and there are like codes of allegiance, emphasising to the Welsh-speaking reader the central relevance of this author's work'.[1] Rather, I mean that Humphreys translates into narrative and story, with searching analysis, what is distinctive and salient about being from, and living in, north Wales.

This chapter is not intended to provide a definitive account of Humphreys's engagement with the history of Wales nor of Welsh history as it is presented in his fiction. It outlines some of the key concepts that inform the way in which Humphreys's fiction employs and interrogates select historical developments. Above all, it seeks to answer the question: what kind of historian is Humphreys?

In attempting to do so, this chapter highlights Humphreys's interest in a number of areas. These include: 'historiography', differing modes of writing about history; his approach to history from a north Wales perspective, offering an alternative to, say, the discourses of the south Wales historians; the heterogeneity of history and the tendency to talk of 'histories' rather than 'history'; how Humphreys might be seen as taking an 'archaeological' approach to history; the importance of the way in which the relationship between language, culture and colonialism is configured; how Humphreys's work may be said to be informed by histories that have been only partially included in the history of modern Wales; how his work shares themes with Welsh anglophone but also European writers; how Humphreys's concern with the intersection of space and time, displaying once again the influences of modernist literature, art and music as well as film, can be more fully appreciated through the work of the well-known Russian theorist, Mikhail Bakhtin; and, finally, how his fiction explores the transformation of space through technology. The chapter includes references to some of Humphreys's key texts, discussed in more detail in part two, but also illustrates some of its arguments with reference to *The Little Kingdom*, a relatively neglected novel. A further important framework, not discussed in this chapter, is feminism, which is the subject of chapter 5.

HISTORY, LANGUAGE AND IDENTITY

The Anchor Tree (1980) opens with a question directed at its historian narrator: 'What kind of an historian are you, anyway?'[2] This is a pertinent question to direct to Humphreys himself. Perhaps the key to his engagement with history and the overarching framework which determines his choice of historical subject matter is the one described in his proposal for a television documentary, 'The Hidden Spring', developed between 1986 and 1988, to which I referred in the previous chapter. His reflections on Welsh history in this proposal make clear how he thought of the first half of the twentieth century and beyond as a

> dramatic conflict between what we choose to call in Welsh our literary renaissance and a world increasingly hostile not only to the local and particular, the rooted and the native, but to most of the civilising habits that gave character to the life of their [the authors with whom the programme is to be concerned] community and what they themselves regarded as an authentic national identity.[3]

M. Wynn Thomas has argued that Humphreys offers a reading of modern Welsh history 'which is both nationalist and Welsh internationalist'. It is also different, he points out, from that which has been proposed by south Wales historians, such as Dai Smith, in which the emergence of an industrial, cosmopolitan and politically radical Anglo-Welsh society in the south displaced 'traditional Welsh-speaking society, which was predominantly rural, Nonconformist and culturally conservative' and 'virtually signalled the end of Wales's already problematic existence as a single entity'.[4]

Within this framework, and from the perspective on Welsh history which he describes above, Humphreys's fiction resists identifying itself with a rural, Nonconformist, Welsh-language society that by the mid-twentieth century virtually ceased to exist. Wynn Thomas maintains that,

> [Humphreys's fiction] consciously departs from the various methods devised for treating Wales in literature as a constituent region of the Anglo-British nation; it explores the major regions of Wales with a view to preparing the ground and establishing the conditions for constructing a separate modern Welsh nation; and it (much more tentatively) reflects on Wales's position in Europe.[5]

The exploration of the relationship between language, myth and power is crucial to Humphreys's fiction, not least the part played by Calvinistic Nonconformity in Welsh history; the perception of Welsh history as colonialist; and the extent to which the history of Welsh-speaking Wales, through its movements for independence, recognition and equality, is characterized by periods of progress and uncertainty. Despite the diversity in Humphreys's engagement with the past, there is a unifying concern with the dialectic between Welsh culture, language and identity as rooted in the local and particular and a globalized, technological world which challenges traditional notions of identity and belonging.

Six years after the publication of Humphreys's first novel, *The Little Kingdom*, one of Wales's most significant anglophone poets, David Jones, who lived most of his life in London but came from a north Wales family, published *The Anathémata* (1952).[6] It demonstrated an important feature of the relationship between fiction and history in mid-twentieth-century English-language Welsh writing. As J. P. Ward observes, Jones's work exhibited a 'purposeful' stance towards history and, in its interrogation of history, might be described as 'archaeological'.[7]

Humphreys's fiction might be similarly described as 'purposeful' and 'archaeological' in its approach to history. With Land of the Living in mind, Gerwyn Wiliams sees Humphreys as a historical novelist 'more determined than his fellow writers in Welsh to uncover the significance of two world wars to Wales and to dissect its effects upon the Welsh'. He provides, Wiliams argues, 'within the novel form, a panoramic and dramatic picture of changes wrought in the Welsh community and the Welsh psyche during and after the Second World War'.[8] However, in the last half of the twentieth century, the homogenizing tendencies of history as a discipline were challenged not only by the Second World War but by decolonization in the post-war years which began with India and Pakistan; migration which boosted many of the ethnic communities that had already been established in cities such as Cardiff and created new communities; the global impact of the movement for black and civil rights in the United States; the increasing complexity of ethnic and national identities which, in Wales, created, for example, awareness of Chinese-Welsh, Italian-Welsh, African and West Indian-Welsh histories; and accelerating globalization which ushered in new lines of communication and exchange.

Growing recognition of the importance of the heterogeneity of history, evident in a newly found interest in histories demarcated along lines of ethnicity and gender, as well as class, was aligned with increased interest in history as narrative. Hayden White's groundbreaking work on the relationship between history and fiction stressed the importance to history of processes, such as selection, editing, invention and emphasis, which had previously been associated with fiction rather than historiography.[9] This mid-twentieth-century emphasis upon the plurality and selectivity of historical discourses is important to recognizing the shift in focus away from the grand sweep of twentieth-century history in Humphreys's work, especially in *Outside the House of Baal* and Land of the Living, which will be discussed in chapters 8 and 9 respectively, and in Raymond Williams's *Border Country* trilogy, mentioned in chapter 1 to more focused sagas.

Humphreys, who has strong affinities with, and was affected by, twentieth-century modernist writers, often presents the reader with diverse 'histories', something that may have been inspired by Virginia Woolf whose influence on *A Toy Epic* has been discussed. Her novel *The Years* (1937) is anchored in the years 1880 to 1937, prioritizing events from a woman's perspective and focusing on those which have been occluded by the agendas of official, often male-oriented, histories. Humphreys takes a similar approach in *Outside the House of Baal* by focusing at one point on a history 'Outside the House of War' instanced by J.T.'s pacifism and the lives of women and men who did not go to war, including the breakdown of Kate's and Lydia's marriages.

Also of particular relevance to Humphreys's concern with historiography is the approach to history, developed through the work of philosophers and cultural critics such as Friedrich Nietzsche and Michel Foucault, which initially had greater impact upon philosophy and literature than upon history as a discipline. Nietzsche's *On the Genealogy of Morals* (1887) laid the foundations for the twentieth-century European interrogation of the truths of history as expressions of power which, again, is a concept that informs Humphreys's work.[10] Indeed, one of the most relevant frameworks within which to read his fiction is Michel Foucault's argument that in Western society, power and knowledge are very closely linked. According to Foucault, everyday authority is exercised through dominant and institutionalized discourses.[11] This is especially pertinent to the examination in Humphreys's fiction of how Welsh cultural experience is distorted and occluded by the 'foreignness' of the English language and by the assimilation in literature and at an institutionalized level of English discourses. At times, although written in English, Humphreys's work seems to aspire to what Kirsti Bohata describes as 'essentialist claims that construct language as synonymous with, or at least the vehicle of, a particular culture ... [claims which] can be persuasive, if ultimately reductive'.[12] In an incomplete manuscript essay on bilingualism, which stresses the importance of the Welsh language, Humphreys argues:

> The roots of the language lie deep in the native soil and in spite of the continuing recession of the language in the face of unrestricted mass-communication vast economic & social change, it is impossible to live in any part of Wales without becoming aware of the language as a strong element in the peculiar colour and flavour of the national life.[13]

However, his own fiction quite often steers towards a view of Wales which Bohata summarizes as an alternative to those which make essentialist associations between language and culture: 'Wales as a culturally composite nation where language plays a great, perhaps paramount, part in the variety of Welsh "cultures", but where it is also recognized that linguistic groups are not culturally homogenous, nor are different cultural groupings always divided along linguistic lines.[14]

The historical consciousness of any nation, like the biographical consciousness of any individual, is constructed around particular milestones. In terms of a particular nation, these milestones contribute to a sense of a collective consciousness. But what actually constitutes a nation's history will vary from community to community and from writer to writer. In Humphreys's fiction, new milestones are conceived and others subjected to scrutiny through his awareness of the inequalities of historical and cultural representation. In this regard, Humphreys may be seen as one of the writers who contribute to a postcolonial view of Wales.[15]

Wales is a country which has only recently begun to be conceived in postcolonial terms. This is partly because, as Kirsti Bohata has pointed out, postcolonialism has been associated with 'a linear-progressive model of colonization, anti-colonialsm and decolonization/independence', which is not entirely appropriate to Wales. Moreover, only recently have Welsh scholars embraced the potential in postcolonial theory to explore fully subjects such as cultural imperialism and hegemony.[16]

At one level, Humphreys's novels address themes which are generally associated with postcolonial critical theorists (including, Bill Ashcroft, Homi Bhabha, Edward Said and Frantz Fanon) such as language, place, exile, imperialism and, of course, nationhood. But Humphreys's view of Welsh history is based around specific concerns, issues and themes which, as suggested in the previous chapter, are part of his own lived experience of Wales. Thus, viewing the history of Wales through the lens of Humphreys's fiction is to experience a particular selection and prioritizing of cultural and national reference points such as the campaigns for the Welsh language to enjoy equal status with English; Nonconformity; technology and modernity; pacifism; fascism; war and gender. In this regard, it may be a little reductive to label Humphreys a postcolonial novelist as such, even though, at one level, he writes within a framework which has much in common with postcolonalism.

WRITING AN ABSENT PRESENCE

Humphreys's work makes an original contribution, even within Welsh writing in English, to wider concerns about the discourse of history and the way in which power and knowledge are linked. Even at its most 'realist', his fiction is haunted by an 'absent presence' which can only be conceived in terms of the absent presence of a Welsh-speaking Wales which seems more potent than the existent Wales. In taking this line, Humphreys risks aligning himself with those who, as Janet Davies has said, have conflated the loss of the Welsh language with 'the realization that the way of life associated with the language in those strongholds [of the Welsh language] has passed away' to the detriment of the need for Welsh 'to anchor itself in modernity'.[17]

The sense of a Welsh-speaking Wales, and especially of a Welsh-speaking north Wales, that is absent provides Humphreys's fiction with not simply a sense of loss, although this is a key theme in many of the novels, but a sense of possibility. It is an aspect of his fiction which, up to a point, is shared by the work of one of his characters, the Welsh-language poet Cilydd More in Land of the Living, and, in some of his novels, it actually becomes a subject of debate. In the last novel in Land of the Living, *Bonds of Attachment*, the nationalist girlfriend of Peredur, Cilydd's son, speaks provocatively about Cilydd's work in this respect:

> She made a gesture of despair towards my father's papers on the floor and tightened the blankets around her shoulders.
> 'They were looking for a people that didn't exist,' she said. 'A country that wasn't there.[18]

The absent centre which Humphreys conceives in his work is similar to that about which the poet Tony Conran has written. Ned Thomas points out that Conran thinks of:

> an egalitarian, Nonconformist culture, embracing Welsh-speaking and non-Welsh-speaking people, that was dominant up to the First World War and exerted an influence on literature long after that, often by producing a reaction against Nonconformity.[19]

Conran thinks of a culture that embraces both Welsh-speaking and non-Welsh-speaking Welsh people. However, the absent centre which haunts Humphreys's work, despite the fact that he has published much more in English than in Welsh, as suggested earlier, is a Welsh-speaking nation. Both Conran and Humphreys are concerned in their writing with the loss of such a past. However, as Ned Thomas maintains, when writing about Conran, 'the invocation of a time when Wales was united by a culture (crossing differences of language) that differentiated it from England has a persisting symbolic appeal'.[20] In Humphreys's work, the absent centre is linked through, for example, Cilydd More's poetry, to what he described as the 'Taliesin tradition'. As conceived by Humphreys, this not only defines and sustains Welsh identity but keeps present what would otherwise be absent from modern Welsh history:

> The Taliesin tradition can be traced through the centuries. What is perhaps less conspicuous is the manner in which at all times it has contrived to be a major factor in the maintenance, stability, and continuity of the Welsh identity and the fragile concept of Welsh nationhood. Indeed it could be argued that this hidden force in Welsh life also served as a catalyst in the creation of the far more robust and aggressive phenomenon of English nationalism, and those changes in the mental and spiritual climate of Europe that gave rise to the dominant power structure of the nation state. But it is in the Welsh experience that we can see most clearly how a poetic tradition can inject into a native language an authority and power that is sufficient to breathe forms of life into the national being even when independent military and political power have long withered away.[21]

The title of Humphreys's proposed television documentary on Kate Roberts, Saunders Lewis, Gwenallt and D. J. Williams, referred to earlier, 'The Hidden Spring', refers to the way in which Humphreys thought of the Welsh literary tradition as a 'powerful underground stream ... about which the vast majority of C4 [television] viewers will know nothing'.[22] Indeed, Humphreys also observes that the Welsh historian Gwyn A. Williams argued that, 'The Welsh as a people were born disinherited.'[23]

In order to understand how Humphreys writes the absent centre of Welsh-speaking north Wales into his fiction, which largely documents the social, cultural, political and economic changes that have occurred in Wales, we may turn to the French philosopher Jacques Derrida, one of the most important late twentieth-century cultural and linguistic theorists. Derrida contrasted history perceived as 'a linear scheme of unfolding of presence' with what, in his terms, is not or has never been fully present.[24] In one of the draft papers relating to the documentary 'The Hidden Spring', Humphreys describes how one of 'the most extraordinary literary phenomen[a] of the twentieth century in the British Isles', a reinvigorated Welsh-language literature, has been what he calls a 'hidden history'.[25]

Derrida points out that the association of history with the 'linear', and what has only been fully present, is only one model of history which is also 'homogeneous, dominated by the form of the now and the ideal of continuous movement, straight or circular'.[26] The alternative way of looking at history according to Derrida is 'pluri-dimensionality', which includes what is hidden or is not fully present. Given Humphreys's emphasis upon moral and social development in 'Protestant' fiction, to which I referred in the previous chapter, we might expect Humphreys to view history in predominantly linear terms. However, his fiction is not, to use Derrida's terms 'homogeneous', only dominated by the present, or informed by 'the ideal of continuous movement'. His work is as focused on the non-linear as the linear and, indeed, the relationship between the two may be seen as providing the necessary creative tension for his writing.

Humphreys's interest in a past that has not been fully unfolded, or has been allowed to unfold, in modern Welsh history is difficult to miss in his work. Two of his novels, *The Anchor Tree* and *Unconditional Surrender*, include characters who want to write history but fail to do so. Indeed, unfulfilled history is the key theme in *The Anchor Tree* in which the historian Morgan Reece Dale, as mentioned in chapter 1, seeks to reclaim a Christian community established by one of his ancestors in eighteenth-century Pennsylvania. While another community, based on different values, has flourished and survived, Cambria Nova is now forgotten. Its site, overgrown with scrub, signifies a past which, like Welsh-language Wales, has never fully unfolded. It is also an important theme in Land of the Living, in which the central female protagonist, Amy, never achieves her ambition of being returned to Westminster and, even later in life when she acquires influence through her wealth and social position, fails to bring to completion female-centred projects in which she becomes involved.

The concept of a history that is not fully present is also suggested in Humphreys's work through its references to the Welsh landscape and Welsh mythology. For example, in *A Toy Epic*, Michael, one of the three boys with whom the novel is concerned, becomes interested in Welsh nationalism at Penmon, the subject of a poem by T. Gwynn Jones, which, together with the poetry of Hywel ap Owain Gwynedd, about which Michael is enthusiastic, demonstrates, Wynn Thomas argues, the power of Welsh-language literature.[27] However, in Humphreys's work, allusions to history and myth should not always be taken at face value. In allying himself with the Normans, Hywel ap Owain Gwynedd did not live up to his poetry and, as such, can be seen as exemplifying a past that, in Derridean terms, has never been fully present.

T. Gwynn Jones's Welsh-language poetry is invoked frequently in Humphreys's fiction. At one level, it may be because of the crucial role he played in the revival of Welsh-language poetry after winning at the National Eisteddfod in 1902 with 'Ymadawiad Arthur' [The Departure of Arthur]. Like much of Jones's work to which Humphreys alludes, it is an important Welsh-language text in so far as it announces the possibilities of a Welsh-language-based nation. However, through its emphasis on the loss of Arthur it highlights what has not been brought to fruition. Jones's 'Argoed' is invoked in *Outside the House of Baal* in the name of the family farm and a lament for a lost culture, as Diane Green has pointed out, the central protagonist, the Reverend J. T. Miles, also repeats a key line from the poem, referring to 'Y mannau dirgel' (the secret places).[28]

While references such as these imply, as Wynn Thomas has said, the continuing cultural presence and power of the Welsh language, the content of the texts often suggests a history that has not fully unfolded. In this case, Jones's poem describes how a people in a remote area of Gaul, with their own language and culture, discover that their language is not understood by their countrymen in the cities. Rather than have their culture and language destroyed by the enemy, they reduce their own country to a wasteland and commit suicide. At one level, the poem underscores many of the themes of *Outside the House of Baal*, such as the decline in the Welsh language, the tension between rural Wales and the city, the rise of a more promiscuous and materialistic lifestyle, the conflict between religion and secularism and the philosophical issues posed by pacifism in a time of war. But, at another level, there is a sense of Jones writing a poem that is as much about what has not come about: the alternative history of Gaul that might have been written if the people of Argoed had been able to develop what was a region into a country.

Derrida's distinction between a past which has unfolded and one that has not been made fully present is particularly pertinent to Humphreys's fiction because pursuing the latter involves engaging with difference, self-division and disruption, as Derrida explains in another work, *Specters of Marx*. In fact, this text explains why Derrida's work provides such pertinent insights into Humphreys's representation of history. Derrida points out, Marx frequently thought in terms of 'spectres', 'ghosts' and' haunting'. For example, on the first page of the *Manifesto of the Communist Party*, Marx talks of communism as 'a specter [that] is haunting Europe'.[29] Thus, it is possible to see the historical themes and concerns in Humphreys's work in the way in which Derrida sees those in Marx's work, as the spectres that haunted him. As was explained in chapter 1, although Humphreys speaks and writes Welsh, which he learned as an adult, and even though he has contributed extensively to Welsh-language culture, he has always been haunted by the fact that he is more proficient in English than Welsh.

The concept of spectre is further appropriate to both Humphreys and Marx because both their concerns, to employ Derrida's words, are like a ghost in that 'a ghost never dies, it remains always to come and to come-back'.[30] There is a strong cyclical dimension, not only to Humphreys's individual novels but in his oeuvre as a whole, in which themes return in ways similar to those in which Marx's ghosts highlighted the 'untimeliness and disadjustment of the contemporary'.[31] Just as readers would find it difficult to overlook Humphreys's interest in what has never unfolded, they cannot fail to miss the way his work is haunted by ghosts and spectres on many levels. Indeed, the preoccupation with such 'presences', as we shall see in the course of this book, comes increasingly to the fore in his work.

Although present in most of Humphreys's fiction, the sense of an unfulfilled past is especially pronounced in the novels *Outside the House of Baal*, *Bonds of Attachment* and *The Shop* and the collections of short stories, *Ghosts and Strangers* and *Old People are a Problem*. Of these, *Bonds of Attachment* is a text which does not simply employ 'hauntology' but takes it as its major theme. In the novel, as explained in chapter 2, a young man, Peredur, seeks to reconcile himself with his mother, the central figure in the Land of the Living sequence, and to gain knowledge of his deceased father, the poet Cilydd More. His narrative is haunted by the past and also by the threat of a future in which he has failed to understand his father or reconcile himself with his by then deceased mother. Through his notebooks and letters, his father speaks in a voice that has not previously been fully present, with a freedom which was not possible in his public and even personal life, as evidenced in the other Land of the Living novels.

At one level, *Bonds of Attachment* is a deeply psychoanalytic text in which Peredur's first-person narrative is interwoven with, and haunted by, his father's own voice in his archived material. But the novel is one in which the son, through his own investigations and through his father's writings, retraces the history which the earlier novels recorded as they moved forwards in time. Thus, it is itself, as a text, haunted by the preceding novels in the sequence. In addition, dealing with what is inside and outside the text, it is haunted by the permeable nature of the insider/outsider boundary. Intriguingly, to any present-day reader of this novel published back in 1991, the novel is not only 'haunted' by the other novels in Land of the Living. Through Cilydd's archive of 'accounts in larger, neater exercise books', it is haunted from the future then and from the past now by the archive of Emyr Humphreys's papers in the National Library of Wales, much of which consists of large, neat exercise books.

The dialectic in Humphreys's work between the unfolding of history and a sense of 'a past which has never been present' but which continuously interrupts it gives his work a noticeable episodic structure. This episodic structure, whereby the historicity of Humphreys's work is simultaneously unfolded and disrupted, is a feature of what is described in contemporary postcolonial thinking as 'subaltern' literatures. These are written by peoples whose histories have been excluded from the official histories, in the writing of which they did not play a part.

In this regard, Humphreys's work has played an important part in reclaiming the unwritten histories of Wales. To appreciate fully the significance of this aspect of Humphreys's fiction, it is illuminating to turn to one of the foremost Marxist cultural critics, Antonio Gramsci. As subaltern, Welsh fiction, Humphreys's novels, in Gramsci's words, are 'markedly fragmented by spasmodically erupting memories, whose anachronic temporalities disrupt the historical trajectory of the characters' stories'.[32]

Thus, Humphreys's fiction takes a complex approach to history which means that, despite his interest in social, political and economic change in twentieth-century Wales, he is much more than a 'historical' writer. More so than critics have previously recognized, Humphreys's fiction is aligned with major developments in the concept of history, emphasizing the heterogeneity of history; history as a narrative involving selection, editing and emphasis; the truths of history as expressions of power; and the operation of power through cultural and institutionalized discourses. Indeed, we have said that it is possible to see Humphreys as a 'postcolonial' subaltern writer, an author from a people excluded from official histories, whose work interrupts conventional, linear histories of Wales and has the episodic qualities associated with subaltern writing. The episodic nature of Humphreys's fiction, and the way in which the 'present' and the narrative of characters' lives are constantly interrupted, are distinctive features of Humphreys's work which may be better understood through a lens provided by Derrida. The reader of Humphreys's fiction cannot but be struck by the extent to which it is haunted by the ghosts and spectres of the past and the way in which it alternates a history of twentieth-century Wales, which is alert to the heterogeneity of history and the determining nature of discourse, with what Derrida calls 'a past that has never been present'.

Thus, writing an absent 'past', Humphreys's fiction is informed by the increasing realization not only of what is distinctive in Welsh culture, history and landscape but of what has not yet been fully realized. Tony Brown and Wynn Thomas have suggested that Humphreys 'set out, by learning Welsh and steeping himself in the history and culture of the language, to see how far a born outsider could become an adoptive insider'. In the process, he aligned himself 'with the radical tradition of Welsh religious Nonconformity'.[33] However, in writing himself into Wales through the Welsh language, which he learned as an adult, and through using the English language specifically as a Welsh writer not simply as an English-language author writing about Wales, Humphreys complicates conventional binaries such as insider/outsider, Welsh/English and adoption/rejection. Analysing Wales's relationships with England, especially the pull of what Brown and Thomas call 'the magnetic, hypnotic, insinuating and seemingly insolent power of England', is important to Humphreys's fiction.[34] But the Wales/England distinction is another binary which Humphreys's work complicates. Equally important to his fiction, and equally complicated, is the European/Welsh binary. Indeed, much of Humphreys's fiction has a distinctly European dimension and, as referred to in chapter 2, draws ideas and inspiration from early twentieth-century European modernism.

PLACE AND SPACE

As observed earlier, one of the principal debates in late twentieth-century cultural criticism relating to Wales was how far the Welsh situation might be described as *colonial*. Ned Thomas recalls that, although many of the features of the Welsh condition mentioned by Anglo-Welsh critics in the 1970s and 1980s 'have much in common with colonial situations, the sharper discourse which actually *called* the Welsh situation colonial, and Anglo-Welsh a colonial literature, came from critics strongly identified with the Welsh language, such as Bobi Jones and myself'.[35] Generally speaking, only a few twentieth-century

English-language Welsh writers thought of themselves in these terms. Ned Thomas maintains: 'The truth is that there was little identification with the colonial hypothesis among late twentieth-century Anglo-Welsh writers themselves, except for R. S. Thomas, Emyr Humphreys, Harri Webb and, in one period, John Tripp, and then always in the context of language.'[36]

In regard to the colonial hypothesis, Ned Thomas is right to argue that Humphreys thought about colonialism largely in relation to language. However, Humphreys also believed that Welsh anglophone literature was stuck in a kind of colonial past, assimilating the culture of the occupying power.[37] His work displays a Janus quality: looking inwards into Welsh culture, landscape and history, but also outwards, to the impact of English upon Welsh culture and politics. But as noted earlier, it also needs to be said that Humphreys's work cannot be seen solely in terms of a Welsh/English binary. In looking outwards, as mentioned earlier, Humphreys, under the influence of Saunders Lewis, mentioned in chapter 1, looks at least as much to Europe as England, believing Wales to have an important place within a confederation of European countries.

There are themes and preoccupations in Humphreys's work which he shares with other twentieth-century Welsh anglophone writers. In general terms, these include the positive sense in which authors who write in English perceive their role in relation to Wales. Although Welsh anglophone authors write in a language which may be associated with the colonization of Wales, they often recognize the potential of the English language to articulate successfully the diversity of Wales and explore the concepts of 'Wales' and 'Welshness'; to conceive and develop an aesthetic that is more distinctly Welsh than English; to rediscover paradoxically a Welsh culture that has been distorted by, or even buried beneath, the disproportionate power of the English language in Wales; and to find the potential, within a version of English that emerged in Wales, to resist the way in which English distorts Wales and Welshness. More specifically, Humphreys's work shares with that of other English-language Welsh writers an intention to examine the emergence and decline of an industrial society; the impact of two world wars on Wales; the depopulation of rural Wales; the politicization of Welsh-language culture; the rise of a consumer, tourism and heritage-oriented society; the public acknowledgement of the ethnic diversity of Wales; and the impact of feminism, post-feminism and gender politics upon the traditional structures and communities of Wales.

Thus, at one level, Humphreys's use of English can be seen as subversive in itself, displaying what the postcolonial critic Bill Ashcroft describes as 'language variance': in Humphreys's case the grammatical/syntactical disruption of English by the Welsh language.[38] The problem with Ashcroft's concept, as Bohata, points out, is that 'to suggest that a word can signify an entire culture does raise some important questions – particularly in a country such as Wales, which has more than one language'.[39] The 'subversive' use of 'language variance' in Humphreys's work has to be seen in the context of its awareness of the complexity of the various communities in Wales which belies its essentialist aspirations, referred to earlier, and the way in which it unravels Welsh history from a variety of language, 'postcolonial' and gendered perspectives.

However, there are also themes in Humphreys's fiction which are more distinctly European to which Tony Brown and Wynn Thomas have drawn attention:

> the plight of conscience when an individual is confronted (even within the self) by the pathology of power; the totalitarian instincts in human nature and in human relationships, manifested in a myriad contexts and ways, including media control; the necessary but corrupting milieu of politics ...[40]

Thus, Humphreys brings a new agenda to Welsh writing in English and new perspectives on familiar themes. Although questions of identity dominate his work because of his own circumstances as a Welsh writer, they are located in a wider context than that in which Wales and Welshness are normally considered. But, additionally, it has to be acknowledged that the emphasis which English-language Welsh writing places on questions of identity is not unique. Erica Carter, James Donald and Judith Squires point out:

> The concern with questions of identity over recent years may at first sight seem surprising, for the consistent logic of modern social and cultural thought has been to undermine the notion of individual identity ... The logic of universalism and, more recently, modernization and globalization have sought to represent localised identities as historical, regressive characteristics, and have worked to undermine the old allegiances of place and community. But the burgeoning of identity politics, and now nationalism, reveal a clear resistance to such universalising strategies. Difference and particularity will not be washed away ...[41]

Generally speaking, Welsh writing in English, especially poetry, has been characterized by a concern with landscape and the natural environment. In an interview with Wynn Thomas, Emyr Humphreys, while accepting his interlocutor's suggestions that he sees landscape as 'the deposit of history', adds that his work is equally concerned with landscape.[42] At one level, he is concerned to raise awareness of the Welsh landscape which bears the imprint of history, often in the form of myth. However, in the same interview, he points out that, as a novelist, his primary interest is in people and landscape, a subject that is imbricated with 'the nature of the form as well as the individual'.[43]

Landscape in Humphreys's work provides the reader with a sense of what is 'real' in an observable, empirical sense but also what is symbolic. Thus, in Humphreys's fiction it provides different levels of context. *The Little Kingdom* begins with a farmer, Richard Bloyd, gazing across the Wirral from a vantage point near Rhyl. At one level, the reader is made aware, as Emyr Humphreys was throughout his childhood, of the physical proximity of England to this part of Wales as well as of the cultural, social and economic power, and hence the attraction, of England. But Bloyd's prospect, in all senses of the word, opens onto a specific landscape and, through its quarries and indus-trialism, onto modernity itself. We are made conscious of the way in which time, in a modernist sense, has a spatial dimension and as such is a discursive construction:

> It was a fine morning but still chilly. Across the water he saw the Wirral emerge from the early morning mist; become once more a solid and substantial rich-green sea-girt land, speckled with red-roofed houses. The tide was out and down the estuary the mud flats gleamed in the oblique rays of the sun like the backs of enormous slugs resting in the low water. Down below on the water's edge the colliery's gaunt cranes emerged from a pall of mist and smoke, in its small harbour a dirty steamer blew its fog-horn into the silence, and after the silence was broken the day awoke. A train raced urgently across the coastal plain, as though all consideration was over, all decisions made, and the execution of plans begun.[44]

This account of the view onto the estuary reads as a poetic preface to a drama which is about to unfold. It depicts an industrial corner of the country coming to life in a new day which seems to be an analogue of the re-emergence of nationalism in Wales. The displacement of the fog and mist creates a sense of intellectual, cultural and social clarity confirmed in the last line, 'and the execution of plans begun'. It also anticipates the idealized optimism of the central character, Owen Richards, drawn, as mentioned in chapter 1, into conflict with his uncle. Owen has some of the qualities of Julius Caesar which highlight the optimism of Owen's nationalism but also turn him into a parody of a national leader: 'You know, I've a strong feeling that there are big things going to happen soon. Very soon. It might be the match to set the whole country ablaze. It gives you an uncommon sense of power. Just a handful of people now, planning ahead' (p. 119). There is, too, a sense of the promise and hope here which, in Humphreys's ideas about the novel, discussed in chapter 2, are frequently aligned with the concept of individual, social and moral progress.

The allusion to *Julius Caesar* and the comparison of Owen to Caesar immediately casts a shadow across the optimism of the opening paragraph. Indeed, it is undermined in two respects. First, the reader might perceive from the paragraph a sense of things starting again but may also wonder why it is not expressed more directly. Secondly, the reader may well question why the novel does not take up the energy and possibility of the opening in a style that is itself more liberating.

The title *The Little Kingdom*, like most of Humphreys's titles, refers to several aspects of the novel.[45] Here, the title refers to Bloyd's property and to Wales in relation to England. But, like many of Humphreys's titles, it both underscores possible readings of the text and disrupts them. Thus, the title cannot be taken at face value. It has an ironic edge to it that highlights the precocious nature of Bloyd's ambitions, in contrast to the country's national aspirations, and emphasizes his scheming and plotting, fit to (dis)grace a Shakespeare play. At one level, Richard Bloyd's view out across the estuary brings into the text a sense of progress. But, in what Humphreys defined in 1953 as 'the Protestant novel', such progress is here linked to dilemma. Thus, after the optimism of the opening of the novel, Bloyd slips into dilemma:

> He could venture to admit to himself that the property had given him cause for anxiety. 300 acres of unproductive flats, too near the colliery for building; still too far from the seaside resort; too flat; too wet; too exposed in winter when the wind blew thin showers of sand over it. Almost 300 acres dead loss, bought admittedly for a song, but still quite profitless. He had plans for it, of course, when buying. He never bought just for the sake of buying. But the plans didn't bear examination afterwards. (pp. 5–6)

As is common in Humphreys's fiction, accounts of present dilemmas echo earlier ones. In this regard, we have suggestions of the dilemma which Bloyd faced when he purchased his property. Thus, the landscape in a new morning, suggestive of post-war optimism, new ideas and forward planning, is a backdrop for a novel that is very much concerned with choice, decision making and dilemma at the level of individuals as well as societies.

THE CHRONOTOPE

The view across the Wirral which opens *The Little Kingdom*, as we have said, is not only a vista onto modernity but modernist in the way in which it makes us aware of the spatial dimension of time and how both time and space are not innocently conceived 'realities' but the products of discourse. This modernist approach to time and space, in which each intercuts the other within a spatial reality, is important not only to the way in which Humphreys conceives the environment but thinks about narrative. His technique, as Wynn Thomas says, of arranging short scenes 'to chime, contrast, crossover and interact', is one which is especially pronounced in *Outside the House of Baal* but it informs much of his work.[46] Thomas suggests that it is a technique which Humphreys developed under the influence of modern drama, especially Brecht's work: modernist music, constructed around the exploration of consonances and dissonances; the language of form and colour in abstract art; and, as Humphreys's own manuscripts make clear, the use of filmic techniques, such as close-ups and cuts. While this may seem a ragbag of influences, the consistent underlying concern is with the way in which form makes meaning.[47]

One way of approaching Humphreys's technique of constructing his fiction through 'scenes', as we shall see in the discussion of *Outside the House of Baal* in chapter 8, is through exploring how meaning is 'moulded' by the interactions between them. Another is to focus upon the nature of the scene and the ways in which time and space interact within them, or rather configure their sense of spatial reality. In order to do so, we have to turn to the work of a Russian theorist, Mikhail Bakhtin, who used the word 'chronotope' to describes a unit of narrative configured by the interconnection of time and space. Although it is important to recognize how Humphreys's scenic structures betray the influences of modern drama, modernist art and music and film, this is only part of the story, for, in a Bakhtinian sense, his work may be described as 'chronotopic'.

Approaching Humphreys's fiction through Bakhtin's concept of the chronotope makes us aware of dimensions to his writing which do not necessarily emerge as strongly if we think of his fiction only in terms of the influences mentioned above. Bakhtin's explanation of what he called the chronotope makes us more aware of the intensity of 'scenes' as pieces of writing:

> In the literary artistic chronotope, spatial and temporal indicators are fused into one carefully thought-out, concrete whole. Time, as it were, thickens, takes on flesh, becomes artistically visible, likewise, space becomes charged and responsive to the movements of time, plot and history. This interaction of axes and fusion indicators characterizes the artistic chronotope.[48]

Bakhtin's stress on the way in which time takes on flesh and space becomes the product of the 'movements of time, plot and history' encapsulates what is at the heart of Humphreys's narrative technique. Indeed, the historicizing of space, to which Bakhtin refers in his definition of the chronotope, is one of the distinctive features of Humphreys's work. Reflecting on the significance of Bakhtin's concept of the chronotope, Deborah Mutnick points out:

> Bakhtin sought to forge in the chronotope an 'historical poetics' that could comprehend and characterize particular sociohistorical epochs and genres. By historicizing that which appears to be given – static, timeless, universal – the chronotope elucidates the dialectic of form and content, text and context, in relation to the time and space of their production and reception. In acts of reading and writing, such historical consciousness permits us to see through or between the given words of a text to the multiple, conflicting ideologies and discourses at work within it.[49]

The chronotopic dimension of Humphreys's fiction is also distinctly modernist because of the way in which it explores, like the fiction of Virginia Woolf and James Joyce, the nature not only of public but of private space. Thus, rooms are a recurring feature in Humphreys's fiction and, as in Virginia Woolf's work, provide a means by which he explores larger issues of identity and social being. The focus upon a sequence of dilemmas in Humphreys's 'Protestant' or 'dramatic' fiction, referred to in chapter 2, is concomitant with its spatial emphasis upon rooms. Humphreys brings to bear upon his representations of interiors the modernist expectation which Charles May describes as the 'essential truth or idea or image that rises above time'.[50]

In Humphreys's fiction, a chronotopic sense of space and time is used in the depiction of interiors to explore the psychology of buildings and

rooms: the extent to which rooms reflect people and ideas but also lock
people and ideas within them. In Humphreys's fiction, rooms are sites
where social realities are formed in a Bakhtinian sense by the interaction of space and time and history and location. In regard to the
chronotope, Mutnick points out:

> As such, the chronotope reveals different social points of view composing
> constituent parts of reality, which are then re-presented through language
> or other symbolic systems. In order to discern these points of view, a
> reader must intuitively, if not consciously, grasp the 'time-space' dynamic
> that underpins them ... To understand historical periods and change as
> systems of social relations, discourses and ideologies that are neither
> given nor immutable but products of complex processes is essentially what
> it means to have a historical perspective.[51]

In *The Little Kingdom*, the intersection of the lives of selected individuals within a specific place and time is subtly developed in rooms which
recur throughout the book. According to de Certeau there are two ways
of focusing upon interiors: either through the way in which interiors
organize movements or through interiors as tableaux.[52] In his fiction,
Humphreys combines both approaches through a realization that the
way in which interiors organize movements and present themselves as
tableaux to the viewer is rooted in social and cultural discourses by which
gender and socio-economic relations are determined. Humphreys's
work engages with space not simply as a material but as a discursive
reality. This may be illustrated by the section which opens part two of *The
Little Kingdom* in which Geraint, a reflective but somewhat self-obsessed
artist friend of Owen, is left alone in the manse while the minister, Rhys
and Rhiannon attend the funeral of Owen's cousin.

The opening sentence of part two of *The Little Kingdom* draws attention to the intersection of time and space: 'The brass-faced clock in the
hall struck four' (p. 59). The clock signifies the objective measurement
of time upon which modernity depends but it is also one of the objects
in the house which create a particular temporal/spatial ambience with
which Geraint interacts throughout this section. The brass face of the
clock signifies a particular period in the manse's history, along with
Anglican respectability and a sense of permanence. The blue curtains at
the window, the 'rather old-fashioned armchairs' and the piano create
for Geraint a sense that 'life here is a calm fugue' (p. 61).

Thus, for Geraint, the manse is outside of time. But his interaction
with the temporal spatial units that are the rooms is very different

from that of those who live there. While he thinks of himself in a 'calm fugue', outside of time, Rhiannon has to cope with her father who loses track of time and whose study evokes not only his authority as head of the house and the family but, increasingly, withdrawal from the world into himself. She has to keep a watchful eye on him, as he forgets to eat his food; has to put out his clean collar on his dressing table; and even has to remember to put his scarf around his neck and his small Bible in his pocket. How Geraint sees her in this role is determined by the picture of life at the manse which he creates in his own mind. As he enjoys watching her, she is for him a 'young goddess' (p. 62).

Geraint's idealization of Rhiannon is expressed through, and is a product of, how he sees her in relation to the house's objects: 'Across the landing in her own room (I have seen it. I slipped in and took in its appearance greedily: the neat single bed, the photographs, the book-shelf, the wardrobe containing her clothes) she lies sleeping' (p. 61). He does not simply see the room but interprets it. For him, it conveys a sense of order and virginity (through the image of 'the neat single bed') and defines Rhiannon in terms of the family (through the photographs displayed in her room). The bookshelf represents her intellect but, as part of the well-ordered room, there is no sense that her books contain material that will be disruptive of anything. In the downstairs room, Geraint most admires her when she is performing the role of dutiful daughter:

> He longed to see her at tea, bending over the silver teapot, her long fingers clutching the handle, her black hair hanging from her bent head, her smile as she handed him his cup, her laughter; to see her walking across the room, her slim, lithe athletic figure. A young goddess. (p. 62)

He does not recognize what for Bakhtin is at the heart of historicized reading. He does not 'understand historical periods and change as systems of social relations, discourses and ideologies that are neither given nor immutable but products of complex processes'. Thus, it is impossible to lift Rhiannon out of her historical context and the way in which to a large extent that historical context, itself defined by particular ideologies which in turn determine social relations, has determined and defined her. The role that Rhiannon occupies at the manse is one which has been socially constructed – as the daughter her role is to become the surrogate mother/wife in the household – and one which limits her opportunities to fulfil her own desires, profession-ally or even sexually. The text interrupts Geraint's unhistoricized and idealized view of Rhiannon when the reader is told: 'She would have liked to have been a doctor' (p. 62). This one line raises a number of issues which encourage the reader to take a more critical view of the manse at this point. Rhiannon, like many women of her generation and class, is confined by family circumstances and familial expectations which are also society's expectations of women.

The tendency to see the natural environment as a significant theme in Welsh literature in English, referred to earlier, has led to its concern with interior spaces, in the work of writers such as Humphreys, being overlooked. This focus upon landscape has been matched by an emphasis upon 'place' as another of the literature's defining characteristics. What again distinguishes Humphreys's work is his concern not only with place, which is in many respects the focus of the traditional English novel, but space. This is no simple matter of semantics. A focus upon place tends to be inward looking, concerned with the way in which identities have been developed within, and in a dialectic relationship with, particular geo-social boundaries. But space requires a more outward-looking perspective and, in regard to modernism, a greater awareness of the possibilities for plural personal and social identities.

Through Geraint's memories, the chronotope of the manse, to re-employ Bakhtin's term, is contrasted in *The Little Kingdom* with two other chronotopes. The first memory occurs when Rhiannon is getting ready to go to the funeral of Owen's cousin. Watching Rhiannon takes Geraint back in time to his childhood:

> The gesture of stretching the glove over outspread fingers was uncomfortably familiar. He could see his mother's fingers working into her glove as she stood in the hall of the house in Mydrin Avenue, one foot raised, balanced on a high heel.
> 'I shan't be long. Be a good boy.'
> 'Can I come?'
> 'No. You stay at home and be a good boy.'
> 'But I want to come with you.'
> Later in the evening, drawing off the gloves and throwing her hat on to the chintz-covered divan:
> 'I'm dead beat.'
> But after supper she is brighter; the front-door bell rings and three gentlemen enter, jocular, masterful, vulgarly courteous, to play cards.

The key phrase in this passage is 'uncomfortably familiar' since it raises questions about Geraint's feelings for Rhiannon. It is not necessarily that Geraint subconsciously sees in Rhiannon a substitute for his mother but that in his creation of her as a 'goddess' he is conjuring an idealized view of the kind of woman that his mother was not, suggested by the men who visit her of an evening. The sudden convergence of the two chronotopes in his mind brings to the fore anxieties in his relationship with his mother, subtly suggested in the text by the way in which she does not allow him to come with her. Of course, while the others are going to the funeral, he is left alone in the manse as he is in this recollection.

> I wish I could see them coming up the road together now, all three in black. Strange to see Rhiannon in black. Let them return. I am tired of being alone. Let them return and bring this room to life again with their voices …Without their presence the house is like an instrument without a player, a dumb symbol longing for expression … (p. 59)

The sudden recollection of his mother at this point may not have been triggered simply by the gloves, but by a new view of Rhiannon. His mother's gloves, together with the reference to his mother's high heels and the jocular, vulgar courteousness of the men who have come to play cards, sexualizes her. By implication, Rhiannon is sexualized, too.

The second memory that interrupts Geraint's imagining of the manse as a 'calm fugue' is his recollection of the time he and Rhiannon have spent two days previously at the Pleasure Palace. Here Humphreys is undoubtedly drawing upon his own childhood experiences of Rhyl. As mentioned in chapter 2, he has recalled that Rhyl 'was unquestionably the place to be. Sodom and Gomorrah had somehow been sanitised and an infusion of English and raucous laughter had been essential to the process.'[53] Unlike Humphreys as a child, Geraint feels uncomfortable with its sense of carnival, possibly because of his memories of the men who visited his mother:

> Down the further end of the dingy shooting range, rubber balls – blue, red, yellow, green – bounced on water spouts, trembling targets, and behind them was hung an old music-hall black curtain: Lord Falldiray on his tweed-covered belly in the painted grass, aiming at a fat, innocent cock pheasant; beside him turning away, Lady Millyfilly (1890 ed.), her hand over her Pre-Raphaelite eyes. Aim. Fire. Miss. The merry balls bouncing calmly, undisturbed. (pp. 63–4)

The Pleasure Beach, like the manse, is a temporal spatial event to which Geraint's reactions are dependent upon the interaction between

himself and his surroundings. But it opens up for Geraint and others
the possibilities of more complex and plural identities, referred to
earlier. The Pleasure Beach mocks the 'respectability' of the manse,
exemplified in the proprietor, 'an aged cockney, with a dyed q.p. and
wax moustache, a bow tie and silver watch-chain' (p. 64). There is a
fleshiness which is repressed in the manse, signified by the 'broad-
mouthed woman with doughy cheeks and peroxided hair, her huge
breast covered by a yellow jumper' (ibid.).

It is in the temporal spatial reality of the Pleasure Beach that Geraint
first tries to tell Rhiannon how he feels about her. However, she discour-
ages him from doing so and it is later, on a walk through the wood
after having tea at Gwern Farm, that Geraint kisses her. Gwern Farm
is another example of how the novel progresses through a series of
chronotopes. The farm appeals to the refined side of Geraint because
Gwilym Blethyn is a farmer-poet: 'Highly cultured in the traditional
way, a good talker, well read, polite and courteous; a good-humoured
wit in the silent laughter that shook his broad shoulders' (p. 66). He
is a keeper of the 'Taliesin tradition', mentioned earlier, and of Welsh-
language Wales. His family participates in the Eisteddfod where his
daughter has already won four firsts.

However, at the Blethyn farm, there is also a reminder of the animalistic, physical side of life celebrated at the Pleasure Beach: 'Hens
scratching in the yard; the old sow pushing her tough snout under the
paddock gate' (ibid.). Once again, Geraint seems inseparable from
the temporal spatial complexities of his environment which he does
not always recognize. His lovemaking with Rhiannon brings out the
animalistic side of him which surprises and disturbs him:

> When Geraint took her in his arms, in the shadow of an oak tree, she
> responded to his kisses and pressed herself against him. For a moment he
> was startled, then her excitement communicated itself sharply to him. His
> love-making was rough and unprepared. He was repulsed by his growing
> desire, as though he were destroying, destroying; sacrilegious destruction
> in a blind drunken ecstasy of the blood. The world was falling, falling,
> torn down by the ravenous woman of all the ages, the mother of us all; out
> of this turbulent primitive womb we fell. (p. 67)

Their lovemaking does not bring, as it does in many of D. H. Lawrence's
novels, release and initiation into a fulfilling sexual reality that has until
now been beyond them. It plunges Geraint into a dilemma in which
he has to resolve what for him are conflicts between his 'cultured' self

and his animalistic desires. The wood is not simply a physical but a symbolic reality. Traditionally, a wood represents the location for what 'civilized' culture represses and denies. Initially, Geraint is startled by the fact that Rhiannon, who up until now has been reticent and protective of her private space, presses herself against him. Together, he and Rhiannon step into what is 'forbidden'. But, for Geraint, the wood is also suggestive of his subconscious. The rhythm and the language convey the abandonment of lovemaking, but the emphasis upon 'destroying', 'falling' and 'the blind drunken ecstasy of blood' suggests ways in which Nonconformity has conditioned his attitude towards sex.

The way in which Eve is represented, as 'the ravenous woman of all the ages' and 'the turbulent primitive womb', conveys his difficulty with Rhiannon as a passionate, full-blooded woman and may even suggest a conflation in his own mind of Rhiannon with his mother. But the wood is a different chronotope from the manse where Rhiannon is perceived and 'framed' in very different ways. On their return to the manse, Geraint counters the dilemma into which he was pitched in the wood by configuring Rhiannon in his mind as his wife in 'a house on the hill': 'It was a pleasurable, literal kind of day-dreaming. His new post at the school, his income, the books they would buy for his library, alone in their house, either side of the fire' (ibid.). Moreover, at this point in the narrative, Rhiannon's bedroom at the manse becomes a very different chronotope from the one Geraint imagined when he peeped into her room. Her lovemaking with Geraint plunges her into a dilemma in which she is caught emotionally between Geraint and Owen: 'She threw herself on the bed and began to cry. It was a relief. Her bare shoulders shook as she sobbed, and her long hair spread over the cool hands she pressed against her face' (p. 69).

PROGRESS AND INTERRUPTION

The chronotope in Humphreys's fiction is often linked, as is the idea of 'progress', to 'uncertainty', which makes for an environment that is itself shrouded in uncertainty and can even be quite menacing. Although, with the exception of the modernist novels, *A Man's Estate*, *A Toy Epic* and *Outside the House of Baal*, Humphreys's fiction often has the kind of linearity that is associated with the nineteenth-century realist novel, the linearity at the level of the story is frequently interrupted by chronotopes involving dilemmas and thresholds that have to be crossed.

Marked as they are by uncertainty and enigma, the chronotopic episodes that constitute Humphreys's fiction create texts which generally demand decyphering. This is certainly the case in the way in which the natural environment is threaded throughout *A Toy Epic*, discussed in chapter 7, a novella narrated through three male voices. In many respects, as will be discussed in detail in chapter 7, the text is based on Virginia Woolf's *The Waves* (1931). Woolf's novel consists of six soliloquies, each in a different voice, and nine italicized pastoral interludes, describing the diurnal progress of the sun. *A Toy Epic* does not have any pastoral interludes but in the alternating voices includes numerous references to the diurnal passage of the sun and also of the seasons. Albie notices how: 'The September sunlight streams through the high churchlike window across rows of singing faces.'[54] Iorwerth remembers:

> Spring, summer, autumn, winter, smartly, slowly, slowly, fast, I walk a mile and a half to school alongside hedges and across fields. Picking the flowers according to the season, a handful of primroses for school, a handful of bluebells home, harebells for Miss Roberts, violets for Mam ... (p. 22)

The relationship of each of them to the environment is chronotopic. Whilst Iorwerth, who lives on a farm, relates to the hedges and the seasons, Albie, who lives in a council house and who walks to school through built up streets, has a different sense of space:

> Passing the little gates and little gardens, the housewives barearmed in doorways, passing the shops and the fish and chip saloon not open yet, I see Mr Pike, the fruiterer, carrying cauliflowers out in round wicker baskets. He speaks to my mother ... I see the assistant brushing in the gloom of the shop towards the daylight door sawdust and bits of paper; I see the newsagent and the tobacconist pulling out the placards for the day, which I linger to look at as I believe he wants me to do. But my mother tugs at my arm. (p. 23)

In both cases, there is a different sense of time and different senses of innocence. For Iowerth, there is a greater awareness of the seasons, while for Albie, time is measured more by the day. Each of them is associated at this moment in time and space with the feminine: Iorweth picks flowers for his female teachers and his mother and Albie is taken to school by his mother. As in Geraint's case in *A Little Kingdom*, they do not understand the systems of social processes at work in their temporal spatial realities. The teachers in the lower schools are mainly women because that was the destiny for most unmarried women teachers while for other women their destiny was to become housewives or secretaries. The references to the newsagent and the tobacconist anticipate a different kind of balance that is to come into their lives as they get older, one that is more masculine.

Although *A Toy Epic* is composed of chronotopes, there is a sense throughout the novel of the 1930s as a complex, single chronotope in which the diurnal progress of the sun, as in Woolf's novel, assumes increasing significance. At the end of the novel, in September 1939, after the boys have been involved in an accident with one of the local buses and Michael has been injured, Iorwerth is left brooding:

> From a hilltop, I have seen night advance from the east across the face of the earth like the shadow of God, neutralizing contours, making hill and valley, town and country one. When it reaches the western sea its movement quickens and finally blots out the horizon. The earth, bearing continents and seas, shows another hemisphere the sun, and another the outer darkness. (p. 121)

This passage has multi-significance for the novel as a whole and brings together its different tropes. At one level, it alludes to the coming war and to the way in which fascism is blotting out the map of Europe and, at another, it invokes, as does the conclusion of *The Waves*, the world moving in the abyss of space. There is a sense of our separate selves being dissolved in the darkness of space and time. The insignificance of human history in the infinite abysses of space was a common theme in popular science in the 1930s, promoted through James Jeans's BBC broadcasts and subsequent publications on astronomy and cosmology. There is also a sense in this final paragraph of the way in which the novel alternately examines the different sides of the 1930s and the lives and minds of the protagonists.

Thus, the references to the natural environment in *A Toy Epic* reflect the significance of the novel's title and the kind of distinction that Bakhtin drew between what he called the 'provincial novel' and what he labelled the 'broad or deep realistic emblematic' novel.[55] In the former, he argued that 'meaning does not exceed the sociohistorical limitations inherent in the images' and that these texts have a 'cyclicity' which 'makes itself felt with particular force'.[56] In its focus upon north-east Wales and its attention to the cycle of the seasons, Humphreys's novel might have become a 'provincial' text. But its meanings, evident in the cryptic representation of the environments, transcend the 'sociohistorical limitations' of the 1930s. However, what makes Bakhtin's distinction so apposite to Humphreys's fiction is the notion of 'progress' in the text. For Bakhtin, the provincial novel was characterized not only by a forceful sense of 'cyclicity' but by a cyclicity that weakened 'growth and the perpetual renewal of life' and was 'separated from the progressive forces of history'. The cyclicity of the provincial novel, in Bakhtin's view, 'made life a senseless running-in-place at one historical point'.[57]

The chronotopic environment in *A Toy Epic*, as in *The Little Kingdom*, is cultural and linguistic. There is a greater sense than in the pastoral interludes in *The Waves*, although these, too, contain cryptic social analysis, of the interconnection of the landscape with social and cultural change. Albie's parents have moved from the rural valleys to a seaside resort. In doing so they have moved from a Welsh-language culture to one that is distinctly anglicized and, in street names and public gardens, not only commemorates English history but marks a subaltern position. Albie lives in Prince Edward Street which mirrors the way in which Rhyl in the 1930s increasingly emulated English culture. In 1937, the Coronation Gardens were created within which was included a memorial garden and playing fields for King George V, who died on 20 January 1936. In 1948, an oak tree was planted to mark the birth of Prince Charles who was to become the English-appointed prince of Wales.

Both *The Little Kingdom* and *A Toy Epic* share uncertainty about the recovery of Welsh-language Wales, at least as far as the north-east is concerned. In Humphreys's novel, there is a vivid depiction of how education has not only prioritized English but led to a prioritization of English in the minds of the community. Michael's mother encourages him to use English rather than Welsh, to such an extent that in Mr Jones's class, in which the pupils are expected to memorize the Creed in Welsh, he refuses to admit that he can read Welsh and in church revels in reading the Psalms in his superior English. This leads to the other children's ostracising him: 'For this the others disliked me and kept me out of their games and conversation' (p. 25). But the divisions which the anglicization of north-east Wales creates are complex, for while the Welsh-language families resent those like Michael they also envy them. Iorwerth, typifying those Welsh-language speakers who forsake the Welsh education system for the spires of England, is proud to tell his mother that he has been moved to the front of the class to sit next to Michael and adds, in a comment indicative of how achievement had come increasingly to be measured against an English yardstick, that, unlike Michael, he got all his sums right.

THE MOTOR VEHICLE, MOVEMENT AND SPACE

The 1930s is a chronotope in *A Toy Epic* that brings together the global mechanization of everyday life in the interwar years with the onset of war. The fact that Albie's father is a bus driver is emblematic not only of a population shift from the rural valleys to the urbanized and anglicized coast but of how mechanized transport was changing the social environment, allowing people access to different communities and to different parts of Wales. Science and technology grabbed the minds of the young in the 1930s. Throughout the text, there are references to small changes and interests which, as the title of the novel suggests, are indicators of much bigger movements and discoveries. When Albie goes to sleep at night, it is with 'a meccano world shifting' in his brain 'like the rails at Chester station' and he dreams of 'shining rails to run through new worlds' (p. 38). But Iorwerth, living in a different chronotope, dreams of himself on the farm. During the week Iorwerth spends at Albie's home, there is an occasion when Albie buys a paper on wireless and Iorwerth buys *The Boys' Own Paper*. When they go to the pictures they watch a serial which, typifying the new fascination with speed, ends with 'a motor-car flying over a precipice' (p. 56).

In both *The Little Kingdom* and *A Toy Epic*, the Pleasure Beach is a significant image, not surprisingly as it was one of the key features of the north-east Wales seaside. In *A Toy Epic*, too, it is a site for personal dilemma. In this case, for Iorwerth who is pulled away from a group of Seaside Evangelists when the Pleasure ground opens: 'I saw for a moment the picture in my aunt's parlour — "the broad and narrow way", and my heart was torn with a painful dissension. In the end I followed Albie' (ibid.). The dilemma is also a societal dilemma, for what the boys taste (literally and metaphorically) on a small and personal level is also society's more widespread consumption and desire for instant gratification: 'My stomach was full, and my eyes still ached. The fumes of petrol from the streets seemed to invade my senses. I felt sick. I vomited in the lavatory. Albie was kind, and I was hot with shame' (p. 57).

Evident in its depiction of landscape and interiors, the modernist environment in Humphreys's fiction is a product not of stasis but of movement. It is not surprising that transport should be a recurring subject in the novels and short fiction. Not only is the bus an important signifier in *A Toy Epic* (recalling how for Humphreys as a child the bus took over from the train 'as the symbol of incontestable progress')[58] but, as discussed in chapter 9, the motorbike is an important feature in *The Best of Friends* and the motor car a significant symbol in that novel and *Salt of the Earth*. There are two ways in which Humphreys develops what is essentially a modernist concern with modes of transport. As I shall explore in chapter 9, *Open Secrets* develops the interweaving in *A Toy Epic* of mechanization and warfare. But, throughout his work, there is a recurring interest, as in Virginia Woolf's fiction, with people in or on a particular mode of transport. Amy and Cilydd seated on a motorbike in *The Best of Friends* is reminiscent of a man and a woman sharing a taxi in Virginia Woolf's *A Room of One's Own*, prompting, as Leena Kore Schröder has pointed out with regard to Woolf's couple, 'a more general speculation on such destructive polarities as male and female, mind and body, self and other'.[59] Humphreys's novels are distinctly modernist in their recognition of how the car 'became one of the key modes for comprehending the very nature of corporeal existence'.[60] As Schröder says:

> The car has a profound effect upon body-image for the essential reason that it throws the body into movement … Constantly propelled forward in time and space, the body is passive in so far as it cannot do anything but sit, yet it exists in a state of pure mobility. In the way that active and passive as discrete subject positions are collapsed by the experience of the automotive self, so does the very language of describing speed twist space into time: *miles per hour*.[61]

In *Salt of the Earth*, Cilydd More and the village mole-catcher, when the former returns to his family home, discuss Cilydd's four tourer in terms of its speed, which serves as a metaphor for the way in which the speed of change is turning observable space into time. One of the intriguing aspects of the first novels in the Land of the Living sequence, discussed in chapter 9, is the way in which a traditional preoccupation with 'place' is superseded by a greater awareness of time or, more explicitly, to adapt Schröder's phrase, the speed of change twists space into time.

Not surprisingly, a group of people travelling together in a car is a recurring feature of twentieth-century fiction. Schröder, thinking of modernist writing, argues that it is through movement that 'the nature of our embodiment is revealed to us more tellingly than in stasis' and that our bodies exist in 'a dynamic relation with time and space'.[62] What is again a distinctly modernist aspect of Humphreys's fiction is the way in which he uses it to trigger wider discussions about change. There is an example of this towards the end of *Outside the House of Baal,* discussed in chapter 8. The two elderly key protagonists in the novel, J.T. and Kate, are driven with the elderly Dan Lew by Aunt Gwyneth along a narrow road leading to Bodafon Hall. At one point, the rhythm of the car imposes silence upon them, emphasizing that embodiment which, in a novel concerned with ageing, is a key theme. The way in which time is changed by speed into space is evident when Gwyneth has to swerve and brake to avoid an approaching driver who blows his horn angrily as she passes. But the house itself, now a training place for boxers, and the mound of stones fallen from the collapsing high wall, also renders time as space and the physical as time. This collapsing of time and space into one another is a trigger for memories which twist the present into the past as Dan Llew remembers how his sister Kate nearly married Archie Griffiths of Bodafon Hall.

The journey along the narrow road to Bodafon Hall in *Outside the House of Baal* may be compared to the journey near the beginning of *Salt of the Earth,* which Cilydd takes with his wife Enid, his grand-mother and Amy Parry, whose life the Land of the Living sequence, of which this novel is a part, traces. In this episode, the make of car, which also features in the previous novel, *The Best of Friends,* when Cilydd, Amy and Enid are students, is actually named: an Austin Tourer. This not only specifically associates Cilydd's car, unlike Gwyneth's, with speed and the 'new', but signals more of a concern with space, as opposed to place, than in the Bodafon Hall episode. Cilydd's car, together with his Homburg hat, suggests his outwardness while the way in which his grandmother is named as 'Mrs Lloyd of Glanrafon Stores' associates her with the inwardness and specificity of place. Her attitude within the car is based on her status and authority within the family: she scrutinizes 'his performance with an uncompromising gaze that did nothing to improve it'.[63] Here, as in the Bronafon episode, the movement of the car emphasizes embodiment. In the latter, the rhythm lulls the elderly into sleep but here the physical experience is more youthful and aggressive: 'The car jumped forward as he changed gear awkwardly …'[64] In both episodes, however, the movement in the car seems to emphasize people's relationship with time. Like Bronafon, Cae Golau turns time into space: 'suburban-looking looking laurels' replace the hedgerows, monkey-puzzle trees have been planted in the lawns, and an 'ill-proportioned portico' breaks up the front elevation (p. 13).

These two episodes featuring a car reflect the respective emphasis in each of the novels on embodiment in relation to the outwardness of space and the more inward perspective associated with place. The same might be said of the car journey which Eddie Lloyd takes with his friend Father Alfonso in *The Shop*, discussed in chapter 12. That novella has a much more developed interest in space as opposed to place and the boundary between these concepts is tested when the central character temporarily gives up her life as a freelance photographer in Europe to redevelop what was once her family's general stores in a rural north Wales village:

> He had a fast car and he insisted I should see the prehistoric stone circle at Almendras, so off we went. The roads were narrow and he drove like a maniac and reassured me by saying that dashing around the world was some compensation for being celibate. We bumped and stumped our way through olive groves.[65]

This passage is much more obviously about speed than the other episodes discussed, but the way in which speed twists time into space stands in contradistinction to the way in which time is turned into space at the Almendras stone circle. The speed with which Alfonso is able to move from the present into the prehistoric past is an index of the way in which the novel itself switches between different temporal perspectives. *The Shop* develops the suggestion present in the much earlier novels, *A Toy Epic* and *Salt of the Earth*, that speed, what is called here 'dashing around the world', will become a defining characteristic of modern life. Whereas in *Salt of the Earth* the Austin Tourer is associated with possibilities, chiming with the optimism of the period, Alfonso's driving suggests a mismatch between hectic global lifestyles and the traditions of the past.

4

Bodies in Time:
Psychoanalytic Contours

The part played by the unconscious is important to many of the novels discussed in detail in subsequent chapters in this book. These include *A Man's Estate*, *Outside the House of Baal*, the Land of the Living sequence, *Unconditional Surrender*, *The Gift of a Daughter*, the collection of short stories *Ghosts and Strangers* and one of Humphreys's most recent novels, *The Shop*.

In chapter 3, we suggested that Humphreys's fiction interweaves historiography, based on recognition of the heterogeneity of history, history as narrative and the way power and knowledge are linked in historical discourse, with a sense, in the French philosopher Derrida's terms, of a past that is not fully present. Derrida's concept is particularly relevant to Wales which, due to its domination by England and the English language, may be regarded as a nation that has always been present yet absent at the same time. But, in Humphreys's work, there is another past that is not always fully present and which is related to the personal in his fiction: the sense that personal narratives have a dimension that is not immediately evident to the observer and not always evident to individuals themselves.

In his first novel, *The Little Kingdom*, discussed in the previous chapter, the young, ambitious academic Owen Richards seeks power through a corrupt and morally bankrupt form of nationalist politics in northeast Wales. He finds himself caught in a moral dilemma that is partly of his own making, through his ruthless pursuit of power. However, as the novel unveils the motivation behind his life, it becomes clear that he is a victim of forces which he barely understands: the bullying he endured in the private school to which his father sent him, his deep-seated need for self-protection and his hatred of his father. In *The Voice of a Stranger*, Riccardo Forli plots against the wife of his friend and commander. However, his apparent conscious behaviour is determined by the psychological effects that the war has had upon him. In *A Man's Estate*, which will be discussed in chapters 5 and 6, one of the central female protagonists, Ada Cwm, is haunted by the fact that she is illegitimate, which determines the nature of her behaviour and her assertive sexuality in ways which she herself only partly understands. Amy Parry, the central figure in Land of the Living, which will be discussed in chapter 9, is an orphan, brought up by her aunt and uncle, whose life is similarly haunted by her childhood, in the form of the poverty and Nonconformity of her upbringing. *Open Secrets*, the third novel in the chronology of Land of the Living, opens with a dream which betrays the extent to which Cilydd More is similarly haunted by his experiences of war, discussed in chapter 9. In *The Shop*, the subject of chapter 12, both principal characters, at a conscious and an unconscious level, are the products of their childhoods and their relationships with a dominant parent: in Eddie Lloyd's case his father and in Bethan Mair Nichol's case her biological mother and her stepmother.

'HAUNTOLOGY' AND THE PSYCHE: *OUTSIDE THE HOUSE OF BAAL*

As discussed in the previous chapter, the French philosopher and cultural critic Jacques Derrida argued that the present is always inhabited by the ghosts and spectres of the past. The spectres are not simply the recorded history but the unfulfilled potential of the past as it is operative on an individual, familial, local or even national level. Since, as discussed in chapter 3, this is true not only of individuals but of the Welsh nation in Humphreys's fiction, what Derrida calls 'hauntology' is a deeply embedded component of his texts. One of the consequences of this, as mentioned briefly in chapter 2, is a tension, or a potential tension, in his work between its primary concern with social and moral progress and the way in which the haunting of the present by the past manifests itself in the individual unconscious. But, within the modernist framework of Humphreys's work, these two elements are not as contradictory as they might at first appear.

Richard Sheppard points out that there is a parallel between modernist theological thought, which we might associate with Humphreys's emphasis upon rational, social and moral progress, and psychoanalysis, which questions the extent to which any individual is aware of his or her motivations. According to Sheppard, modernist theological and psychoanalytical thought each seeks to place the embodiment of human identity within a wider scheme of things. Within this broad framework, both 'God' and the unconscious in modernist thinking have the capacity to interrupt and disrupt self-motivated, rational being. Sheppard maintains that 'God is said to irrupt cataclysmically into the human world' to make humans more aware of their 'place in the scheme of things' and paradoxically to make them 'anew'. This may be compared with the way in which human beings, according to psychoanalysis, are 'governed by and [are] at the mercy of irrational, primitive powers'.[1]

Characters in whom modernist theological thought and psychoanalytic ideas are brought together, such as the minister J. T. Miles in *Outside the House of Baal*, recur in Humphreys's fiction. Often, the view that such characters have of themselves, as will be shown in chapter 7, is disrupted by being shocked into an awareness of how individuals are subject to forces, social and psychoanalytic, beyond their immediate control. These characters are also often haunted by their pasts.

Humphreys's interest in such characters does not mean that we should read his work as if there is a distinction between literature and psychoanalysis which suggests that the latter is a superior form of critical knowledge. As Sue Vice points out: 'It is now often agreed among writers on psychoanalytic literary practice that the relation between criticism and text should be not masterful but mutual.'[2] Thus, psychoanalytic criticism of Humphreys's work must acknowledge that the primary focus is not the psychoanalytic but the way in which the text explores subjects that may be illuminated by psychoanalytic perspectives.

However, the nature of the relationship between the text as a literary creation and the psychoanalytic is complex and has been the subject of debate. In some criticism of literature, psychoanalysis seems to be regarded as superior to literary critical analysis in the sense of being more insightful. Drawing on the work of Shoshana Felman, Vice maintains that contemporary literary practice involves not simply reversing 'the usual priority of psychoanalytic discourse over literary', as mentioned above, but 'a deconstruction of the whole relation' between the literary and the psychoanalytic.[3] At the heart of this wider deconstruction of the relation between the literary and the psychoanalytic is a concept of *implication*, or suggestion. This refers to the way in which psychoanalytic themes and issues are often suggested rather than boldly stated in a literary text. The notion that the psychoanalytical discussion of a text is often presented cryptically in Humphreys's fiction, with the exception of the boldly psychoanalytic novel *The Gift of a Daughter*, which will be considered in chapter 10, is particularly applicable to the way in which his work explores human behaviour and motivation from a psychoanalytic perspective.

Humphreys's employment of the concept of 'implication', that is the way in which the text suggests rather than insists upon the relevance of the unconscious, can be aligned with his interest in the way Beckett's work illuminates the dark, mysterious places of the self, mentioned in chapter 2, and his use of what one reviewer of Virginia Woolf's work labelled 'substitution-symbols', to which I also referred in chapter 2. Humphreys's interest in implying a psychoanalytic aspect to character, without prioritizing it, is commensurate with the diverse range of approaches he adopts to the subject of human motivation.

However, 'implication' – the way in which the psychoanalytic themes are incorporated subtly into a literary text – does have a bearing on the way in which the reader responds to the work. Vice, quoting Felman, explains: 'Instead of applying to the text a scientific knowledge, the interpreter will allow the rather different activity of *implication* to take place, in which each of the two domains will find itself "enlightened, informed, but also affected, displaced, by the other".'[4] The concept of not 'applying to the text a scientific knowledge' means that the reader does not bring a plethora of predetermined psychoanalytic theories to the text but responds to the way the text presents human behaviour, suggesting that there is something beyond what is observed that is complex, almost mysterious. Thus, Humphreys's fiction may be seen as operating on a more subtle level than simply offering crude psychoanalytic explanations of human motivation. Bringing Vice's and Felman's concept of psychoanalytic reading to bear on Humphreys's work highlights the extent to which his fiction is suggestive in ways that have not been fully recognized. Through the psychoanalytic issues and themes with which his fiction is concerned, Humphreys illuminates, complicates or even renders disturbing human motivation and behaviour.

Notes that Humphreys made at the back of one of the exercise
books in which he began writing *Outside the House of Baal* suggest
that initially he thought of the novel in terms of two frameworks, one
Marxist and the other Freudian:

> The world's end supernova
> Marx – society – economy
> Freud – sex- violence[5]

On the same page is the following additional reference to Freud, sexuality and violence:

> Thea – Brophy
> Sexuality & violence
> Her reading of Freud[6]

These notes clearly betray Humphrey's interest in the way in which
Freud, through key works such as *Studies on Hysteria* (1895), *The
Interpretation of Dreams* (1900) and *Three Essays on the Theory of
Sexuality* (1905), configured the modernist individual, driven as
much by unconscious desires and forces as conscious, rational decision making. But the way in which the notes are written suggest that
Humphreys's thinking, although inspired by Freud, had moved away
from Freud's type of psychoanalytic literary criticism which, as Vice
says, 'attempts to "analyze" the text's author or its characters', to one
more closely aligned to the more subtle presentation of psychoanalytic
issues and themes which Vice, drawing on Felman, calls 'implication'.[7]

Further notes which Humphreys made in his *Outside the House
of Baal* notebooks suggest that, through the kind of psychoanalytic
literary activity which Vice describes, he was interested in exploring
the origins of violence and how they may find expression in sexual
behaviour:

> the seeds of – sexual – B. Brophy's – ...
> will
> violence[8]

Moreover, his notes indicate that at the time he was contemplating a
parallel Marxist and Freudian framework for the book, he was also
considering a narrative based around fear:

> FEAR – of castration
>   of death
>   of starvation
>   of the unfamiliar

of someone taking what you have got
or of craving more [9]

It is clear that Humphreys was thinking of writing a novel that was far more Freudian in some of its concepts than the novel which he eventually published, but also one based upon 'implication' as opposed to Freud's cruder model. The extent to which Humphreys thought in terms which anticipate contemporary psychoanalytic literary criticism is evident in the published novel, though less so than Humphreys had at one time envisaged.

However, before considering how 'implication' is employed in Humphrey's fiction through more detailed discussion of *Outside the House of Baal*, it needs to be pointed out that Humphreys's approach to reading also anticipates contemporary psychoanalytic literary criticism in its interest in the relationship between language and meaning. In Humphreys's fiction, the psychoanalytic, as in contemporary literary criticism, is never singular or definitive. As Vice says of contemporary practice, referring to Barbara Johnson's work, 'every "framing" commentary … leaves itself open to further analysis'.[10]

There is evidence in the notebooks that Humphreys added episodes and details to *Outside the House of Baal* to suggest, by 'implication', further ideas about human motivation and call into question rational models of human behaviour. The text at these points brings together modernist theological and psychoanalytic thinking around, as Sheppard maintains, a disrupting awareness of the 'primitive', referring to the way in which it has not been totally displaced by so-called sophisticated, civilized behaviour. Through this disrupting awareness, the text encourages the reader to question interpretative, and especially 'rational', frameworks for human behaviour. At a broader level, these episodes and details added later to the text encourage the reader to recognize, as Barbara Johnson points out, that every framework invites further analysis. Thus, reading Humphreys's fiction through psychoanalytic frameworks provided by Vice and Johnson suggests that Humphreys's fiction is more thought provoking about human behaviour than has often been recognized.

One of the later additions to *Outside the House of Baal*, according to Humphreys's notebooks, is the account of Lydia, the wife of the central protagonist J.T., and her friend Jenny Leyshon with Lydia's children, Vernon and Ronnie, which opens chapter 19 of the published novel. In the first draft, the chapter was to begin: 'Wynne Banister walked

backwards from the stairs.'[11] In this new scene, inserted into the manuscript, Ronnie is sitting with his finger in his nose, a childish act of
self-comfort, reading *The Boy's Magazine*. It is a magazine that with
its pink cover inculcates boys into a type of masculinity that is aligned
with institutionalized violence, war and empire. It betrays Humphreys's
interest, pursued in *A Toy Epic*, in the discourses of masculinity and
war:

> On the pink cover of the magazine there was a picture of British Tommies
> with fixed bayonets leaping down into a German trench. At the bottom of
> the page German soldiers in their sinister steel helmets cringed and their
> shaded faces crumpled with abject fear.[12]

By 'implication', the Tommies are associated with rifles and bayonets, two phallic objects with which men, as soldiers, are traditionally
associated more than are women, and which, as in the dream of one
of the central protagonists in the later novel *Open Secrets*, which will
be discussed in chapter 9, define masculinity in terms of war and
violence. According to the unpublished manuscript, the phrase 'with
fixed bayonets' was an even later addition.[13] It is a phrase which not
only emphasizes the violence of the event which is being described but
plants the seed for a further level of commentary through introducing
a phallic element.

At one level, Humphreys, as a pacifist, is pointing out the way in
which the discourses of war, boyhood and masculinity in popular children's magazines are interwoven and, connected with each other in this
way, influence the consciousnesses of their young readers. At another
level, the graphic images and the language do not simply articulate the
interconnection of these discourses. They imply that the subconscious
and language work in similar fashion.

In this regard, the psychoanalytic critic Jacques Lacan's work is illuminating. Unlike Freud, Lacan's work emphasizes that children enter
a world of language which constitutes what in European linguistics is
referred to as the 'Symbolic Order'. Entering the Symbolic Order, girls
and boys, Lacan argues, see their gender identities determined and
defined differently. Sue Vice, developing her argument that contemporary psychoanalytic literary criticism is based on the activity of
'implication', or suggestion, as we have said, draws on Lacan's concept
of a 'Symbolic Order', constituted by systems of language, particularly his notion that language and the subconscious work in similar
ways along the two axes of metaphor and metonymy.[14]

Thus, the above passage from *Outside the House of Baal* may be read metonymically; that is to say, by emphasizing the accumulation of referents: the rifle (implied), the fixed bayonet, the trench and the steel helmets. But it also functions metaphorically in the sense that one signifier is substituted for another. Thus, the act of impalement suggests sexual thrusting and the trench suggests not only the mutilated German body but the violated sexual body and the unconscious primitive into which the Tommies are leaping.

Ostensibly, the passage seems to be structured around binaries: Tommy/German soldier; bayonet/steel helmet; and bravery/fear. These binaries signify, by 'implication' rather than overt statement, how the Tommy is glorified for his bravery in an act of liberation and the German soldier is condemned as a cowardly oppressor. But there is also an absent or denied presence here. This act in war, and of war, may be seen, certainly in the eyes of a pacifist, as involving the magnification of cruelty and callousness. The unconscious surfaces to interrupt and distract from so-called acts of bravery in war and links them to primitive instincts which are part of a complex power/dominance/sex paradigm.

The account of Ronnie reading is juxtaposed with a description of Vernon drawing:

> A draught from the back door had started a black patch on the glowing mantle of the Aladdin lamp and a tongue of yellow flame was edging through it, but Jenny was too intent on Vernon's pencil to notice. He was drawing a castle, the walls of which ran so close to the edges of his paper that the pencilled men who covered the battlements were very tiny, and the flags on top of the towers at each end were squashed squares with crossed lines on them. Across the bottom of the sheet arrows flew through the air in broken arches, and two lumps with four lines sticking out of the larger of them represented a dead horse.[15]

Although the drawing is described in the third person, the reader is conscious that it is being studied carefully by Jenny. Reading the passage through the activity which Felman described as 'implication', her female presence may be seen as providing a further level of interpretation. Jenny's interest in a child producing such an obviously violent picture implies also her interest, as a woman, in how war magnifies the violence associated with masculinity which has oppressed many women in their own homes for centuries.

The black patch on the ceiling is ominous, suggesting violence and death which may be hanging over the boy together with the darkness of the unconscious itself. The entry of the flame into the black patch would appear to imply the entry of violence into the boy's unconscious. Whereas, at one level, the magazine which Ronnie is reading magnifies the British soldier and invests him with an individual grandeur, the men in Vernon's drawing are dwarfed by the castle which, in terms of the span of history, may be standing long after they are dead and forgotten.

The arrows flying through the air suggest the shells of modern warfare. Read metaphorically, Vernon's drawing highlights the slaughter of war, the insignificance of the individual within the massed ranks, and the abjection of death, encapsulated in his configuration of the dead horse as 'two lumps with four lines sticking out of the larger of them' which bears little resemblance to the living animal. The drawing presents the reader, and Jenny who is observing Vernon, with war, violence and death without compensatory symbolism, such as the glorification of death in battle. But it also implies the darkness within Vernon's own unconscious in which Jenny may be interested. When she first enters the house where one boy is reading a war comic and the other is making a drawing of a castle under siege, she tells Lydia about J.T.'s sermon, the subject of which has a direct bearing on Vernon's drawing and Ronnie's comic: 'Against the madness of war. And the childishness of it. And the pointlessness. It settles nothing. One war sows the seeds of another' (p. 252).

The new opening to the chapter is structured in such a way as to encourage the reader to consider how each activity in the drawing room is enlightened, informed and affected, if not displaced, by the other. The relationship between the various parts of the room highlights how the two children are together but also separate from each other. This is underscored by the different ways in which the two boys relate to Jenny. Noticing that Lydia has fallen asleep, Jenny indicates to Ronnie not to make a sound: 'The boy looked down and continued reading without returning her smile' (p. 279). Ronnie's reaction implies that the seeds of the kind of cruelty and callousness which is a part of the heroism about which he is reading have already been sown and that this will affect his relationships with others, especially women. Vernon, on the other hand, does not show the same contempt toward Jenny. He returns her smile, but, disturbingly, he then begins to 'draw deep lines into the paper' (ibid.). Thus, the section inserted in chapter 9 of *Outside the House of Baal* emphasizes how suggestions of the unconscious in Humphreys's work tend to remain as *suggestions*. But these suggestions are often such that, as in the accounts of Ronnie's reading and Vernon's drawing, they trouble not only the reader but the process of reading itself. Ronnie's magazine and Vernon's drawing are open to different interpretations and because different readers can move the boundaries of the text at such points, through the different knowledge and insights that they bring to it, there are questions raised about the nature of the literary text in general.

Barbara Johnson points out, in a discussion of Edgar Allan Poe's 'The Purloined Letter', that, although Derrida argued that a text is 'literary' because 'it remains inside certain definite borders', the 'frame', as she calls it, can never be as definite as Derrida maintains.[16] In other words, the boundary which defines the literary text as distinct, say, from the world to which it refers and the body of knowledge upon which it draws as well as between the text and what the reader brings to the text is always 'permeable'.[17]

Episodes, or chronotopes, in Humphreys's fiction, such as those considered above from *Outside the House of Baal*, that call into question the frame of the text, also question our understanding of the boundary between the conscious and the unconscious. *Outside the House of Baal* is especially challenging in this regard because, as will be shown in chapter 8, the text is structured through a complex inter-mixing of themes, tropes and signifiers. Thus, the reader may recall the earlier episode in the novel when Jenny visited Lydia while she was breastfeeding. In this earlier episode, it is notable that Lydia returns Jenny's smile while in the later passage Vernon returns Jenny's smile. It would seem as if these references to smiles being returned to Jenny were placed in the respective passages to complicate the reader's interpretation of them and to call into question the framework or boundary of each. The earlier of the two passages we are comparing observes that Lydia 'turned slightly so that her pale breast was not so fully exposed to Jenny's eager gaze' (p. 279). That Humphreys thought of this as a key sentence in the passage is evident from the fact that, according to the manuscript, he continued to make later additions – 'pale' and 'so fully' – to make it more vivid.[18] Although Lydia tries to turn her breast from Jenny, Jenny makes a point of commenting upon them – 'Wonderful nipples you've got' – and contrasting Lydia with her sister who 'had a lovely figure' but nipples so small that she could not breast feed (p. 253).

Such is the permeability of the 'frame' around these episodes, of the borders which the reader might cross to compare them with other episodes in the novel, and of the boundary between the conscious and unconscious, that they are open to numerous interpretations. Indeed, there are a number of possible unconscious forces at work, including Jenny's possible interest in Lydia; her own designs on J.T.; and the fact that her own marriage is without children.

There are further possible readings if we think of the boundary between the literary text and psychoanalytic ideas as permeable. Jenny's interest in Lydia's breasts is not the only aspect of this episode which invites the reader to think about what is *implied* in the text. Lydia's son bites her nipple causing her pain. The theory that the origins of a child's personality lie in its experiences at the mother's breast was a feature of psychoanalysis in the first half of the twentieth century associated with psychoanalysts such as Melanie Klein and Joan Rivière. For this school of thought, the child's experience of the mother's breasts was both positive, identified with the breast which the mother offers her child, and negative, referring to the breast which is withdrawn from the child. These experiences were perceived as important in how a child was later to develop. But equally important as an indicator of the child's future personality was the way in which it took its mother's breasts in its mouth. The infliction of pain, as Lydia experiences here, was seen as an index of a future bullying or even violent personality.[19] Thus, according to mid-twentieth-century theory, the infant in turn seeks, finds, obtains and loses the mother's breast, alternating between contentment and distress. Through the echoes which interconnect these two episodes in *Outside the House of Baal*, Humphreys seems to be implying the possibility of a link between a child's experiences at the breast and its later relationship to violence and pain. Again, according to the manuscript, the line which stresses the experience of Lydia's baby son at the breast – 'His mouth pulled at it greedily' (p. 253) – was a later insertion, reflecting Humphreys's continued interest in making this idea explicit.[20]

PSYCHOANALYSIS AND SEXUAL IDENTITY

Anthony Giddens has argued that 'the encounter between feminism and psychoanalytical theory has proved to be the source of important and original contributions to psychological and social theory' and particularly in relation to the 'fragmentary and contradictory character of sexual identity'.[21] This is an area which is explored in Humphreys's fiction, by 'implication', to use the term discussed earlier, especially in regard to same sex-relationships.

Relationships between women is a subject which is often rendered cryptically in Humphreys's novels, relying more on implication than overt statement, as in the above episode involving Jenny and Lydia. A further example is the suggestion that is made in the later novel *The Best of Friends* regarding the relationship between the central protagonist Amy Parry and her prospective employer, Miss Eirwen. The episode in which Amy and Miss Eirwen meet for the first time is focused on tension between the two women, arising from the ambiguity of Miss Eirwen's interest in Amy. Before Miss Eirwen makes herself known to Amy, the latter sees her watching her from 'an open window'. In the manuscript, an additional detail that the window is on the second floor is added, creating the impression that Amy is being spied on.[22] In the first manuscript version, the complexity of Miss Eirwen is strongly suggested:

> She was wearing a painting smock. She raised her hand to wave shyly at Amy to indicate she would come on over to meet her. Amy waited in the large entrance hall until Miss Eirwen appeared wiping her hands with a rag one leg dragging slightly as she made an effort to walk briskly towards her. Her pale face was strained with a nervous determination to be friendly.[23]

This passage is then deleted and replaced by the eventually published version in which the emphasis is on what Miss Eirwen observes and less on her physical appearance:

> Amy smiled back politely and made for the front door which was wide open. She stood on the broad mat and considered her wet Wellingtons. She pulled them off and walked into the hall in her bare feet quieter than if she had been entering some exclusive archiepiscopal chapel.[24]

Amy is shown around the house by Leo Galt and the deleted description of Miss Eirwen is reintroduced, with very minor amendments, when Amy is shown to her studio. When she is shown to the sitting room, her bare feet appear to attract Miss Eirwen's attention, as Lydia's breasts appeared to interest Jenny: 'She had begun to stare at Amy's feet' (p. 335). Like Jenny actually mentioning Lydia's breasts, Miss Eirwen comments upon Amy's feet: 'Really I shouldn't keep you standing in your bare feet' (ibid.). The manuscript version is amended by the insertion of a sentence, only slightly modified in the final published version, that underscores Amy's nervousness: 'Amy's chair creaked as she moved it' (ibid.). Eventually, Amy becomes more relaxed in Miss Eirwen's company and this is suggested through reference once again to her feet: 'Amy stretched out a bare foot towards the fire. Her cheeks were flushed with the warmth of the room and her eyes sparkled' (p. 336). Within the context of Miss Eirwen's interest in Amy, her bare feet are possibly a metonym for her naked body.

Although Miss Eirwen is happy to have Amy in her employment, Amy eventually decides to give up the post to preserve her independence. Throughout the Land of the Living sequence, Amy attracts psychoanalytic interest because she is an orphan who starts out from a poor background but ends up a lady of the manor. She is a figure that traditional, conservative Wales, represented in *Open Secrets* by her husband's family, finds difficult to accept, other than as Miss Parry, the county secondary schoolteacher that she becomes in *Salt of the Earth*. When she reveals to them that she is an orphan, Cilydd's grandmother, Mrs Lloyd, is shocked that she knows little of her father other than that he was killed in the First World War:

> 'I used to have a photograph of him in a white suit,' she said. 'I think it was a white suit. It was a bit of a secret really. My Uncle Lucas couldn't stand the sight of him.'
> She laughed, but Mrs Lloyd could not accept such disturbing information as subject of laughter.
> 'I used to hide the photo under my mattress when I was a little girl. What happened was, after my mother died, my father went off to sing with Carl Rosa on a tour of Canada.' [25]

The absence of Amy's father means that her husband's family feel that they cannot get to know her because they do not know her lineage. In a close-knit community and culture which values genealogy, in the form of the 'cofiant' (or biographical memoir), for example, the orphan is a liminal figure. But Amy is also a boundary figure in that she is the stepmother to her best friend's child who is, in turn, a permanent signifier in the present of the especially close and enigmatic relationship between Amy and Enid as women.

Humphreys's later fiction develops psychoanalytic themes which are present to some extent in his early work. This conveys the impression that his later work deals with subjects towards which his fiction had been moving all along. One of these subjects is the relationship between father and daughter, explored in *Unconditional Surrender*, which will be considered in chapter 10, and in the most explicitly psychoanalytic of his novels, *The Gift of a Daughter*, which is also examined in more detail in that chapter. In the first of these novels, set, as mentioned earlier, in the final years of the Second World War, the daughter of a rector of a rural north Wales parish disrupts the way in which her father thinks about her through her relationship with two suitors, a local conscientious objector and a German prisoner of war. The conscious way in which the rector thinks about his daughter is brought into tension with unconscious forces within his psyche of which he is not fully aware. The contrast between the conscious and the unconscious in the father-and-daughter relationship, which is treated subtly in this novel, is brought to the fore in *The Gift of a Daughter*. Both novels involve a father who becomes estranged from his daughter because she becomes involved with a lover of whom he disapproves. However, in *The Gift of a Daughter*, the daughter's death not only causes her father to think about his relationship with her but brings to the fore his unconscious feelings for her. These emerge through a relationship which he develops with a young woman in Tuscany who reminds him of her.

The second psychoanalytic theme which dominates Humphreys's later fiction, but which occurs in a more embryonic form in his early work, is the extent to which people, including those who enjoy the most intimate relationships, can ever really know each other. While it is not suggested that Humphreys has ever read the work of contemporary British psychoanalytic critic Jacqueline Rose, he shares her concern with what mourning can tell us about our relationship with others.[26] It is a theme to which we will return in subsequent chapters and it pervades Dylan Thomas's *Under Milk Wood*. In that text which Humphreys is assumed to have known well, the community, mainly of women, elderly men and children, reflects the kind of communities which existed during the Second World War, permeated as they were by a sense in which everyone was a stranger to each other. Much of Humphreys's fiction, especially *Outside the House of Baal*, is concerned with this difficulty of really knowing another person. But what is a secondary theme in the earlier work is the principal focus of his short-story collections *Ghosts and Strangers* and *Old People are a Problem*, and of his twenty-first-century novel *The Shop*. These texts are discussed in relation to this theme in part two.

5

Women, Feminism and
Post-feminism

As we have observed, Emyr Humphreys's novels were written over a period of about half a century and in their content span the twentieth century from before the First World War to the present day. Thus, they cover different periods in the recent history of feminism and place women within a variety of cultural contexts. The development of feminism per se is not in itself a major theme in Humphreys's work. However, in his fiction there is a recurring interest in independent, and radical, women and also in women who do not fulfil their potential because of social and cultural barriers. If one were to summarize the 'feminism' of Humphreys's fiction three features, at least, would need to be identified: its concern with the social, cultural and political advancement of women and how to reconcile this with independence and fulfilment in their private and personal lives; the novels' pursuit of the diversity, complexity and even contradictoriness of female identity as distinct from the tendency, in the 1970s and 1980s, to essentialize or simplify female experience; and their exploration of the tensions between the historical and social forces that determine female identity and individuals' capacity to invent and reinvent themselves in gender terms. Moreover, in Humphreys's recent writings, an assertive female presence provides a vehicle for examining a female identity that seems somehow beyond 'feminism'.

PERFORMATIVITY, GENDER AND DESIRE

Humphreys's representation of complex and contradictory female characters across a range of historical and cultural contexts takes us to the heart of his thinking about gender which is anticipated even in his fiction of the 1950s, 1960s and 1970s, and is best discussed through late twentieth-century critical ideas on gender and sexuality. The first of Humphreys's representations of radical, independent women is the illegitimate daughter of the local MP for a north-east Wales community, Ada Cwm, in *A Man's Estate*, a novel that is set in the early twentieth century and is discussed in chapter 6. As mentioned in chapter 2, *A Man's Estate* is one of Humphreys's earliest modernist novels which was influenced by the work of the American, Nobel Prize-winning novelist William Faulkner. Indeed, one of the influences upon Ada Cwm may have been Faulkner's character, Temple Drake, an independently minded and sexually 'fast' university student in Faulkner's *Sanctuary*. She is one of a number of sexually active women who populate Humphreys's fiction including Dilys and Frida in *A Toy Epic*, Polly in *The Gift* and Peredur's girlfriend in the Land of the Living sequence. However, as will be shown in chapter 6, Ada Cwm is a figure who also betrays the influence of the illegitimate character in Elizabethan theatre. In the 1940s and 1950s, as we have seen in regard to *The Little Kingdom*, discussed in chapter 2, Humphreys's work was substantially influenced by Shakespeare.

Ada Cwm is more sexually independent than even some of Humphreys's subsequent women characters, some of whom, such as Amy in Land of the Living and Judith in *The Anchor Tree*, use sex as she does to manipulate men for their own advantage. Although Humphreys's early novels include women who take lovers outside their regular relationships, such as Rhiannon in *The Little Kingdom* and Lucy in *A Change of Heart*, female characters do not have a strong voice in *A Toy Epic*, much of which, as explained in chapter 2, was actually written before *A Man's Estate* although it was published subsequently. But in *A Man's Estate*, women's sexuality, perceived as dangerous and shameful, is part of a duality which does not always bother Humphreys's male characters, with the exception of Michael, and certain types of loose women. Although Michael begins to feel guilty in *A Toy Epic* for having sex with Dilys, his friend's girlfriend, Humphreys's fiction generally presents men and promiscuous women as accepting of casual sex (as, indeed, is the case with Dilys who has

a number of sexual relationships) or, in the case of women, as being
sexually dangerous.

In its general representation of female sexuality, however,
Humphreys's fiction anticipates some late twentieth-century thinking
about the nature of female gender and sexuality. Thus, although *A
Man's Estate* is concerned with the first half of the twentieth century,
it also explores ideas which are generally associated with the end of the
century.

Of the late twentieth-century ideas about gender identity and
sexuality that are anticipated in *A Man's Estate*, the most important is the concern with gender identity as 'performance'. Thirty
years after Humphreys's novel was published, this is a familiar and
much theorized concept, principally associated with the feminist
cultural critic Judith Butler who has argued that 'gender is performa-
tively produced'.[1] In other words, gender is not simply the product of
biological determinism or cultural forces. It is at least partly produced
by a 'performance' which everyone undertakes in order to assume a
gendered identity. This element of performance, through which a
gendered subject is created, allows women to assume conscious roles,
sometimes mimicking and/or mocking what society and culture
expects of them as women. Thus, as is discussed more fully in chapter
6, performativity enables women, such as Ada Cwm, to resist, and
even mock through mimicry, what male-dominated society demands
of them. Indeed, the mocking female presence and/or voice is a recurring feature in Emyr Humphreys's work from *A Man's Estate* through
to his later fiction, such as *The Shop*.

The basic concept of female gender as performativity, as Butler
defined it, is anticipated in Ada's perception of her own ability to
assume roles. At one point, when she is having sex with Dick, a member
of the Elis family which refuses to acknowledge her as an illegitimate
daughter of Felix Elis, she muses:

> He could do anything to me. I was his slave and being his slave was the
> only happiness in my heart. A happiness I had the sense to cover. I tried
> to appear a quiet sensible girl, anxious to get on, studious, polite, hard-
> working, so as to hide the laughter in my heart that shouted my love and
> my enslavement through the moments when I gazed with silent concen-
> tration at Trallwm, the maths Master, in the decorous sixth-form room.[2]

In this passage, the performative element in gender identity is reflected
in Ada's consciousness that women assume roles to meet the male
gaze: 'I *tried to appear* a quiet sensible girl ...'

However, although it anticipates late twentieth-century ideas, the above passage also reflects early twentieth-century thinking. While Butler theorized the concept of gender as performance, it is an idea that has its origins in the 1920s and informs the work of modernist writers such as Virginia Woolf, with whose fiction, as mentioned earlier, Humphreys was familiar. In fact, Ada Cwm reflects further ideas about sex and desire from this period. Catherine Belsey points out that 'Love is a Victorian value. The nineteenth century supposed that the problem was repression: desire released was therefore desire fulfilled.'[3] Ada's juxtaposition of 'my love and my enslavement' reflects the way in which nineteenth-century 'feminist' thinking influenced early twentieth-century thought. But the early twentieth-century, through the influence of Freud, prised 'apart desire and love'.[4] This inevitably resulted in a schism in thinking about sexuality, summarized by Belsey, which is reflected in *A Man's Estate*. Belsey maintains: 'There is a metaphysics of romance, of love as presence, licensing, legitimating and authorizing sexual pleasure. And there is another metaphysics of the body, of nature as presence, as absolute, as outside culture.'[5]

Thus, at one level, *A Man's Estate* reflects the boundary position of early twentieth-century writing, between nineteenth-century ideas about love and repression and the separation of desire and love which characterized early twentieth-century psychoanalysis. But, at another level, it betrays a later strand of thought, which feminist cultural critics such as Butler sought to theorize long after *A Man's Estate* was written. Again, it has been summarized by Belsey who argues that it is possible that 'love, desire, the body are all meanings. As meanings they are conditions of our experience; and at the same time, as meanings they are culturally produced and historically limited.'[6]

More rounded female characters than Ada Cwm populate Humphreys's later novel *Outside the House of Baal* which was written in the 1960s, a period which is generally perceived as the beginning of what critics associate with what is called 'second-wave' feminism. The term 'second wave' was coined by Marsha Lear to refer to the increased feminist activity of the 1960s. At the time *Outside the House of Baal* was written, 1960s feminism was characterized by a particular emphasis which emerged in that decade. Contemporary feminists maintain:

> The slogan 'the personal is political' sums up the way in which second-wave feminism did not just strive to extend the range of social opportunities open to women, but also, through intervention within the spheres of reproduction, sexuality and cultural representation to change their domestic and private lives.[7]

CONTEMPORARY AND CONTEMPORANEOUS PERSPECTIVES

The principal female characters in *Outside the House of Baal* are the sisters Kate and Lydia, discussed in chapter 8. Although what was happening in terms of feminism in the 1960s does not explicitly enter the novel, it is clear that the way in which the novel depicts the changes in the conditions for women from the 1920s onwards has been influenced by Humphreys's experiences, writing during the 1960s. Humphreys himself has observed: 'All historical writing is an extension of a point of view, which is itself fixed in its own present.'[8] Post-1960s feminism is evident in the extent to which the novel, through the life histories of Kate and Lydia, emphasizes the rights of women in their private relationships as well as in their public lives.

In many respects, Lydia and Kate both represent different perspectives on the first half of the twentieth century. Lydia rebels against the oppressive Nonconformity in which she grew up and, in the early stage of her relationship with her future husband, demonstrates an awareness of herself and of her sexual needs which recalls D. H. Lawrence's fiction. Indeed, the episode where, to her sister's horror, she takes her mother's picture apart, convinced that there is a secret image of her early lover hidden behind it, is emblematic of her awareness of suppressed discussion of women's desires and experiences. Her radical behaviour and views stand contrast with those of her sister. Kate is an example of those women who remained at home to take their mothers' place when they died and, following their fathers' deaths, found themselves with few opportunities to obtain their ideal husbands. Indeed, it is clear from the novel that despite the achievement of women's rights, many women in the first half of the twentieth century found it difficult to survive as single, independent women. In Kate's case, things are made more complex by the loss of her eye, suggesting self-maiming and sexual castration. This happened in an accident when she was a young woman and attracted to J.T., but realized that Lydia and he were attracted to each other sexually.

The tension in the representation of independent women and feminism in *Outside the House of Baal*, arising from the way in which the novel elides perspectives from different historical periods, occurs throughout Humphreys's work. One of the reasons for this is that while his novels, especially those in the Land of the Living sequence, span periods of modern history, they are also philosophical works, serving as vehicles for the debates in which Humphreys was engaged at the time of writing. The early novels, such as *A Man's Estate*, reflect Humphreys's interest at the time of composition in how female behaviour gives expression to the performance element in gender identity. In his later work, he shifts the emphasis from female behaviour as an expression of gender and sexual identity to the way in which gender is constituted by behaviour. This is evident from a comparison of the scene from *A Man's Estate*, discussed earlier, in which Dick and Ada make love, and the scene in the later novel, *The Best of Friends*, in which Amy and Val Gwyn make love for the first time.

Stephen Knight describes Val Gwyn in *The Best of Friends* as 'romantically handsome, deeply nationalist, with a special yearning for the beautiful Amy', which makes him sound, not unfairly, like the mysterious romance lover transferred to nationalist Wales.[9] But, in making love to Gwyn, Amy is assertive and in control: 'Lie on me'; 'I'm not made of glass'; and 'I won't break'.[10] Here, the short, almost terse commands, do not simply express Amy's sense of herself as a woman. Her gender identity is constituted through what she says and her lovemaking with Val does not simply express but shapes her desires for him. The type of lovemaking in which she engages, and the way it constitutes her identity as a woman, echoes non-sexual scenes in the novel, in which Amy's feminism is configured in her behaviour. In Humphreys's work, the need for women to assert themselves and assume a 'performative' role in order to find sexual satisfaction and be taken seriously as lovers is mirrored in the public life where they similarly have to work against preconceptions of the female. In seeking Amy's support for his working-class socialism, Val's friend Pen Lewis addresses her: 'Well it's your lucky day, girlie.'[11] The word 'girlie' is not only patronizing, suggesting that Amy is intellectually and politically 'fragile', but reflects how Welsh socialism failed to liberate Welsh women.

This is not to suggest, however, that either Amy or Ada are idealized representations of independent women or even female characters with whom either their author or the reader would wish to identify. Knight comments that 'Humphreys does not deal in unexamined simplicities'.[12] Amy is a complex and somewhat contradictory character. While her husband in *Open Secrets* uses the family property to 'protect' conscientious objectors, Amy becomes involved in the war and, as a Welsh socialist, as Knight points out, becomes concerned about the damage he is doing to her public reputation.[13] She becomes an increasingly less sympathetic protagonist as the Land of the Living saga progresses because her contradictions become even more startling. In *Open Secrets*, Amy the Welsh socialist is pro-investiture and even plans to involve Brangor Hall in what Knight calls 'this confirmation of colonial continuity'.[14] Knight shrewdly suggests that we should look on Amy 'as a symbol of the people of Wales who, during the 1920s and 1930s, did face bravely the major mystifying challenges, in both the north and the south'.[15] However, it is possible to go further and suggest that she encapsulates the contradictions, particularly around nationalism, identity and independence, which pervaded much of Wales in the mid and late twentieth century.

Indeed, one of the key themes in *Outside the House of Baal* and the collection of short stories *Natives*, published three years later, is the way in which men oppress women. A theme in two stories from this collection is the betrayal of women by men. 'Mel's Secret Love' in *Natives* is concerned with a female employee having an affair with her male boss that has to be kept secret. The affair has to be concealed, from Mel's perspective, because of the conservative attitude towards sex outside of marriage in the era in which the story is set and, from the man's perspective, so that he can protect his reputation and marriage. However, the relationship with which Mel is involved is typical of extramarital affairs in which married men take advantage of women because they have no intention of leaving their wives and families. Although written in the third person, the story's narrative voice sympathizes with Mel and underscores her loneliness and the lack of prospects for her in the situation.

As a collection of stories, *Natives* depicts the way in which personal relationships in the 1960s were often situated on the cusp of traditional ways of thinking, which were restrictive for women, and new cultural attitudes, which ostensibly offered more opportunities for them. Whether the 1960s privileged female rather than male sexuality is a moot point and is the subject of the story 'The Suspect'. On the surface, the marriage depicted in this story, which will be discussed in more detail in chapter 11, might be described as 'modern', in so far as a husband and wife agree to continue living together while she has an affair with the unmarried optician in the town. However, whilst she initially believes that she has found someone who really loves her, it turns out that she is not the only woman with whom he is having a relationship and that he may even be a rapist.

FIRST-, SECOND- AND THIRD-WAVE FEMINISM

As mentioned at the outset of this chapter, Humphreys's concern
with gender and sexual identity is matched in his work with interest
in the social and cultural forces that determine, and have configured,
female identity across diverse social and cultural contexts. This area of
concern in his work is evident in the texts discussed above in regard to
gender and sexuality: through the struggles and experiences of Amy
and the more politically principled Enid in Land of the Living and,
in *A Man's Estate*, not only through Ada but her half-sister Hannah,
who wished to become a doctor but was prevented from doing so by
the social and familial expectations placed upon her. The compromise
which she is forced to make, working in a pharmacy, epitomizes the
disadvantaged position of women generally at this time, and subsequently, and the way in which few women were able to fulfil themselves
professionally. This aspect of Humphreys's fiction will be explored in
the readings of select texts in part two of this book. However, within
this wider discussion of the critical frameworks in which Humphreys's
work may be placed, it is important to acknowledge the different ways
in which feminism itself has been configured and reconfigured, not
without a great deal of debate and disagreement, over recent decades.

Indeed, Humphreys's novels set in the first half of the twentieth
century make an especial contribution to our understanding of
feminism in twentieth-century Britain and, most particularly, Wales.
Elizabeth Meehan has observed:

> It is commonplace now to see feminism in Britain as arising in the 1960s,
> flourishing in the 1970s and achieving a clutch of legislative victories, then
> dying in the 1980s under the assault of the New Right. This underesti-
> mates what was going on before the 1960s ...[16]

First-wave feminism is generally seen as the 'first concerted movement
working for the reform of women's social and legal inequalities in the
nineteenth century'.[17] Thus, the term is generally accepted as referring to the way in which women's movements responded to specific
injustices and is perceived as including rights for married and divorced
women, such as property and child custody rights, the opening of
educational opportunities for woman in secondary and higher education, and opportunities for women to enter the professions.

The division of feminism into periods, such as first, second and
third waves, is not unproblematic and Humphreys's novels suggest that

first-wave feminism, being primarily concerned with women's rights and the social injustices affecting women, extends from the nineteenth century to well into the twentieth century. In this regard, Land of the Living, which spans the first half of the twentieth century, is especially significant. The dilemma/dissident narrative, which as argued in chapter 2 was the distinct mode of fiction that Humphreys developed, proved a particularly appropriate vehicle for giving voice to women's political consciousness and expression to debates about their role in society.

This type of political feminism is explored within historical contexts throughout Land of the Living, through the principal female protagonist Amy Parry and, in the earlier novels, through her close friend, the politically committed Enid Prydderch. The early novels from the sequence make a particular contribution to our understanding of first-wave feminism in a Welsh context. Martin Pugh has pointed out that 'by the 1930s the optimistic spirit of reconstruction engendered in 1917–1918 had largely evaporated' and the 1930s 'fostered a climate rather hostile to feminists, which was due, fundamentally, to the pervading sense of shrinking economic opportunities'.[18] It is this transition in feminist opportunities from the end of the war, from the 1920s to the 1930s, which Humphreys explores in *The Best of Friends* and *Salt of the Earth*. *The Best of Friends* is concerned with Amy Parry and her school friend Enid Prydderch going to university in Wales in the 1920s. The novel explores the complexity of the situations in which the young women find themselves and the way in which they become more politicized, from not only a feminist but a nationalist and a socialist perspective. An episode from *The Best of Friends* which explores the involvement of women in political protest in early twentieth-century Wales depicts a demonstration over Sunday golf. The protest at the golf links by the Lord's Day Observance Society brings together university students and a variety of church groups. Amy, who steps forward to confront the golfers, finds herself up against an English-speaking, privileged, professional, male power base which fills her as much with frustration as rage. Very different is the response of her college friend Mabli who undertakes a silent, obstructionist protest on the golf course. Indeed, she and Amy represent two faces of protest in the 1920s and 1930s: silent, passive resistance and assertive, violent action. In undertaking the latter, Amy presents a face of feminism which disturbs even her supporters in the conservative Welsh community.

The contrast that is drawn between Amy and Mabli at the golf links epitomizes wider expectations about female behaviour: 'Mabli could be openly commended for playing the passive and reasonably mute part of a female martyr to the church cause. But this young woman was something else: vehement, aggressive, dangerously disobedient and undemure.'[19] The language employed here reflects the views of the ministers, and of much of the community. Mabli's mute protest is contrasted with the way in which Amy screams in the face of Major Lightfoot, who leads and epitomizes the patriarchal privilege associated with the golf club, and rouses the crowd to anger. Despite being a protestor, Mabli ironically exhibits the passivity which was expected of women. On the other hand, Amy, who displays qualities of the male protestor, is criticized not simply for her anger but for being 'undemure', that is 'unfeminine'. There is a fine line between the patronizing attitude of Lightfoot and the conservative view of women which is held by members of the community who appear to support Amy. Her smashing of the clubhouse window seems to signify the breaking of the glass ceiling of what is acceptable in this Nonconformist region of Wales in the 1920s

Although the focus in the golf-links episode in *The Best of Friends* is upon Amy, there is interest, too, in the way in which Major Lightfoot's confrontation with her produces unexpected reactions from the protestors. Once again, the text stands at the boundary between contemporaneous ideas about gender identity and notions that became more prevalent at the end of the century. The way in which the novel represents the different types of female protest in the 1920s and 1930s is indicative of its historical dimension, but the examination of how patriarchal attitudes and discourses produce unpredicted responses reflects late twentieth-century thinking about the relationship between colonizing or patriarchal discourses and the sometimes unforeseen verbal and/or physical violence to which they give rise. Thus, Lightfoot did not expect the kind of rhetoric Amy turns on him: 'These people are foreigners. They've taken our country and they want to impose their will on every inch of it!' (p. 210). Amy's speech introduces a colonial paradigm into the protest while Lightfoot's words and actions – 'You'll hear from me again, young woman' (p. 213) – underscores the patriarchal motif in the text.

The unanticipated consequences of dominant discourses are used here to critique the Symbolic Order of which the golf club is a part. The uncertainty in the link between intention and discourse, which is explored here, is a key subject in late twentieth-century, feminist theory. Contemporary feminist theorists, such as Judith Butler, have overturned ideas about a stable causal link between the discourse of the patriarchal oppressor and the female victim. Butler, thinking primarily about patriarchy, has coined the term '*promising ambivalence*' to refer to the breakdown in this chain.[20] The word 'promising' emphasizes how women can, and should, take advantage of the way dominant discourses are often undone by what they did not anticipate. Thus, Lightfoot is taken by surprise by Amy, whose speech takes advantage of the unpredictable, and in Butler's word the 'ambivalent', consequences of Lightfoot's discourse. However, Humphreys's work is distinct from the later theoretical, feminist writings in the way in which it places Amy in a dilemma which she did not foresee any more than Lightfoot foresaw the consequences of his actions and his patriarchal speech: 'She would like to have been a prophetess but she was losing control of her voice. She was sinking in her own weakness, groping for sympathy and support, blinded with salt tears of frustration' (p. 211).

Humphreys's perspective on Welsh women as embodied in the character of Amy Parry cannot be seen as a reflection of the status of women generally in Wales at this time. At one level, his work, echoing at times *Young Wales*, a vehicle for the Home Rule movement, explores the role that liberated women might play in constructing a new and independent Wales. But, while the cause of female emancipation is linked to an independent Wales, as Bohata suggests was the case in *Young Wales*,[21] the cause itself is downplayed in terms of many of the practical barriers facing women at the time, such as the marriage bar facing women teachers which was not abolished until the Education Act of 1944, in favour of exploring competing nationalist and feminist ideologies. While there are aspects of Humphreys's work which may be read through a postcolonial perspective, as suggested in chapter 3, in one respect his work is at odds with postcolonial theory. Bohata points out:

> If (anti-colonial) nationalism and imperialism are generally presented as binary opposites in much postcolonial discourse, then feminism and nationalism are often also seen to be in competition rather than in alliance, since anti-colonial nationalism has often proved too overtly patriarchal while women's rights may be viewed as subordinate to the primary aim of achieving national independence.[22]

Humphreys's Land of the Living sequence conspicuously avoids presenting feminism and nationalism as binary opposites while maintaining a critique of how women were perceived as occupying a subordinate position, often linked to the family.

Throughout Humphreys's fiction, from *The Best of Friends* to *Unconditional Surrender*, which is set in the closing years of the Second World War but written in the 1990s, there is a recurring concern with the way in which women – in *Unconditional Surrender*, a mother and daughter – become more independent of their husbands and fathers. As we shall see in chapter 11, the collection of short stories *Old People are a Problem* is actually concerned with women of different generations who are a 'problem' because they are independently minded. But, in the later work, too, female independence is aligned with the unanticipated consequences of oppressive discourses. Thus, dissidence in Humphreys's later fiction is a product of female protest but is also connected to the way in which oppressive discourses can be seen as containing the seeds of their own undoing. Although, as discussed in chapter 2, Humphreys has come to think of himself as a dissident rather than a Protestant novelist, his concern with the subject of moral and social progress is as important to his later work as his earlier fiction. Throughout his writing, such progress is linked to feminist awareness, on the part of men as well as women.

While *Outside the House of Baal* and Land of the Living are concerned with women growing up in an increasingly politicized, feminist context, Humphreys's novels and short stories of the 1990s and the first decade of the twenty-first century are concerned with women who have grown up in a cultural context dominated by feminism. In one regard, it may be possible to associate these women with what is sometimes called third-wave feminism or even post-feminism. It is a complex and controversial concept and it is a moot point as to whether in the latter half of the twentieth century 'feminism' evolved into or came into conflict with 'post-feminism'. Inevitably, the prefix 'post' is as ambivalent in 'post-feminism' as in 'postmodernism'. Does it signify a movement beyond feminism but one which has nevertheless developed out of feminism? Does it signify a break with feminism? If it does suggest a departure from feminism, then it poses inevitable questions such as 'how' and 'in what respect' is it a departure? Or, as in the 'postmodern', does the prefix suggest the relative nature of cultural meta-narratives, arguing for a multiplicity of 'feminist' perspectives? Benjamin Brabon and Stéphanie Genz argue:

> On the one hand, post-feminism is perceived as a pro-patriarchal, anti-feminist stance, a backlash against feminism and its values, whereas, on the

other hand, it is seen to denote a postmodern and post-structuralist feminism that discredits discursive homogeneity and a unified subjectivitiy.[23]

Notwithstanding that post-feminism is a subject of debate, the lines of thought which see post-feminism as addressing 'the concerns and experiences of women today' and which stress the heterogeneity of the female subject are appropriate to Humphreys's later fiction.[24] Genz and Brabon summarize post-feminism in ways which chime particularly with the 'feminism' in this phase of his writing. They shrewdly argue that 'postfeminism can be considered as a movement of feminist pluralisation and diversification', in the process opening up 'the feminist realm for the articulation of "other" voices and identities'.[25] One of the contributions which Humphreys's fiction makes to our understanding of twentieth-century feminism and to modern Welsh history generally is its emphasis upon diversity. In seeking to reclaim the role of women in Western society there was a tendency in late twentieth-century feminist theory, as Genz and Brabon argue, to essentialize 'female' experience. Thus, drawing on the work of anti-essentialist feminists such as Deborah Siegel, they argue that post-feminism can be discussed 'in relation to deconstructive theories that undermine the concept of an essential female/feminist "identity" in which "woman" as a monolithic term is unable to address the complexity of gender in relation to other aspects of identity, including race, ethnicity, class, sexuality and age'.[26]

The emphasis upon the concerns and experiences of women at the end of the twentieth and the beginning of the twenty-first centuries in Humphreys's recent work, such as *The Shop*, is part of a wider preoccupation with the fluid nature of the relationship between meaning, identity and culture in fiction generally over the last twenty years. In some respects, *The Shop*, concerned with a late modern and at times even postmodern relationship between two lovers, develops Humphreys's concern, first expressed in *The Best of Friends*, with analysing subjectivity. Humphreys's fiction, especially his later work, is populated with women for whom unpredictability is liberating. Genz and Brabon, drawing on the work of Alcoff, argue that post-feminism has been perceived as a liberating theoretical position: 'For feminist theorists, the attraction of postmodern critiques of subjectivity can be found in the promise of an increased freedom for women and "the 'free play' of a plurality of differences unhampered by any predetermined gender identity" as formulated by either patriarchy or feminism

itself.'[27] The appropriateness of this 'free play' not only for Bethan in
The Shop but for her relationship with Eddie in the novel becomes
clear if we turn from Genz and Brabon's discussion of post-feminism
per se to Belsey's examination of love and desire within a postmodern
framework. Viewed through Belsey's analysis of love and sexuality in
postmodern culture, as well as the concept of post-feminist, Bethan's
unpredictable verbal exchanges with Eddie and her equally unpredictable behaviour acquire a wider significance. Writing generally
about the place of love and desire in postmodernism, Belsey suggests
that: 'Knowledges inscribed in language collide and clash, producing
alternative forms of understanding; resistances generate new developments; reputations efface old convictions.'[28]

Thus, Humphreys's fiction, concerned with radical, independent
women, benefits from being read through a number of feminist lenses.
However, it interweaves historically situated debates and subjects
with ideas that were more prevalent at the time particular novels and
stories were written than in the period(s) in which they are set. Because
Humphreys's fiction spans the twentieth century, it dramatizes and
explores the development of feminism in Wales, especially north
Wales. But, in his work, feminism is configured as part of a complex
nationalist and socialist political landscape. While his earlier work,
especially the novels written in the 1960s and 1970s, concern women
growing up and living as adults in an increasingly politicized feminist
and nationalist environment, his later work, written in the 1990s and
the first decade of the twenty-first century, is focused on women who
have grown up in an era configured by feminism. These subjects are
discussed in more detail in part two.

PART TWO

READINGS

6

Resistance, Gender and Performative Identity:
A Man's Estate

As far as the chronology of publication is concerned, *A Man's Estate* is Humphreys's first modernist novel. As indicated in chapter 2, there are two obvious frameworks within which to discuss it: as a modernist, dissident text and as a work which has a sexual/psychoanalytic theme.

As mentioned earlier, and as I have argued elsewhere, the influence of William Faulkner's *The Sound and the Fury* (1929) and *As I Lay Dying* (1930) on *A Man's Estate* is clearly evident in the way in which the narrative is told through a number of points of view.[1] Three of the four sections of *The Sound and the Fury* are ascribed to characters who tell the story from their particular perspective while the fourth section has an omniscient narrator. *As I Lay Dying* consists of fifty-nine sections, each narrated by one of the fifteen characters who alternate in telling the story. *A Man's Estate* is narrated by four characters: Hannah Elis, Hannah's brother Philip Esmor-Elis, the minister Idris Powell and Hannah's father's illegitimate daughter Ada Cwm, who, unlike the others, narrates only one section. Originally, Humphreys had conceived of the novel as having four narrators and consisting of ten books, opening with a book narrated by Hannah to a brother she had never seen.[2] The narrative by Ada was a later and, as will be discussed shortly, significant addition to the novel.

A Man's Estate is centred on a farm, Y Glyn, near a small town, Pennant, which Wynn Thomas in an interview with Humphreys suggests is based on places like Cricieth and Pwllheli.[3] It is set in post-First World War north Wales, but memories and reports of earlier events take the reader into the pre-war years. Although *A Man's Estate* looks back to the depiction of a stagnant and corrupt society in Humphreys's first novel, *The Little Kingdom*, its depiction of north-west Wales betrays a more self-conscious attempt to write a Welsh novel in the style of Faulkner. Begun when Humphreys was staying in Austria, *A Man's Estate* reflects how this critical distance from his native north Wales had allowed him to see the similarities between north Wales and the American South. Thus, despite the obvious differences between Faulkner's Yoknapatawpha county in northern Mississippi and north Wales, Humphreys suggests that there are profound similarities between them, not least their shared emphasis upon patriarchy, obsession, bloodlines, inheritance, covert sexual relationships and betrayal. As in narratives of the American South, families in *A Man's Estate* are joined by illegitimate bloodlines.

In the nineteenth century and the early twentieth century, north Wales and the American South shared a biblically based culture and some of the common features in their literatures – patriarchy, inheritance, bloodlines and betrayal – are indebted to the Old Testament, if not in origin then in the manner in which they are approached. *A Man's Estate* concerns 'inheritance' and property in a way that is somewhat Hebraic. In the Hebrew culture which informs the Old Testament, property, as opposed to personal possessions, belongs to the family rather than to the individual. This concept originated with the notion that the land was given by God to His people. The firstborn son possessed the 'birthright' to the family land, a custom that, as far as *A Man's Estate* is concerned, has some resonance in Nonconformist north-west Wales also. Elis's son, Philip, is sent away by his mother Mary Felix Elis in order for her to retain what otherwise he might lay claim to after his father's death. In fact, Philip is sent as far away as possible from Y Glyn to be brought up by his aunt Gwendoline, with whom his father, according to the midwife Mrs Aster, also had a sexual relationship, creating doubt as to who really is Philip's birth mother. Brought up by Gwendoline in London, Philip eventually attends medical school and qualifies as a doctor.

The strawberry birthmark which Philip, on his return to Pennant, shows the midwife who delivered him, is both a symbol of his birthright and, given the nature of the Elis family, also the mark of Cain. However, it is the desire to protect the estate, and not simply to claim it for herself, that motivated his mother to send him to Gwendoline and, despite the differences between them, to keep her daughter Hannah at home and unmarried. It was a principle in Hebrew society that if there were no sons who could inherit the property, it would pass to a daughter, providing she did not marry outside the tribe, or, in the case of this novel at the end of which Hannah becomes the sole owner of Y Glyn, remains unmarried.

Despite the numerous differences between Ada and Hannah, Ada, too, desires property. Whilst having an affair with Mary Elis's other son, Dick, mentioned in chapter 5, Ada recalls: 'The idea of property came into my mind then. To have my own place, my own castle, my own plough and pasture, woods, gardens, hills, rivers, my own domain.'4 The slippage in language here between castle, plough and estate, and between owning and working the land, encapsulates the ambivalence of Ada's position within the community and within the text. However, it is difficult to understand fully this ambiguity in her relation to the family and the wider community without acknowledging that there is an additional influence to that of Faulkner on *A Man's Estate*.

ILLEGITIMACY AND THE 'PERFORMATIVE'

Like Humphreys's first novel, discussed in chapter 2, *A Man's Estate* is redolent of Shakespeare's family tragedies, hingeing on the warring relationship between two local clans, the Elis family and the family of their maid by whom Felix Elis has his illegitimate daughter. The novel looks behind the respectable Nonconformist society of north Wales and discovers a dark labyrinth of intrigue, plots and secrets. Felix not only has sex with his maid but seduces his wife Mary away from his cousin, Vavasor, who owns the chemist shop in Pennant. Before Ada's birth, Felix dies from pneumonia, partly as a result of his wife's depriving him of medicine and water, after which she marries Vavasor who played a part in the murder.

If the complex plots in *A Man's Estate* are redolent of Elizabethan theatre, Ada Cwm is typical of the illegitimate character in Elizabethan drama. The Elis family is 'respectable' and 'legitimate' whilst the Cwm family is of lower social status and is the Other in Pennant. As in Renaissance drama, Ada, as an illegitimate figure, is able to move between the warring families and between different classes in the community.

Ada appears to have inherited Felix Elis's hearty appetite for sex. She has a relationship with Mary's son by Vavasor, Dick; with the new minister, Idris Powell; and with Wally Francis, the garage owner. Her relationship with the latter breaks down when she discovers that it was he who was responsible for the charge against Dick that got him sent away to the war in which he was eventually killed. She also enters into a relationship with Dr Pritchard in return for the financial backing that she needs to purchase the guest house, Bronllwyn. Like the illegitimate character in Elizabethan drama, she is motivated partly by hostility towards the 'legitimate' family which decries its responsibility for her illegitimacy. She seeks to persuade Dick to oppose his mother and join the Cwm family where the Elis family are like a running sore in daily conversation. Ada remembers how 'Frankie knew he could always make us laugh. Hate the Elises and laugh at their dependants' (p. 169). Ironically, when Philip returns to Pennant from London, Ada helps him find his father's grave, one of the places where she and Dick have made love.

Ada's sense of her female identity might be described, as explained in chapter 5, by the term 'performative', coined by the contemporary feminist cultural critic and theorist Judith Butler. In Butler's view, identity is not entirely determined by socio-cultural discourse but is also the product of individual agency. She recognizes, as Kathy Dow Magnus says, that 'The fact that the subject is *constituted* by social discourse does not mean that the subject is *determined* by social discourse'.[5] Through performing his or her own 'truth', the individual subject can be the agent in his or her emancipation from determining discourses.

The Victorian hymn which the title of the novel partly invokes (it is also keyed to a Welsh hymn) refers to different classes born into and confined within their social place.[6] It highlights the social order, and more particularly the socio-cultural ideologies and structures that maintain it, which many of the characters in subtle and not so subtle ways seek to overturn. The most obvious of these is Ada who, like the illegitimate character of the Elizabethan stage, resists the way in which the Elis family and the community try to define her through the way in which she 'performs' her identity. In this respect, she anticipates, to varying degrees, independently minded women in some of Humphreys's later novels, such as Lydia in *Outside the House of Baal*, Amy Parry in the Land of the Living sequence and Bethan Mair Nichols in *The Shop*, as well as some of the characters in the short stories and novellas to be discussed later in this book.

However, Ada's behaviour does not simply give expression to how she configures herself. Based upon the different roles that she seems able to assume, Ada is, for the most part, constituted by her behaviour. This is evident in the different ways in which she engages with a range of individuals within the community. In this regard, the influence of Elizabethan theatre on the text is especially appropriate. Alison Findlay points out that in the seventeenth century the theatre and the illegitimate were perceived as occupying an equivocal area, spatially and ideologically.[7] In Humphreys's novel, the 'performative' and the illegitimate, in the person of Ada, are interwoven as they were on the Elizabethan stage.

Kathy Dow Magnus points out: 'Butler proposes an understanding of agency in terms of the process of resignification: the subject who is produced in and through discourse can act by articulating words in contexts that invest them with new meaning.'[8] In many respects, this is the understanding of agency which Humphreys develops through Ada Cwm, a woman who relies heavily upon resignification and developing new meanings. Indeed, Ada, like the illegitimate person in Elizabethan drama, is something of a 'shapeshifter' which suggests that, like Amy Parry in Land of the Living and Eve in traditional Christian interpretation of the Bible, she is also manipulative.

In *A Man's Estate*, Humphreys's emphasis is upon bodily behaviour as much as language. Magnus points out that Butler has come to place a greater emphasis upon language in her later writings than she did in her early work, which stressed social discourse in a broader sense. As was suggested in chapter 5, a similar transition occurs in Humphreys's fiction which is evident if the importance of language to performative gender identity in *A Man's Estate* and the later novel *The Shop* is compared.

However, it is not simply Ada's body language and Bethan's noticeable verbal wit that distinguishes *A Man's Estate* from *The Shop*. Another important difference between their respective forms of performative identity is that Ada seems much more reactive than Bethan. Thus, while Ada through her 'performativity' is able to resist patriarchy and the forces that oppress women she never achieves the degree of freedom which Bethan does. Her sense of independence comes from quarrelling with and mocking what Pennant expects of her and as such is always defined by what she reacts against. Indeed, Magnus argues that Butler herself came to see that 'performative identity' was too reactive, too much a product of what it mocked and mimicked, to be a totally effective mode of resistance for the oppressed. Humphreys's novel anticipates Butler's concept of 'performativity' in the way in which it approaches gender identity and also in the manner in which it explores the effectiveness of 'performance' as a mode of resistance when it is always determined by what it is a reaction against. Ultimately, the novel is sceptical about performativity in a woman's pursuit of liberation, as is Butler in her later work. As Magnus says, where performativity is reactive, 'the subject can do nothing *but* resist'.[9] Both Humphreys, through characters such as Bethan in his later novel, and Butler come to place more emphasis upon the importance of 'proaction' and upon the importance of women's achieving control of the language and discourses which oppress them.

Thus, at one level, Humphreys clearly recognizes what Ada achieves through 'performance'. But, at another level, he is sceptical about performativity as a totally effective mode of resistance for women in an oppressive environment. One reason, as we have now seen, is that performativity, for all its liberating creativity, can be too reactive, as opposed to proactive. However, Humphreys is also sceptical about performativity as an effective means of resistance for women because it may, as in Ada's case, become synonymous with exaggeration.

In critically examining Ada's actions as a product of Pennant's repressive environment, Humphreys's novel is sceptical of the manner in which her appearance and behaviour appear overdramatic. Thus, at different points in the novel, Ada appears to assume a reactive, creatively liberating performance in which she seems to have freed herself from what oppresses her. But, in other parts of the novel, she seems to have become so exaggerated in her performance that she turns herself into something that is not real. Under such circumstances, Butler, in her later essays, suggests 'exaggeration reveals its fundamentally phantasmatic status'.[10] The drafts of *A Man's Estate* indicate that, in developing Ada, Humphreys had difficulty in establishing the right degree of psychoanalytical 'realism', since Ada needs to appear as a woman who has attained independence, and yet needs to represent in a sufficiently controlled way (such as in the scene in the graveyard) the exaggeration to which her performances are prone.

The passages which describe Idris Powell's initial meeting with Ada were rewritten a number of times. The drafts suggest that Humphreys was seeking to create an impression of Ada that does not so much convey her stunning features as exaggerate the performance on which her relationships with others is based. Humphreys later added the following sentence to the earlier drafts of this scene: 'To many she would appear too hard and combative; but what I saw that morning was the softness and ready affection that young women who appear too ready to defend themselves by attacking often have.'[11] Powell is eventually forced to admit 'It seemed absurd to think that she was this old man's mistress' (p. 68). The drafts of this episode convey the impression that Humphreys was seeking to integrate the exaggerated extremes of Ada's performativity – that she is more beautiful than most women in Pennant and yet is the mistress of an elderly man. The key to this is Idris's comparison of Enid and Ada:

> Enid was a dark copy book beauty; neat, gentle, meditative, loving. Ada's looks were not gentle. Her chin was too large, and her grey blue eyes too watchful. She was taller than Enid, more ample-breasted. Her taste in clothes was more uncertain but her manner more confident and more questioning. (p. 69)

The description of Ada suggests the liminality and ambivalence of the illegitimate figure in Elizabethan drama – 'her taste in clothes was more uncertain' – but displays the confidence which more conservative parts of male-dominated society at the time would have found disturbing. Her eyes – 'grey blue' and 'watchful' – indicate the 'knowledge' which the illegitimate have and could one day use against the legitimate.

The published version of Idris's meeting with Ada is noticeably less ambivalent than the early draft which acknowledged Ada's beauty but also suggested a more cowed figure: 'Her head was slightly lowered and her short dark hair hung forward.'[12] The phantasmatic quality of Ada at this point in the final version is captured by some subtle revisions of this earlier draft. Her 'watchful eyes' are more threatening and are more suggestive of her power, derived from knowledge of what is hidden. The original phrase, 'enquiring eyes', was more closely aligned with the hesitancy suggested by her 'slightly lowered' head in the early draft.[13] Indeed, a line deleted from one of the earlier versions strongly suggests that Humphreys was thinking in terms of Ada's sexuality as a projected phantasm: 'Her features were inclined to thickness, her nose was slightly too big, but the whole was beautiful as though beauty were a quality projected and showered [over grey eyes] over her person.'[14]

The phantasmatic quality which is evident in Idris's account of Ada characterizes the way in which sexualized female and male bodies are described in the novel. This is evident in two scenes in which Hannah, a representative of the 'legitimate' family, spies on members of the 'illegitimate' family. The first of these incidents occurs when Hannah unexpectedly sees Ada's brother Frankie sleeping in the loft, wearing only an open shirt. Hannah fantasizes about touching him – 'A touch upon his smooth eyes that would not wake him or disturb him' (p. 55) – while he seems able to read her mind: 'Want to touch me? You can if you like' (p. 56). The entire episode may be read in Freudian terms. Frankie's leg is symbolic of the phallus which Hannah desires, almost in fairy-tale terms, in order to 'break the spell' in which she is 'cruelly caught' so as to acquire 'new power' (p. 55). The 'spell' is the role in which she has been cast as a spinster in Y Glyn while her powerlessness and sense of 'lack' result from the male domination of the society in which she lives and against which her mother and illegitimate half-sister struggle. What Hannah requires is the equivalent of the power which she perceives as associated with men but denied women.

Later, in glimpsing Ada making love to Dick on her father's grave, Hannah once again sees and desires the power which is denied her. In pointedly making love to Dick at this particular spot, Ada mocks the phallus which abused her mother and the phallocentricity which has labelled her in a particular way. At the same time, through having sex with Dick, the heir apparent of the Elis family, she seeks to acquire the power which that clan denies her. Her ambition is suggested by the way in which Ada has brought her bicycle (which, consisting of two wheels, may even function as a vulval image) further than anyone else into the graveyard.

The picture that Hannah has of Ada making love to Dick is a fetishized one in that Ada is presented in male fetish terms: 'She was wearing her school uniform and between her skirt and long black stockings I could see exposed part of the white young strength of her thighs' (p. 57). In Ada's case, the image of the fetishized schoolgirl is turned into an actively rebellious sexual image, reminiscent of the St Trinian's Girls' School cartoons from the late 1940s. The flesh which Hannah glimpses between Ada's skirt and stockings signifies the 'illegitimate' that the novel unveils within 'legitimate' society, suggested by Ada's uniform. But the description of Ada's legs – 'the white young strength of her thighs' – implies the sexuality and power which threatens the Elis family and their place in the community. A marginal note in a draft version of this episode in Humphrey's notebooks reads: 'insert page fears of Cwm family'.[15]

ADA AS SOCIALLY DISRUPTIVE 'SUBALTERN'

Reading Ada Cwm's performative identity through Butler's theorizing of agency and gender provides insights into Ada Cwm's dilemma in *A Man's Estate*. Constituted of social discourses, especially the discourses of illegitimacy and independent female sexuality, Ada resists being determined by them through performing her own 'truth'. But while she seeks, and achieves, a degree of emancipation through her performativity, the fact remains that her performativity is tied to resistance. This limits the extent to which she achieves proactive agency over her own life.

Since Ada's actions are substantially concerned with resisting the way in which women's identity and sexuality were determined at that time, as a character, as discussed earlier, she is mainly 'reactive'. In this regard, she reflects the illegitimate figure of Elizabethan theatre which was equally largely resistant. This does not mean, of course, that they were wholly resistant and it is their perceived capacity for socially disruptive behaviour which places the illegitimate figure, like Elizabethan theatre itself, outside the 'law'.[16] As a woman daring to encroach on a 'man's estate', and as an outsider in the community, Ada, the illegitimate daughter of Felix Elis, is metaphorically outside the 'law' of the father.

Like the illegitimate character on the Elizabethan stage, Ada represents the Other. She makes the point in the narrative that she is allowed to speak only late in the novel:

> In me I carried my father and my mother's blood. Blood does not speak, you may say, So why be afraid? But there was their history inside me, grown from the wounding accident that made me, all the darkness of it; and there was Dick, related to me through my father's blood, the mirror in my heart in which I watched the world move. (p. 182)

As mentioned earlier, one of the tropes of the novel is the threat which the illegimate poses for the legitimate estate. Ada recalls her mother's drunken tirade against the Elis family:

> You had a fine father. A Member of Parliament he was. But he didn't live to do anything for you or your poor old mother. Died and left me in the lurch. And I can't swear he would have done even if he had lived. He was a slippery customer when you come to think about it. Just remember, my girl, that Dick's the same breed. (p. 172)

The way in which Ada's mother quickly changes her view of Felix Elis gives us an insight into the dilemma in which she probably found herself when he tried to seduce her; flattered by the attentions of a respectable MP, hopeful that this would be the chance in life for which she had been waiting, but recognizing underneath it all that he was 'a slippery customer'. At the end of the novel, it is the illegitimate blood that destroys the Elis family because it is Ada who takes Philip to see the midwife who reveals to him the truth not only about the murder of his father but what he was like as a man.

Since *A Man's Estate* is a Welsh novel, published in English and then later in Welsh, concerned with rebellion and resistance, it raises the question as to how far Ada's role may be illuminatingly discussed in Marxist as well as feminist terms. Ada and her family may be seen as representing what the Marxist cultural critic Antonio Gramsci called 'subalterns'.[17] Subalterns, he argued, were affiliated to dominant formations, a position exemplified by Ada's mother Winnie in her role as a maid at Y Glyn. But, like Winnie, who saw her affair with Felix as an opportunity to reverse her social position, the subaltern seeks social position and influence.

In applying the concept of subaltern to Ireland, Colin Graham points out that it is important to distinguish between 'subversity from below which seeks only to subvert, and that which seeks to topple and replace "the dominant"'.[18] Ada and her mother, like the illegitimate character in Elizabethan drama, are concerned to topple those who occupy the dominant positions in order that they may themselves achieve social 'position'. They are not concerned to topple the social system per se. This is evident in Ada's dream, while in a sexual relationship with Dick, of becoming a farmer's wife, her mother's ambivalent attitude towards the fact that her daughter's father is a man of standing, and the Cwm family's mocking of the Elis family. In bringing together subversion and illegitimacy in Ada, the novel poses questions about the nature of class and the gendered subaltern within Welsh-language, Nonconformist society which, in turn, raises questions about women within patriarchal society generally.

The dissenting, subaltern female voices in *A Man's Estate*, such as those of Ada's mother, the midwife and Ada herself, are not uniformly counter-hegemonic. The ambivalence within Ada is evident when she reflects on her father's relationship with his wife at his graveside with Philip: 'There must have been a streak of weakness in him. I mean he let her win, so easily in the end. She had everything her own way. He should have dealt with her in the beginning' (p. 216). She also remembers how her mother changed:

Since we had moved to *Hyfrydle* she had begun to go in for respectability. She was Mrs Evans, *Hyfrydle*, the quiet widow who had done so well for her children, whose language was restrained, who did not drink and could be, when the occasion arose, taken by her daughter into the best hotels of Wales and England and no disgrace to her at all and could be a model mother-in-law to her son Frankie's wife, however rich she turned out to be. (p. 180)

Humphreys, possibly drawing upon Shakespeare and Elizabethan theatre, suggests that, whilst the illegitimate is a visible symbol of subversion, it may be oriented not only towards subversion, but towards power and homogeneity as well.

In this regard, the novel explores the dilemma in the representation of the illegitimate figure, such as Ada, as a subaltern. Colin Graham suggests that there is 'a serious intellectual danger of celebrating the subalternity of subaltern groups' because it 'easily slides into a continuous and necessary restatement of their oppressed position'.[19] Rather than celebrate Ada's subalternity, *A Man's Estate* examines the complex power relations associated with the gendered subaltern and the complex relation of the subaltern to the Welsh-language, Nonconformist community. Whilst gender is the subject of domination and stratification within Nonconformist society, Ada, as the illegitimate, gendered subaltern, has no fixed or fully determined status.

SEXUAL DILEMMAS

The title of the English-language version of the novel is ambivalent, suggesting that it is what a man owns which, as in the case of Felix Elis, gives him power and influence. But it can also be seen as referring to a man's sexual prowess as Philip at one point suggests: 'I couldn't ignore the influence of the place because the whole occasion seemed an unworded powerful direct challenge to my manhood' (pp. 213–14). In other words, the title may be read as referring to both the male body and the principal patriarchal institutions that privilege it. In *A Toy Epic*, the three principal male protagonists who enter the sixth form together admit that 'We walk boldly towards a man's estate, not only to study but also to possess the world' (p. 73). The pun in the title, *A Man's Estate*, is appropriate because the novel is centred as much on sexual relationships as it is on Y Glyn. In her affair with Dick, Ada has her own map of Pennant based on the different places in which she and

Dick have made love. Her 'map' mocks the way in which family names in Wales are often associated with a place, as her mother becomes known as 'Mrs Evans, *Hyfrydle*':

> At different places I waited for him as often as he waited for me. The sea shore, the Hen Eglwys [the Old Church], the Middle barn, the Lime Kiln near Miss Aster's cottage, the waiting room of the railway station at Derwen, and most exciting of all, Bronllwyn Wood, and the West Lodge and when Bronllwyn became empty sometimes even inside the house itself. (p. 170)

The title of the Welsh-language version of this novel, *Etifedd Y Glyn* (The Heir of Y Glyn) places the emphasis on Y Glyn (the name of the farm) and, thereby, on the complex manoeuvrings in and through which individual, social and moral progress can occur. In the course of the novel, Ada defines her dilemma in different ways: negotiating entry into the culture which designates her as Other; struggling with socially induced gendered dependence; and extricating herself from discourses that render her insignificant. Even her relationship with Dick, whom she professes to love, is complex and problematic. It is not always clear how much he loves her as opposed to needing her as a kind of sexual toy. This becomes evident when Dick returns from the war in uniform and tries to persuade her to have sex with him even though she has recently had an abortion, having been made pregnant by him. In line with the punning in the title of the novel, he arrogantly suggests that, if she agreed to sex, he could teach her the new erotic skills he has learned while in the army:

> 'No,' I said. 'Dick. No. Just kiss me. That's all.'
> 'No,' I said. 'I mean it. No. How can you be so selfish?'
> 'I don't care what you learnt,' I said. 'Or who you've learnt it with.'
> We were sitting up and quarrelling, bitterly and foolishly.
> 'I'm just something for you to play around with while you're on leave,' I said. (p. 178)

What Dick does is to turn their 'love' into a dilemma. She is caught between wanting him sexually and being afraid of having sex with him and, as the above exchange makes clear, between her love for him and her growing suspicion that she may be no more than a plaything to him. This is compounded, as her rebuke 'Or who you've learnt it with' makes clear, by the fact that she does not know how sexually active he has been with other women including, possibly, prostitutes.

With Dr Pritchard, Ada finds herself in a situation and dilemma similar, we may suppose, to that in which her mother found herself with her employer. Dr Pritchard wants her as a mistress but he is really asking her to prostitute herself in order to be able to purchase the guest house. In what he says to her, reported to us by Ada, the reader can almost hear Felix speaking to his maid:

> But I want to be honest about this love business. If it means I'm completely infatuated with you and can think of nothing else but you, that isn't true. Wanting you doesn't disturb my work. It doesn't make me any less patient with my wife. But I do want you. (p. 197)

For Dr Pritchard, the notion of the affair is straightforward and businesslike, as Felix Elis's affair with her mother probably was. In these relationships, the novel demonstrates how the early twentieth century prised apart love and sex. Dr Pritchard's phrase 'love business' is contemptuous because it grinds so negatively with the true meaning of the word 'love' and, because everything is underhand, with the word 'business' which is drained of any suggestion of integrity.

What really makes Dr Pritchard – and by implication Felix Elis – so contemptible is that there is no hint of any kind of moral dilemma as far as he is concerned. In contradistinction to the image of the oak-panelled room which opens the novel, Ada refers to the rotten woodwork in the room in which they talk which suggests the moral malaise of Pennant and of the wider world in which they are living. At one point, Ada says contemptuously: 'The silly young idiot gaped at me with what he imagined was an attractive look. I wondered what dance-hall he had used to develop his technique' (p. 195). While Dr Pritchard's proposal creates no moral dilemma for him, it presents her with a dilemma on many levels. She is aware of the fact that she is prostituting herself and allowing herself to become, in an image Humphreys develops later in *A Toy Epic*, his 'toy'. Ada herself says: 'Bronllwyn was another toy to him and having a bar there, and a drinking club of which he would be the power behind the scenes where he could bring his friends and where they would see me and quietly realise that I was another one of his toys' (pp. 199–200). But she is also ruthless and is prepared to sell her body and soul to obtain what she wants:

> I thought afterwards that my willingness was what he wanted most. He was paying for me to become a new department of his life and he liked the idea of it more than the reality. He was paying to have his own way with a toy he had fancied: a rich child who wanted the brightest in the window. He wasn't impotent but his interest in love-making was very slight. What he paid for, I decided, was the notion that I had become his mistress and that he was a man who lived a very full and very interesting life. (p. 197)

Ada invokes the central theme of *A Man's Estate*, suggesting that it is not simply sex that men want but a fantasy of themselves as men. As is the case of many men's relations with mistresses and prostitutes, Dr Pritchard is buying an illusion which he then expects Ada to help convince him is a reality. Ada, revealing once again how performativity and manipulation are linked in her character, comments: 'I took some trouble to cultivate the aspects of our relationship that pleased him' (ibid.). Like most rich men's mistresses, Ada is able to rationalize what she is doing and recognizes the performance and masquerade involved in being part of a man's estate.

Thus, the novel is centred on a series of dilemmas, some of which are alluded to through reported events while others are 'enacted' in the text. These include dilemmas to which the reader is not directly privy but which are an absent presence in the novel. The most important are those in which Mary would have found herself when Felix Elis enticed her away from Vavasor and when she discovered her husband's cruelty and his sexual use of their maid. The mentally broken Mary at the end of the novel gives us insight into the turmoil into which she was thrown when she is confronted by Philip, accompanied by Hannah: 'I sent you away to save you from knowing. I saved this girl from knowing. Wicked. Abominable. Wicked. Too wicked to live. I put a stop to his tricks. A woman here, a woman there. Lies. Lies. Lies. Lies' (p. 236).

This is one of the few occasions in the novel when Mary is given a voice and, whilst her confusion and rambling are meant to suggest her breakdown, they also suggest the dilemmas in which she found herself and about which the reader up until this point in the text has heard only from others.

The novel opens with the dilemma in which Philip finds himself in relation to his marriage plans because he has failed to obtain the research fellowship that he wanted: 'Three years in Greenland. I don't give a damn where. But I want Margaret with me. I don't give a damn what her old man says' (p. 12). Towards the end of the novel, the dilemma has become that of his Oxford girlfriend, Margaret, as the first account of them together at the beginning of the novel when he coldly criticized her poetry had suggested might be the case, although he had failed to recognize it:

> I can't marry you, Philip. It would never work. I must tell you at once. I tried to tell you at the station … Physical attraction isn't enough, Philip … and it isn't as if I don't admire your work, I honestly do, as much as I admire you, but I don't understand it any more than I understand you … My father's right basically. Marriage is something between families. It's

got to be, in order to be a success ... Romantic love is one of the things
that's gone wrong with the world ... Your kind of anarchistic rationalism
is out of date, Philip. Much as I like you, I couldn't live with it ... You see
I'm too conservative for you ... but you'll say I've just talked myself into
doing what Daddy wants. (p. 221)

The letter conveys the different levels of the dilemma in which
Margaret now finds herself through the broken sentences, the ellipses,
the rapid changes in tone and subject, the repetition of his name and
the shift from the formal, almost distant 'My father' to the more intimate and almost childlike 'Daddy'. The explanations for her behaviour
range from the personal to the more philosophical: 'Marriage is something between families.' Ironically, the latter invokes the very theme of
internecine conflict which is, of course, central to Philip's dilemma.

   Of the characters in the novel, Philip is one of those who make the
most individual progress, coming to a more realistic understanding of
his relationship with his fiancée and of his aunt and his parents.
Although he has returned to Pennant to obtain the money that he
needs in order to marry, he comes to recognize that he was also motivated by the desire to understand the mother who had sent him
away: 'I had hated her with varying degrees of intensity all my life; but
now I didn't hate her any more' (p. 236). However, within the wider
scheme of the novel, Philip also represents the return of the repressed
and, as something of a 'trickster' figure, he forces others to confront the
truth which brings about Vavasor's suicide and his mother's mental
breakdown. It is apposite that he is himself a haematologist, for his
function in the text is to reveal the truth about his family bloodlines.

   The other people who make individual progress in the novel are Idris
Powell, the minister, who begins to resolve the conflict between his spiritual calling and the yearnings of the flesh, and the Elis's eldest child,
Hannah, who is a thirty-year-old spinster when Philip returns home.
Idris's sexual passion for women is contrasted both with Philip's almost
scientific coldness and with the minister's own Christian love for his
parishioners. On resigning from his church, Idris becomes somewhat
dishevelled, his outward appearance, as is the case with the Reverend
J. T. Miles in the later novel *Outside the House of Baal* (1965), reflecting
his inner turmoil. Hannah notices how 'His collar was unclean and his
shirt was worn into a tear at the neck. I was genuinely troubled about
him' (p. 254).

   Hannah achieves some kind of progress in that she is able to win her
brother's affection and becomes the sole owner of Y Glyn. However,

the tension between this concept of individual 'progress' and the psychic and societal complexities that bedevil it is still present at the end of the English-language text. It is difficult to be certain how much Hannah tells us is 'real' and how much is still shrouded in illusion. When she says farewell to her brother and he promises to write to her, there is still something of the former Hannah in her words: 'But I felt it was the noise of the train that was spurring me on too fast to declarations of intimacy. Between such as Philip and myself, intimacy grows very slowly I was thinking ...' (p. 254). Here, there is a suggestion of the love and hope which, as discussed in chapter 2, was important to Humphreys's concept of the 'Protestant' novel. But in Hannah's case, the resolution seems to be only in her own mind: 'Wherever Philip wandered, I knew he would come back. I was something he wanted to need, and not to forget' (p. 254).

Ioan Williams has suggested that one of the loose ends of the novel is the way in which 'Ada has faded out' by its conclusion.[20] In the final section of the novel, narrated by Hannah, Ada has disappeared: 'Driving home, I passed a notice of Bronllwyn Sale— For Sale—*with Vacant Possession. Delightful Country Mansion Suitable for Conversion to Guest House* ... She wasn't wasting any time' (p. 255). Ironically, Ada's departure plunges Hannah into the final dilemma of the novel: 'Should one buy it to prevent strangers coming and upsetting our way of life? That was exactly what Uncle Vavasor would have said' (ibid.). The fact that the reader is informed of Ada's departure almost as a postscript to the novel is commensurate to the marginal position of the mistress in 'a man's estate', as Dr Pritchard makes clear to Ada when he says that wanting to have an affair with her does not make him 'any less patient' with his wife.

The focus throughout *A Man's Estate* on a character who is at the periphery of so many lives only serves to highlight the moral, or amoral, centre of Pennant. At the end of the novel, there is a subtle hint that, while Hannah has possibly come to a more realistic vision of things, which is presented with a degree of ambivalence, she has also assumed some of the characteristics of Ada. The dilemma that the sale of Bronllwyn creates for her is rooted, like so many of Ada's dilemmas, in self-protection, albeit reflecting the way in which Welsh-language-speaking communities became increasingly concerned in the later decades of the twentieth century with the purchase of holiday homes and local businesses by an influx of non-Welsh-speaking English people. Moreover, there is a new hard edge to her. Although she is

'genuinely troubled' by Idris's appearance, she comments upon him
with a candidness which is associated in the novel with Ada: 'I had not
seen him before in so clear a light; so absolute and pathetic a failure.
Ready for a shabby protracted martyrdom' (p. 254). In passing judge-
ment on Ada, she does not recognize how like Ada she sounds: 'Don't
think me hard, Idris. But I can't see her as you do. As a sort of special
case. Everybody gets hurt. She can look after herself. I wish I could
say as much for you' (p. 255). The fact that Hannah, despite the individual progress that she has made, only half-recognizes her own
self-contradiction – 'Don't think me hard, Idris' – together with the
'threat' which strangers pose to the community undermines the expression of hope in the last lines of the English-language version of the
novel: 'The air was warm and a lark rose out of the half-grown grass
and disappeared slowly into the sky, singing' (p. 255).

7

Contested Masculinities: *A Toy Epic*

In chapter 6, we discussed *A Man's Estate* as a modernist novel which eschews the grand historical sweep of conventional historical fiction in favour of a more localized and individual narrative. Through its different voices, it examines history at this level as a product, in a Foucauldian sense, of institutionalized discourses. These discourses included the way in which gender and sexuality, as discussed also in chapter 5, are locked in binaries such as legitimate/ illegitimate, normal/deviant and respectable/lewd.

A Toy Epic, which, as mentioned earlier, was begun, albeit in embryonic form, during the Second World War, is also focused, not on the grand sweeps of history, but on personal and localized narratives. But a significant difference between *A Toy Epic* and *A Man's Estate* is the greater extent to which the former looks outward to globalized historical events and examines how they impact on individual lives in their localized contexts. These themes are aligned in *A Toy Epic* with a stronger awareness of the politics of space. By the 'politics of space', I mean the extent to which authority is maintained through dominant and institutionalized discourses that are embedded and codified in spatial relations. The difference between *A Toy Epic* and *A Man's Estate* in this regard may be attributed to the fact that, whereas the latter was largely influenced by William Faulkner, *A Toy Epic*, as mentioned earlier, betrays the influence of a further modernist writer, Virginia Woolf, interested in the relationship between power, meaning and discourse and the discursive construction of space.

Like *A Man's Estate*, *A Toy Epic* is told through a number of voices. In this case, the novel is narrated by three boys from different

backgrounds in north-east Wales. But the technique which introduces
the voices and by which a change in voice is signalled is identical to
that used by Woolf in *The Waves*. Her novel, as explained in chapter 3,
consists of soliloquies by three males and three females, describing
their progress from childhood to maturity, and nine italicized pastoral
interludes. As we have seen, although there are no pastoral interludes
in *A Toy Epic*, the influence of the diurnal passage of the sun in Woolf's
interludes is evident in the alternation of day and night and light and
dark which is threaded through the different voices in Humphreys's
text. We have already seen that Humphreys appears to have turned
to Faulkner in depicting north-east Wales from the First World War
through to the Second. He also derived from Faulkner's fictional
Yoknapatawpha county, supposedly part of northern Mississippi, an
emphasis upon patriarchy, obsession, bloodlines, inheritance, covert
sexual relationships and betrayal. But, as the similarities between *The
Waves* and *A Toy Epic* reinforce, in the latter novel Humphreys was
concerned with exploring a different set of themes.

A *Toy Epic* is set in Flintshire, in what one of the protagonists,
Michael, calls 'one of the four corners of Wales'.[1] Wynn Thomas points
out that the other corners are south Wales, west Wales and north-
west Wales.[2] At one level, the boys, and hence their different narrative
voices, are symbolic of the polarities in Wales and of the different
forces that shaped the country during the first half of the twentieth
century. Michael, the son of an Anglican minister, who at one point
denies that he can read Welsh, embodies the anglicization of Wales
from without and also from within; Iorwerth, the son of a farming
family who belongs to the Nonconformist chapel culture, represents
two 'traditional' aspects of Wales which seemed to be losing their influence and significance in an increasingly secular and 'modern' country;
and Albie, the son of a family who have moved from the rural valleys
to the coast to try to make a better future for themselves, represents a
significant internal migration within the country and the reorientation
of the north-east towards the emergent coastal urban centres.

However, the three narrators are not simply analogues of patterns
of social change and cultural polarities in north-east Wales. The novel
is centred on what Humphreys, as discussed in chapter 2, saw as one
of the lynchpins of the 'Protestant' or 'dramatic' novel – progress on
a social or individual level – and is concerned, like *The Waves*, with
the narrators' development from childhood to maturity. In this regard,
the novel is also concerned with subjectivity, especially contested,

incomplete and multiple subjectivities. One of the most obvious parallels between Woolf's and Humphreys's texts is the way in which they interweave these with contested and multiple masculinities. In both texts, the emphasis is upon the social and cultural significance assumed by the male. Even in fiction like *The Waves* in which the women, unlike in Humphreys's novel, are assigned a narrative voice, they are more schematic and symbolic as characters than the men. *A Toy Epic*, like *The Waves*, examines the notion of hegemonic masculinity from the perspective of different types of masculinity, exploring the societal and imaginary boundaries between it and femininity and what is presented in the novel as an existential crisis in masculinity.

Throughout his early work, Humphreys employs a number of different methods to convey the way in which the male perceives the liberated, sexualized woman. Michael watching Frida diving sees her as 'more radiant than Arethusa arising from the river' (p. 89). The reference is to Ovid's Arethusa whom the goddess of chastity, Artemis, changed into a pool to protect her from the god Alpheus. The comparison says much about Michael as a product of a particular anglicized, classical education and underscores his lack of sexual experience with women compared with Frida's experience of men. However, the episode turns the Arethusa myth on its head. The emphasis is not upon her entering or being changed into water to be hidden from male pursuers but on emerging from the water in a way which heightens her visibility and sexual attractiveness to men. In this regard, she is more 'The Lady of the Fountain' from *The Mabinogion* than Arethusa.[3]

Although Humphreys's novel is set in a later period than Woolf's, in the 1930s, the focus for the examination of hegemonic masculinity in both texts is a chronotope moulded by war – the First World War and its impact in Woolf's case and, in Humphreys's novel, the anticipation of the Second World War. In this regard, *A Toy Epic* can be seen as exploring subjects with which Woolf became most fully concerned when writing *Jacob's Room* (1922): namely, the extent to which masculinity continued to be moulded in the first half of the twentieth century by war and the place of war in the male psyche. On entering the senior school, like the pupils in *The Waves*, Humphreys's three protagonists encounter the roll of honour:

> In the Assembly Hall there is a Roll of Honour, said Albie, a black wooden image, stretching like a totem pole from the ceiling to the floor. Upon it there are names inscribed in gilt lettering, thus — JOHN ED. JONES, Burton School, U.C.N.W., 1899. This is the first name, at the top

of the list; the last, almost on the floor, is FLORENCE HAYES, Cohen Exhibition, Liver. University, 1927; and after her honourable pupils such as myself must pass without mention. (p. 50)

The roll of honour is intended to socialize the pupils into the world view and values which the school represents. But there is an absent presence here; the title 'Roll of Honour' invokes another roll of honour, found in schools, chapels, churches and town and village centres, of those who have lost their lives in war: 'And here in faded sepia are the pupils of the school who were killed during the war of 1914–1918, boys in uniform, with sad surprised faces' (ibid.). The comparison of the roll to a totem pole is significant, since a totem pole is a symbol of death and of a particular, Native American perspective on it. The carvings of animals on a totem pole signify the animal with which the spirits of the remembered dead in Native American thinking are associated.

One of the experiences that the boys encounter, individually and collectively, is the experience of the sudden death of someone they knew related to war. In *A Toy Epic*, as in *The Waves*, it is the death of someone who is not assigned a narrative voice in the novel but about whom the pupils talk with mixed feelings. In Humphreys's novel, it is Jac Owen who joined the air force but was killed six months later during a training exercise over the North Sea. Iorwerth, who narrates this section, remembers his last sight of Jac:

Early this summer, before the exams, he came with Michael to Maesgwyn. He was wearing his new uniform. When he went for a walk after tea I remember him gathering bluebells. That is how I see him now, a small blue figure, bending among the trees. (p. 107)

There is a poignant contrast here between the uniformed military figure and the 'feminine' activity of gathering flowers in which he is engaged which brings to mind Iorwerth as a child gathering flowers on his way to school. In Iorwerth's case, the act linked him to the female teachers and his mother for whom he picked them, but it seems to link Jac to a more 'feminine' type of masculinity and to the reality of nature from which his uniform separates him. Although Jac had not remained in school for very long, a remark made by Michael suggests that the decision to join the RAF was a product of the school's culture: 'Used to look back on his brief schooldays as the Golden Age. Always used to ask after the teachers and talk about them as if they were mythical figures, odd sort of heroes. There's something so pathetic about dying young, so innocent' (ibid.).

In one respect, what Michael says here provides a commentary upon the 'sad, surprised faces' in the school's photographs of those pupils killed in the First World War. Now they do not appear heroic, only 'innocent' and 'pathetic'. However, Michael does more than challenge the notion of death in war as heroic. He challenges the normative male role in relation to war without being made to feel inadequate and insecure himself. In school, Jac was associated with an ostensibly radical, daring masculinity based on breaking rules. But, despite the rule breaking that the particular type of masculinity with which Jac was associated entailed, it remained aligned to the larger, hegemonic masculinity which took men into war as conscripts. In the account of their early schooldays, Jac is contrasted with Albie who displays the qualities of the officer class which the school is designed to nurture:

> He does not bend over the paper with his tongue sticking out and following his pen like a dog following his master. He sits upright, eyes only cast downwards, his pen held firmly in his hand moving steadily over the paper.
> Equally confident and capable on the football field he is the undisputed captain of the football team. He coolly plans out tactics, commanding his team with quiet authority which has to be obeyed. (pp. 53–4)

The language here – 'tactics', 'commanding', 'authority' and 'obeyed' – is that of the military. Whilst there is nothing new in linking the playing field and the battlefield, it did have a particular resonance in north-east Wales in the 1930s where the playing field which was laid as a memorial to King George V in Rhyl was one of 426 playing fields across the country intended to prepare the British people, mainly men, for the possible conflict with Germany.[4] The kind of confidence which these playing fields were meant to inspire was ironically a product of uncertainty.

Jacqueline Rose has argued that war is intricately linked to uncertainty: 'The familiar destructiveness of war represents not, as is commonly supposed, finality but uncertainty, a hovering on the edge of what, like death, can never be totally known.'[5] Not only is this the note on which the novel concludes, but the passage of both personal and 'historical' time is repeatedly linked in *A Toy Epic* to uncertainty. For Iorwerth, particularly, uncertainty and new knowledge are interleaved:

> The short service is in English. We sing a familiar tune to unfamiliar English words. The headmaster reads a portion of the Scriptures and then reads a prayer out of a small blue book which he opens on the open Bible.

This is the first time for me to see a prayer read; no one in our Chapel reads his prayer. Now it is clear that I am on the threshold of a new world. (p. 51)

Although Albie is not popular with the other boys – 'His accomplishments are too many; his superiority too definite' (p. 54) – he seems more secure in his identity on 'the threshold of a new world' than Iorwerth who, trusting only in his Nonconformity and his farm life, finds it difficult to relate to him:

To him I am strange and foreign; he does not understand my excited talk of farm or Chapel. I cannot bring with me to school fresh news to excite him. My father buys a new horse; twin calves are born to the cow 'Seren Wen'; the fox is about again; such things do not interest him. I cannot recount to him stories of missionaries I have read in *Y Cenhadwr* or *Y Trysorfa Fach*, nor can I explain to him my ambition to preach, to make long speeches woven from beautiful words, to see the light of heaven descend upon my hearers' upturned faces. (pp. 54–5)

Albie's mind is one that is intensely contemporary and up to date. But, despite his interest in scientific developments, his perspective is paradoxically static. As Iorwerth notices, he is, to quote Bakhtin, 'running-in-place at one historical point':[6]

Albie's talk is all of wireless and motor cars, the mysteries of engines, also the exploits of famous footballers and cricketers. His world is a swiftly moving pageant that never leaves the main streets of towns, always hedged between tall buildings, moving through crowds and congested traffic. (p. 55)

That last oxymoronic sentence neatly captures the coincidence of movement and stasis. Although Iowerth can suggest that Albie is interested in 'the mysteries of engines', they are not 'mysteries' to him in the sense that his Bible-reading friend Iorwerth understands the word. Albie's blinkered pragmatism runs counter to the dynamic suggestiveness of the language and of the imagery in the novel. When he hears of Jac's death, even though it occurred on a training flight, Iorwerth's response is ominous, sensing that something dreadful is coming, and anticipating, though he does not know it, the Second World War: 'I feel chilled on the street corner in spite of the sun, as if there were a cold wind blowing' (p. 107).

Jacqueline Rose draws attention to one of the key paradoxes of war which is at the heart of *A Toy Epic*: 'War not only threatens civilization, it can also advance it.'[7] Throughout *A Toy Epic*, war, injury and scientific and technological knowledge are implicitly or explicitly related. Injury and machinery are first linked by the way in which Iorwerth has lost some of his fingers in farm machinery. This is recalled again after Mr Phillips, the Welsh master, tells Iorwerth and Michael that the war could begin 'as soon as the corn harvest is over in Eastern Europe', an image which implicitly invokes farm tools and machinery. Half a page later, machinery, war and the maiming of Iorwerth's hand on the farm are linked in a more explicit image, this time of a machine in the Rock Shop: 'looking inside I see the shining steel arms twist the stiff toffee' (p. 109). In regard to the ambivalent view of mechanization in the novel, an important signifier at several points is petrol. At first Albie's father delights in his new job as a country bus driver but eventually the petrol fumes begin to affect his health; Michael and his friends are made to feel sick by the petrol fumes of the bus they take to school, and Iorwerth, prior to witnessing an accident between a cyclist and a car, whilst on holiday with Albie in the seaside resort of Llanelw, complains: 'The fumes of petrol from the streets seemed to invade my senses' (p. 57).

Mr Phillips's explicit talk of war – 'You know, don't you, that the scientists say that it is possible now to build a bomb big enough to completely destroy a single city' (pp. 108–9) – follows the episode in which the barber, implicitly invoking for the reader the execution of the leaders of the 1916 Easter Rising in Ireland, declares how he would pick out the Welsh nationalist leaders and shoot some of them as an example to others (p. 105). However, he does not simply recall the Easter Rising, he anticipates the way in which the German occupying forces dealt with insurrection. Indeed, Iorwerth's description of the barber invokes the rise of totalitarianism across Europe in the 1930s: 'Any moment, it seems to me, he can … swell greater still into the shape of a Monster of Unreason, able to crush whole streets of cities under his blind merciless boot' (ibid.). The word 'Monster' here is remembered later in the novel in the description of the bus which collides with the young people's car at the end of the novel: 'The great bus came suddenly into view, a roaring monster with its wicked headlamps pointing straight at us' (p. 119).

In *Outside the House of Baal*, the Reverend Joe Miles contemplates the prospect of a Second World War: 'It occurred to me, you know, this is one dilemma of our times. The way science makes it possible for unbalanced people to realize their fantasies' (p. 258). The reference in *A Toy Epic* to the barber becoming a 'Monster' who will 'crush whole

streets of cities under his merciless boot' may be read also as a reference to how fascism was able to recruit ordinary people who did indeed
become this kind of 'Monster'. Iorweth's reaction offers us a partial
explanation of this phenomenon: 'He seems to me the white-overalled
emperor of a seething maggoty world in which I want no part. A man
like this couldn't exist on our farm. The farm is the place for me; so
long as it remains hidden and does not offend this monster' (p. 105).
Unwittingly, Iorwerth seems to signify those in the 1930s who saw the
potential consequences of fascism but chose to look the other way.
Such an outlook seems to characterize Iorwerth's position as an individual and the novel connects his implicit responses to the domination
of fascism in 1930s Europe and to the anglicization of Wales:

> I am the traveller between two worlds, learning by experience the slow
> lessons of tolerance, which every foreigner must learn. At school I am
> the Israelite in Babylon, resistant to foreign influences, and careful of my
> household gods, conforming outwardly in every detail to the pattern of
> a Llanrhos County School boy, but inwardly firm in my own upbringing
> and persuasion. (p. 67)

Thus, Iorwerth is able to ignore the barber because he sees him as
outside his world. He is able to survive, as his following Albie to the
Pleasure land demonstrates, by conforming outwardly to one set of
values and behaviours and inwardly to another.

However, there is also a suggestion in *A Toy Epic* that rhetoric is not
to be trusted. The reference to fascism in the figure of the barber is
anticipated in the earlier account of the sermon preached by a minister
'well known for his fervour' (p. 86). Characteristic of Humphreys's
work, this passage is multilayered. In the reference to the 'iron fist' with
which he strikes the pulpit and the measured beat with which he seems
to recreate 'the tramp of the Roman legions' conquering Wales (p. 87),
the preacher anticipates the coming war – the 'horrible unknown' –
and the march of the armies of the Third Reich. But, in its rhetoric,
inflammatory language and hand gestures, his preaching is ironically
redolent of the oratory of Hitler himself.

Perhaps under the influence of the war poets and novelists but
undoubtedly drawing upon his father's experience of the First World
War and his own observations from reports of the Second World
War in which he was a conscientious objector, Humphreys explores
the way in which the language and rhetoric of war fails, or refuses,
to embrace its reality. Rose, alluding to Clausewitz's theory of war,

argues that the very concept of war 'is incapable of calculating, or mastering, the chaos, inconsistency, and randomness of the object it is meant to predict and represent'.[8] *A Toy Epic* turns on inconsistency and randomness. Injury and death – Iorwerth's maiming, the cyclist's possible fatal accident, Jac's death and the final accident – are the products of chance. But Rose also maintains, with even more relevance for Humphreys's novel: 'The particularity of war is a moral factor which slides and deceives.'[9] By this, she means that the idealism and moral principles that are employed to justify war are hardly ever fully adhered to in the operation of the war itself. Thus, the experience of war, what Rose calls its 'particularity', is one in which the moral framework, its justification, 'slides and deceives' for those caught up in it. In this regard, Jac's death is dubious, rooted in illusory concepts of heroism and masculinity which are undermined by his youth and innocence. The barber, as an analogue of fascist thought and action, raises questions about ordinary people becoming 'monsters', losing all sympathy for fellow human beings and becoming more like those they will end up fighting. Even more disturbingly, he raises the issue as to why he does not see the enemy in himself. Iorwerth demonstrates what can happen to moral convictions when he turns a blind eye to what he can see the barber may become.

Because of its persistent references to war, we could argue that *A Toy Epic* is a war novel in the sense that Dylan Thomas's *Under Milk Wood* is a play about war. Of its many themes, one of the most significant is that which is unfurled from the early mention of the 'sad surprised faces' of the young men killed in the First World War. The novel seems to ask at this point: why are we 'surprised' by the chaos, randomness and inconsistency of war? Rose points out: 'But to suggest that war is in some sense the repressed of its conceptualization – that is, of any attempt to think it – might be one way of explaining why we are never prepared for the full horror of war.'[10] If *A Toy Epic* raises the subject of war, it also raises the issue as to why war is not thought through in terms of its 'reality'.

8

Time and Being: *Outside the House of Baal*

As discussed in chapters 2 and 3, Kate Roberts was an important influence on Humphreys's work and it is not difficult to see the parallels between his one-volume family saga, *Outside the House of Baal*, and her *Traed Mewn Cyffion*, which he saw on the surface as 'in the mould of the "three generations sagas" of popular fiction'.[1] One of the most important parallels between the two texts from Humphreys's reading of the latter is the preoccupation with time which determines the structure or, to employ Humphreys's word, 'pattern' of each of them. Indeed, he finds in Roberts's novel,

> a profoundly feminine understanding of the nature of Time. Because of her peculiar awareness of the passage of the seasons, of the characteristic rhythms of daily life in a given era, it would not be unreasonable to claim that Time itself, Welsh Time, was the chief character in the novel.[2]

Avoiding Humphreys's rather essentialist concept of a 'feminine understanding of the nature of Time', which raises many questions, both texts are structured around the passage of the seasons, the rhythms of daily life and different concepts of time. While one could confidently argue for 'time' as a character, if not the 'chief character', in each novel, Humphreys's concept of 'Welsh Time' is more enigmatic and problematic. Yet the phrase summarizes how each novel approaches the concept of time through contrasting the way in which Welsh language and identity are rooted in the local and particular with a wider modernist understanding of time, linked to science, technology and globalism.

More than any of Humphreys's other novels written in English, *Outside the House of Baal* explores the creative tension between different perpsectives on history, and ultimately time, into which the French philosopher Jacques Derrida provides pertinent insights, as discussed in chapter 3. Although Humphreys, according to his own concept of the Protestant novel, outlined in chapter 2, recognized the importance of linear development, he avoids focusing exclusively upon it in *Outside the House of Baal*. Indeed, he also avoids the kind of linear versus cyclical binary which tends to dominate narratives that reject a purely linear approach to events. The structure of the novel is based upon a concept of history and time which Derrida has termed 'pluri-dimensionality', an alternative to conceiving of 'a linear scheme of the unfolding of presence, where the line relates the final presence to the orig- inary presence according to the straight line or the circle'.[3] The focus of this chapter will be on reading *Outside the House of Baal* through its 'pluri-dimensionality' and on how it avoids simpler linear or cyclical connections between events in favour of a complex pattern of seemingly endless returns, (re)readings and alternative interpretations.

As I suggested in chapter 3, the title of the novel highlights the notion of being an 'outsider'. At one level, this refers to the sense of being literally outside of the *House of Baal*, which is the situation in which the Reverend J. T. Thomas and his sister-in-law Kate find them- selves, living near a public house.[4] But it also challenges the reader to think of the novel more generally in terms of being an outsider and to consider the different ways in which it might be applied to different characters, outside, say, history, time, language, war, Christianity, family and Nonconformity. Frequently, characters refer to themselves as outsiders but none more than J.T. who feels himself an outsider in respect of his pacifism and his quarrels with the bigotry of traditional Nonconformists and with the 'modern' world. Wynn Thomas suggests that J.T.'s characterization is based on George M. Ll. Davies, 'a char- ismatic, if controversial, personality during the inter-war period'.[5] As Thomas points out, there are strong similarities between the two ministers. Davies was imprisoned as a conscientious objector during the First World War, thereafter embarking upon a 'pilgrimage of peace', and, like J.T. , attracted the disapproval of his denomination.[6]

However, as described in chapter 3, the title should not be taken at face value where the word 'Outside' is concerned because, in the course of the novel, it can refer to those who may be outside but are still influenced by what they are outside of. Thus, Lydia may be outside the Second World War in so far as she has not gone overseas but she is, nevertheless, killed by a bombing raid on Liverpool. In this regard, the novel, which, as I have suggested, is concerned with people who are outsiders on many different levels, also questions the very concept of 'outsider'.

There are several ways in which the title of the novel may be read. It refers to the killing of the worshippers of the god Baal, a Canaanite fertility god, in the Old Testament (Kings 2: 10). In the Bible, Jehu (the king of Israel infamous for his brutal killing of Queen Jezebel) tricks them into attending a great sacrifice to Baal in their temple and, when they are trapped inside, all are put to death. It is an incident which raises questions about violence (and, implicitly, war) because Jehu might have avoided killing Baal's followers and exiled them or even tried to convert them.

The phrase 'House of Baal' cannot help but bring to mind 'House of God', too. In other words, the novel could be interpreted as exchanging the 'House of God', referring to the time when the chapel and the ethics of Nonconformity (epitomized by the former family home Argoed) dominated Wales, for the modern secular age dominated by the House of Baal (associated by the minister J.T. with the pub onto which his and his sister-in-law Kate's small home looks). The drunkenness, promiscuity and immorality (or amorality) in mid-twentieth-century Wales which the pub symbolizes is a recurring motif in the novel.

Although published in the mid-1960s, *Outside the House of Baal* anticipates the interest in late twentieth-century fiction, such as in the work of Ian Sinclair, Ian McEwan, Christopher Meredith, Stevie Davies and Sarah Waters, in the nature of time while Humphreys also looks back to the exploration of time in the work of writers such as Kate Roberts, William Faulkner and Virginia Woolf. The novel incorporates many of the different concepts of time in Western thinking, including Newtonian abstract mechanical time; Kantian notions of time as the product of human intuition; Bergson's concept of 'duration' (lived time); and Marcel Proust's internal time consciousness. But there are two aspects of twentieth-century thinking about time that frame *Outside the House of Baal* more than any others: Henri Bergson's late Victorian critique of Newtonian mechanistic time from the perspective of lived time, published in 1887, which had an important influence upon early twentieth-century modernist narrative;[7] and time consciousness as a concept shared by all human beings but experienced differently by individuals.

Outside the House of Baal is primarily focused on the retired Methodist minister, J.T. and his sister-in-law, Kate, who share a house, their lives up until that point and the lives of their family, friends and acquaintances. In many respects, it is one of Humphreys's most successful 'dramatic' novels, effectively integrating the two principal features which characterized this type of novel as he defined it: the theme of progress on an individual or societal level and a recurring concern with personal, social and moral dilemmas. It also successfully interweaves a modernist text with a realist, or semi-realist, aesthetic.

Compared with *A Man's Estate* and *A Toy Epic*, *Outside the House of Baal* is more traditional in that it is a third-person narrative. However, it is modernist in the way in which the narrative alternates between a present, in which a day in the life of the two central protagonists unfolds, and past episodes in their lives, conflating the boundaries between the past and the present. Time in the text, as already noted, is explored as an individual, cultural and spatial concept.

TIME, MODERNISM AND MEMORY

The narrative of *Outside the House of Baal* is framed by time. In chapter 16, J.T. receives news that his boyhood friend Ivan Cole, who has been ill for some time, has died aged seventy-eight and left him his watch. This is the watch he had when they worked in the village forge together as youngsters. The chapter ends with J.T.'s buying a bus ticket for a mystery tour to Ynys Môn (then called by its English name, Anglesey) so that he can go and collect the watch while, unbeknown to him, Kate has persuaded her niece to embark on a day out in Anglesey to the same end. As Wynn Thomas points out, 'of its twenty-six chapters, ten are set in the present and sixteen in the past, but the latter are given four pages to every one of the former'. Moreover, although 'there is a regular pattern of alternation between past and present' in the first quarter of the novel, thereafter, 'the arrangement is irregular, with the maximum disparity occurring after chapter 18, when there are four chapters in succession dealing with past events'.[8]

As suggested in chapter 3, movement was an important modernist metaphor for examining embodiment in the twentieth century. The interconnecting of time and physical, spatial awareness is an important trope in *Outside the House of Baal*. The narrative opens with J.T.'s awakening to a new day: 'Somewhere in the room a clock was ticking, showing what time it was.'⁹ But, in this opening chapter, it is not simply the clock that indicates the time and the text encourages the reader to ask what time is being referred to here: the time of day; the time in J.T.'s or Kate's life; objective, bodily or mental time; time in the twentieth century; or time in the history of a particular culture or nation?

The mechanical time which the clock signifies is contrasted with the biological time that J.T. feels in his body. It is an effort for him to move the eiderdown on his bed so that it avoids a chamber pot which, in another indication of his bodily age, he has used twice in the night. The way in which he then lies back in the bed suggests death: 'When it was done his head sank back and his mouth closed' (p. 5). These two different measurements of time, the relentless linear, steady tick of the mechanical clock and the physiological body clock that advances and reveals itself in different ways at different times even within the same body, are in turn contrasted with further concepts of time. They are juxtaposed with the marking and prioritizing of events from the lives of J.T. and Kate through the objects displayed in their home. Some of these, such as the worn poker and Kate's faded pinafore, signify time passing in a sense which is not so easily measured as that conveyed by the ticking clock and, like the changes over time in our bodies, is not so immediately observable. Meanwhile, the Grecian urns which emboss the iron fireplace suggest a 'historical' perspective in which the larger sweep of time is divided into periods of differing significance as if history were the product of objective scholarship instead of partial subjective perspectives. Moreover, the Greek vases on a presumably Victorian, or at least early twentieth-century, fireplace eliminate the distance between the ancient and modern worlds. They now stand in a dialectic relationship to each other that belies the use of terms such as 'ancient', 'modern', 'present' and 'past' and emphasizes a spatial rather than temporal link between the two objects from different periods.

Although the mechanical clock appears to mark linear time, the circular movement of the clock's hands suggests that time is essentially cyclical and the individual life is marked by events and ceremonies that repeat themselves in generation after generation. But, as noted earlier, the novel avoids even this linear/cyclical binary. Various perspectives on time are examined through the structure and content of the novel which, like time itself is, in Derrida's phrase, 'pluri-dimensional'.

The narrative alternates between the day in which we are introduced to J.T. and Kate and select events from their past, initially their childhoods, and that of Kate's sister Lydia. The effect of the narrative structure of *Outside the House of Baal* is to eliminate the distance between old age, childhood and the earlier stages in one's life (informed by a linear concept of time), placing them in a dialectical relationship to each other, just as the vases and the fireplace in J.T. and Kate's room erase some of the distance between 'ancient' and 'modern'. I use the phrase 'dialectical' relationship to refer to the way in which the novel's concept of a plural dimensional time works in practice. The connection between events changes for characters and for the reader as the novel reconsiders and alludes to different episodes in ways which change their significances.

Humphreys uses a plural dimensional concept of time, through the intermixing of two people's old age and their earlier lives, to explore larger topics around identity and subjectivity including the significance of particular cultural epochs, changing notions of masculinity and femininity, and different perceptions of the relationship between mind and body. The chapters set in the past also pursue the contrast, introduced in chapter 1 of the novel, between a subjective, corporeal awareness of time and an objective one, introducing a further theme in the novel concerning the nature of memory and the part played by it (particularly its changing character) in creating and maintaining identity.

The opening chapters present us with snapshots from J.T.'s and Kate's respective childhoods which are linked in more complex ways than just chronologically. The passages are linked spatially as well as temporally and interlinked through recurring images, subjects, people and tropes. At one level, they are experiments with the chronology of narrative itself and, at another, with the nature of memory. At the time that Humphreys was writing this novel, the dominant model of memory was Freudian, in which memory was linked to the subconscious, and the selective nature of memory in turn connected with repression. Humphreys's conceptualizing of J.T., Kate and Lydia is Freudian in the sense that they are motivated by subconscious drives and desires, not all of which they are fully aware of, and of which the reader is made more conscious as the chapters unfurl. However, Humphreys's model of memory is different from Freud's in that it is less dependent upon the dialogical relationship between the conscious and subconscious mind. Humphreys appears to believe that events, incidents and images are not primarily connected chronologically in the mind but spatially. In other words, if one were to model Humphreys's concept of memory it would be one in which events from different periods in an individual's life are linked by something they have in common.

In *Outside the House of Baal*, this model of individual memory is applied to cultural, familial and national memory so that events that are invoked at different points in the narrative are similarly linked by what they have in common. Reading this novel is akin to experiencing memory because it is based on what is triggered by various events connected spatially, and not only temporally, in the text. This concern with what is triggered as one moves from one part of the narrative to another is employed as a means of questioning narrativization itself. The novel is a typical modernist text in that, through its questioning of national narrative, it examines what is meant in this and other connections by identity. In particular, the Freudian model of memory which is based on what is repressed and distorted in consciousness is challenged by Humphreys's model of spatial juxtaposition, enabling the text to explore what has been suppressed in individual, cultural and national consciousness in new ways.

NARRATIVE STRUCTURE

As has been suggested, the preference in *Outside the House of Baal* for spatial connection rather than temporal sequence is one of the principal modernist features and determining factors of the narrative itself, as is evident from the alternation of chapters dealing with old age and childhood. The first seven chapters of the novel, linked as mentioned earlier through shared images, themes and places, reflect the way in which different events might be arranged in our own memories. One of the most significant subjects which link these sections is time itself. As already noted, the first chapter opens by juxtaposing a ticking clock with J.T.'s awareness of ageing in his own body. As the novel moves back in time from this particular morning in the life of J.T. and Kate, it develops the multidimensionality of time suggested by the clock and the body.

The first event of Kate's childhood, with which the second chapter begins, develops the concern with ageing found in the first chapter with reference to the frail body of Kate's mother in a wheelchair. This representation, once again, is contrasted with the objective mechanical time by which we live our lives when Kate's eldest brother, Ned, consults his watch and reminds the family that if they do not hurry they will miss the train. Kate's aged mother in one generation is cryptically linked to the ageing J.T. in another, since the way in which she tugs at Ned's trouser leg is similar to Joe's tugging at the eiderdown. Through these carefully selected details, the narrative contrasts the traditional meas- urement of time (signified by the pocket watch), both with the way in which modernity, as I mentioned in chapter 3, twists time into space (through speed signified by the train), and with biological time signi- fied by the ageing body.

Throughout the novel, the reader is made aware of the plural nature of time in scenes, or chronotopes, that intermix, for example, biolog- ical, mechanical and institutionalized time as well as different types of memory. Like Ned's pocket watch, the clock in J.T.'s room main- tains the emphasis upon the way in which the objective measurement of time has become fundamental to modernity, since it made the industrial revolution possible. The pocket watch signifies the way in which individual life in the modern age is increasingly lived according to socially determined timetables rather than reflecting the natural and communal rhythms which for generations prior to the twentieth century determined the pace of life in north Wales farming communi- ties. The introduction of the train is an image not only of how speed has become a key feature of modern life but of increased mobility. It represents the way in which modernity has transformed spatial rela- tionships and the individual's awareness of his or her embodiment.

A significant moment at this point in the novel, as it moves back- wards in time from J.T.'s and Kate's 'present' as elderly people to their childhoods, is one which may appear minor. This is when, as a boy, J.T. is in the school classroom of standard two. Movement through school life, which is measured in terms of years linked to educational phases, represents a further societal, and hence individual and familial, way of measuring time in terms of stages that are perceived as important milestones. These milestones locate the individual life according to a particular concept of progress, based on educational attainment. Through this process, the individual is aligned with and measured against the lives of others who pass through the state educa- tion system in different parts of Wales. But, once again, Humphreys interweaves linear time (informing the concept of progression through various school years or 'standards') with a more complex concept of time suggested by the sense of different generations moving through the same classroom. The latter encapsulates Derrida's thinking about 'hauntology' (discussed in chapter 3), where individuals from the past are like spectres, being absent yet present at the same time.

The way in which the passage of time in the first chapter of the novel is revealed through references to fading clothes, such as Kate's pinafore, is echoed in the schoolroom episode in J.T.'s childhood by the detail of the darned knees of his stockings. As a child, J.T. embodies the possibility of the future but already, as his darned stockings suggest, he is caught up in the passage of time. Moreover, the movement in the text from the present to the past implies that the seeds of the future into which we think we are travelling have already been sown in our past. There are a number of key images in this episode of the passage of time: the reference to the school bell, the discoloured string tied around the neck of the jar in which tadpoles were brought to school, and the school yard worn by the feet of generations of students. This first incident in the child J.T.'s life, like the first one from Kate's early life that involves her elderly mother, picks up the suggestion of death in the first chapter of the novel in which the elderly J.T. lies in bed after the exertions of moving the eiderdown. The bell heard by the schoolboy J.T. suggests not only the way in which days and weeks are divided into blocks of time but the funeral bell. Thereby, it also suggests the absent presence in the schoolyard of generations of children. When J.T. touches the jam jar in which, concealed by its dark water, a tadpole is supposedly turning into a frog, mirroring his own transitional adolescence, he is initiated into biological time and with it an awareness of his own mortality.

In the third episode from Kate's and J.T.'s childhood, Kate watches her father taking the house clock apart to clean it. The stopped clock makes the house unusually quiet, underscoring the silence which follows the absence of her mother. Her father's dismantling of the clock seems to signify both his attempt to understand 'time' in regard to ageing and death and the way in which the narrative itself is structured around an examination of time. Paradoxically, the house and Kate's mother now stand outside of time but it is at this moment, when time has momentarily stopped, that Kate and her father become most conscious of it. She sees him now as an old man and, insisting that Kate look after her sister, he envisages the family without him. The expectation that Kate will assume the maternal role in relation to her sister sows the seed of her future in which she will never be happily married and have a family herself.

Through the reference to the Welsh-language newspaper on which the clock's parts have been placed, this episode in Kate's life introduces the way in which time is measured, and history recorded, in regard to Welsh-language culture, which has a different narrative from English-language culture in Wales. The former has a history of peaks

and troughs in which it loses and regains its cultural and civic significance. At the time when Kate's father spreads the clock's parts onto
the newspaper, the Welsh language was being lost in many parts of
Wales, a process that also involved the decay of assumptions embodied
in the culture, such as the importance of genealogy and the localizing
of identity in a particular place, which in turn determined how time
was perceived.

The way in which time expands and contracts, as it were, at different
moments is developed in the fourth episode from J.T.'s childhood
in which he watches the village children playing a game of fox-and-
hounds. The energy and vibrancy of the language reflects that of the
play itself and contrasts with the ponderous J.T. in the classroom where
his father is working for an external BA from London University. This
incident is linked to Kate's previous memory of her father after the loss
of her mother through J.T.'s hearing the news that his father is about
to remarry. Although at the heart of this episode there is an intense,
spontaneous childhood experience of life, the game of fox-and-
hounds, which runs counter to the prevailing sense of time passing,
the narrative is primarily characterized at this point by a brooding and
philosophical sensibility. This is highlighted in the way in which the
game is preceded by a reminder that the schoolyard has been worn by
the feet of generations of children and the discovery that the frog in the
jar is dead. Here, J.T. is beginning to emerge as an 'outsider'. He seems
more aware of time than of living it and, not having been told that his
father is about to remarry, seems something of an outsider even within
his family itself.

The next episode from Kate's childhood which introduces Lydia,
and the immediate episodes which follow it, are concerned with
perspectives on death and echo the serious, reflective sensibility with
which even the young J.T. is associated in the novel. The reference to
time, implicit in the worn surface of the playground in J.T.'s school, is
echoed in the detail of the granary where Lydia finds an old newspaper:
floorboards are worm-eaten and there are remnants of winter oats. In
the old newspaper, Lydia finds an advertisement for a quack medicine
which she believes will cure her mother who, so Kate tells her, has gone
away to die. In the next section, the fiancée of J.T.'s father, recalling
the impact that the death of his wife had on her prospective husband,
comforts herself with the belief that burdens are lightened by love; and
Lady Glanadda's son invites Lydia and Kate to watch a skeleton dance
in what could be a carnivalesque parody of the medieval march of the
skeletons.

Consistent with what modern psychoanalytic theory would term the process of abjection, these seven chapters introduce us to the repugnant physical avatars of death manifest in extreme old age, of which Lady Glanadda's father is an example. Her son admits: 'He just sits there all day, looking through the window, until they come to put him to bed' (p. 27). This sense of the abjection of old age is even more pronounced in the next chapter, which returns to the 'present' in which J.T. and Kate share a house. Kate, who lost an eye when she was much younger, looks at herself in a mirror: 'There was an area of darkness around her eyeless socket, like a ragged hole torn in a white mask' (p. 34).

In the first chapter of the novel, the relationship between J.T. and Kate suggests how time progresses through the complexity and dilemmas of human relationships. Chapter 2 closes with Miss Dowell discovering the 'reality' of her fiancé's drinking. Waiting for her drunken husband-to-be to return home, she finds comfort in sharing a bed with her prospective stepson. As they hold hands beneath the bed sheets, he feels her engagement ring digging into him, symbolic of the dilemmas by which he will find himself trapped in his future marriage to Lydia. In the next chapter, his future sister-in-law, who could for a time herself have been his wife and who ends up marrying a drunk, notices how 'the wedding ring on her finger was out of all proportion, thick and heavy, and yet it could no longer be passed over the swollen knuckle' (p. 34).

THE CHRONOTOPIC STRUCTURE

The episodes in *Outside the House of Baal* are effective because of the way in which Humphreys interweaves time and space and subtly juxtaposes different temporal frameworks. This is evident in the account of the confrontation between Lydia and her father when she is exposed over lying about her whereabouts one evening. The initial descriptive elements – the low kitchen fire and the buffeting wind – signify the larger ambience of Argoed House but also flesh out the 'hour' as Pa, along with the apprehensive Kate, awaits Lydia's return.

In chapter 3, I noted that Humphreys conflated the way in which the interior of buildings and rooms may be thought of simultaneously in terms of movement and of fixity (tableaux), and I suggested such a fusion was the product of the dominant cultural discourses of the time that determined spatial relationships. The relationship between Kate and Pa, and subsequently between Pa and Lydia, is reflected in the special organization of life at Argoed which is both 'realistic' and, to employ Bakhtin's phrase, 'realist emblematique'. The father's position in the parlour and Kate's in the kitchen signify their different respective statuses within Argoed. This is reinforced by the father's Welsh label – *merch i* (my girl) – for both his daughters which is an expression of his endearment but also of the position which they inevitably occupy as daughters in his eyes. In this regard, their spatial relationship to their father is significant. He occupies a room at the centre of the house where he might expect to receive family and visitors. They are associated with the kitchen and laundry rooms which are closest to the outside of the house and adjacent to the doors to which tradespeople might be expected to make their way. Whilst he remains seated in what is really his room, Kate waits on him, as does Lydia when she returns and falls on her knees to take off his boots. Kate is subject to his commands, as is evident when he orders her to bed, and, even as an adult, she is positioned between childhood and maturity. This in-between position is re-enforced in this 'scene' by her exhaustion at the end of a tiring day and the need, nevertheless, for her to prepare herself for the equally punishing morrow.

Of course, at the centre of the scene is the tense confrontation between Lydia and her father which is rendered all the more dramatic by being narrated in a time frame which nearly equates to that in which the episode unfolds. Like a spider waiting for its prey to enter its web, her father leads her on by asking questions about the chapel that evening, knowing full well that she has not been there. As she undoes the knot of his boot laces – the difficulty in doing so symbolizes the difficulty in untangling herself from her Nonconformist family and community – she ties a larger knot for herself. Simultaneously, her father is surreptitiously folding his paper, aptly entitled the *Christian Companion*, into a phallic, cylindrical weapon with which to strike her. I say phallic, because her father's authority comes not only from his position as head of the family but also from the social status which men at this time enjoyed.

It is significant that the *Christian Companion* with which Lydia is struck is an 'old copy' (p. 83), because the confrontation is not simply between father and daughter but between the sober past which has moulded him and the more liberated present for women which is evident in Lydia's appearance: 'her cheeks rosy with the fresh wind, her eyes shining and small curls falling away under her hat' (p. 84).

The interior of Argoed, like the interiors of rooms in Humphreys's first novel, *The Little Kingdom*, discussed in chapter 3, excludes certain ideas and people but also locks individuals and certain ideas in together. Here, Lydia literally brings the 'outside', in the sense of what is outside the physical and spiritual boundaries of the house, into Argoed. But to her father's eyes, she might as well be bringing into the house what in biblical terms is outside the House of Baal. The outside is initially associated with 'the buffeting wind' p. (83) but subsequently, as Lydia comes back, with 'the fresh wind'. Lydia's greater sense of freedom is signified by her removing her gloves and unbuttoning her coat. Even in unlacing her father's boots, where one could emphasize the love rather than the servitude in the act, there is a sense of the part she could play in bringing her father from the past into the present. But, of course, such a present would be hers rather than his.

At one level, the blow struck by the Nonconformist paper is a strike against the emergent secular and amoral present which, in her father's eyes, Lydia represents. But there is also a sense that in its death throes, Nonconformity will become more removed from the Welsh-language family and community. This is suggested here not only in the blow to Lydia but by the way in which her father chastizes her in English: 'my girl'. And while Pa speaks to her in a way which reflects the ideal of the Nonconformist family – 'soft, gentle, unthreatening, calm, fatherly' (p. 85) – he is all the while calculatedly preparing to strike her. This contradiction is explicitly referred to again later in the novel, when Lydia, now a mother herself, is holidaying with her sister-in-law Bessie. Listening to Bessie's 'warm and friendly tremulo' (p. 294), Lydia declares: 'It's a better house than Argoed, Bessie, I always thought so' (p. 295).

In all the episodes involving intimacy or confrontation, narrative time in *Outside the House of Baal* conforms to the actual time of the events themselves, as tends to be the case in drama. The breakup between Kate and Wynne Bannister begins on a night when she waits in bed for his return. As mentioned earlier, this episode echoes the earlier one in the novel in which Miss Dowling, sharing a bed with her future stepson J.T., waits for the return of the young boy's father whom she is to marry the following day, and sees him drunk for the first time. The Kate and Wynne episode further develops the imagery of time which is woven into the fabric of the whole novel. As Kate, woken by Wynne's noise, looks at the clock, she holds it close to her hip, pulling up her nightdress in the process, so that it signifies not just mechanical time but biological time. Because of the years that she has given to fulfilling her own father's promise to care for the family and Argoed, Kate is in danger of ending up childless at the end of her childbearing period.

On hearing her husband at the bedroom door, Kate tries to lock it but there is no key. When he enters the room, Wynne tells her that he has heard a ripe apple fall, continuing the interest in organic time and Kate's biological age. However, the reference to the apple places both of them, as a couple, within the wider context of nature and also invokes the biblical myth of the Garden of Eden. Kate's marriage to Wynne is her induction into sexual knowledge, an experience which is for her aggressive and crude: 'Come down to old Wynne and he'll give you something you like. Something very tasty' (p. 304). His choice of phrase reduces love and sex to appetite. When Kate surprises Lydia in telling her what Wynne was really like, before learning the full truth, Lydia calls him 'The old fool!' (p. 349). This establishes a link with J.T. for, at the beginning of the novel, Kate, now sharing a house with J.T. in the 1960s, blames him for making her break Aunt Addy's butter dish, and calls him under her breath 'You soft old fool!' (p. 9). In the novel as a whole, the expression acquires a larger significance, reflecting the perceived failings of the male-oriented society of north-east Wales. At one point Dan Llew bemoans the fact that 'both my sisters married fools' (p. 275), adding that Archie Griffiths of Bodafon Hall, whom Kate at one time considered marrying, was, also 'a bit of a fool' (ibid.).

OUTSIDE THE HOUSE OF BAAL AS A DILEMMA NOVEL

At one level, J.T. may seem to be an odd choice for a 'Protestant' or 'dramatic' novel in which the idea of progress is an important feature. The work eschews the chronological approach of the *Bildungsroman* which follows a character's progress from childhood to maturity, since it begins with the central protagonists in old age and moves backwards in time. It is also challenging as a story because, as Wynn Thomas points out, there are times when it is strangely silent on key events, such as 'Ma's death, Kate's reaction to losing her eye, the marriage of Lydia and J.T., the death of Pa, [and] J.T.'s reaction to the death of Lydia'.[10]

Ioan Williams argues that the old age of J.T. 'witnesses the decline and defeat of every one of [his] cherished beliefs':

In the first place he lives outside the house of Baal – the large public house which he identifies every morning from his bedroom window as a witness to the defeat of Temperance. He has lived through two world wars which effectively defeated the tradition of pacifism, and now inhabits a world increasingly governed by the standards of English suburbia, where the Welsh language is in retreat. He has failed as a minister and as a father and husband. Even now in his relationship with Kate, his sister-in-law, he is unable to break through the barriers of non-communication.[11]

However, in moving back in time and in alternating past and present, the novel is structured through numerous personal, social and moral dilemmas which deconstruct, rather than describe, what we mean by 'failure'. Early in his life, J T. declares: 'I am a stranger in this world … My home is outside of time' (p. 112). The novel explores how far this is true and questions whether he is deluding himself in thinking in these terms for, at one level, he is certainly not outside of time and society. As the novel unfolds, his self-image as a stranger is also explored in his relationships with others, especially his father, his wife and Kate, and in his values and beliefs in regard to the changing and emergent world around him.

The death of Joe's father exemplifies Jacqueline Rose's argument that in mourning we come to realize how little we know those with whom we are most intimate. Drawing on Freud, she argues that 'Death is a problem, not because we cannot surmount its loss or imagine our own death, but because it forces us to acknowledge that what belongs to us most intimately is also a stranger or enemy, a type of foreign body in the mind'.[12] A single, seemingly innocuous detail when the curate informs J.T., now a theological student, that his father is dead brings to mind the earlier scene when J.T., then in standard two at school, waited while his father worked for his BA: 'There was a frog in Joe's throat when he spoke' (p. 82). A commonplace colloquialism assumes a new-found significance at this point in the text. It reminds us of how in the earlier episode he had to flush a dead frog from a jam jar in which it had been brought to school, supposedly as a tadpole. What is meta-phorically in J.T.'s voice is his first close encounter with death. The idea of death in the voice occurs again when we learn that Bessie has a goitre in her neck so that 'she laughed unsteadily in her throat' (p. 295). In J.T.'s case, it is his engagement with Christianity, to which I will return below, that begins to clear his voice. In an argument with Griff over whether there is an afterlife, we learn that Joe begins 'to clear his throat excitedly' (p. 112).

The sense of distance between J.T. and his father in the earlier episode, when he did not know that his father was about to remarry, is repeated more dramatically when he learns that his father took his own life, a suicide which is echoed later in the novel by Archie Griffiths's death. As mentioned earlier, in the episode in which Lydia as a young woman is struck by her father, her removing her gloves signified the desire at that time in her life to cast off some of the dictates of Nonconformity. However, when J.T.'s maternal grandmother wears gloves to his father's funeral, she is highlighting the Nonconformist respectability that has become lost to her through his 'shameful' end and interment in unconsecrated ground. In contrast to the symbolic significance of Lydia removing her gloves, those worn by J.T.'s grandmother represents the values of the traditional Nonconformity on which she has always relied but which now, through the disgrace of her son-in-law's burial in unconsecrated ground, puts her in a dilemma.

The lock of faded hair which J.T.'s grandmother tries to push from her eye brings to mind Lydia's small curls falling rebelliously from under her hat prior to her confrontation with her father. This echo serves to link Lydia and the grandmother in what at this point in the novel might seem an unlikely coupling. But the grandmother's moral indignation – 'the effort of looking [into the grave] sketched a grimace of disapproval on her face' (p. 85) – might be seen as anticipating the stance which Lydia will assume towards J.T. in the later years of their marriage. Once again, the past, present and future are linked at different levels. What the grandmother whispers to J.T. is both literal and metaphorical: 'Move on' (p. 85) and 'keep to the path' (p. 86). She invokes many tropes from the novel, including Nonconformity, J.T.'s father's ambition and dilemmas faced by individuals struggling in unsuccessful personal relationships. In the process, what she says exemplifies the way in which moments of time are always multidimensional.

Given that J.T. proves as distant in his own family as his father was in his, it is ironic that the first major theological debate that he initiates is over that part of the Nonconformist creed which believes that the sins of the fathers are visited on their children (p. 294). Since J.T. is very much the son of his father, an example of inherited traits repeated elsewhere in the novel, this creed seems to reflect not only the multidimensional concept of time in the narrative but the way in which moments of time and events are, to use Derrida's term, 'haunted' on many levels by 'spectres' and 'ghosts' from other moments and events including those with which the individual is not directly involved.[13]

Thus, in some instances in the novel, the sins of the father seem to be visited across families. The accusation of Lydia's father that she has lied over not being in chapel, in the episode discussed above, is mirrored in the occasion when J.T. accuses her of lying about where she had obtained a necklace he has found among her possessions: 'The word "lie" seemed to touch off a fresh burst of anger' (p. 339). The discovery by J.T.'s stepmother that her new husband is an alcoholic is replicated in Kate's discovery that her husband Wynne Bannister is an alcoholic too. The reasons for the failure of Kate's marriage – Bannister's secrecy, different lifestyle and (mis)management of money – act as a commentary upon the reasons for the failure of her sister Lydia's marriage to J.T. It also underlines the dilemma at the heart of the latter case: to what extent is J.T. to be admired for his social and pastoral conscience and his moral commitment and how far is he to be regarded as selfish, too wrapped up in his own pursuits? When Lydia turns on J.T., echoing her brother Griff's earlier criticism that he merely throws out quotations like a defensive shield, she accuses him of being 'Full of words and phrases as if they have mattered more than anything else. You aren't like a normal man at all. You live on words and phrases. That's all you are about. You don't care about me or about the children' (p. 339).

The novel is centred on a principal dilemma found not only in Wales but in Western society generally in the twentieth century which involves two fundamentally different ways of looking at the world: the Christian and the modern, secularist perspective. In some respects, the secularists give expression to a particular scientific world view which Christianity has for centuries repressed. When, in the novel, the secular voice makes itself heard in the society of north-east Wales, it is often exaggerated in terms both of what it says and what it is perceived as challenging. This is evident in the way in which Griff, who wants to become a lawyer, attacks Christianity: 'Organise the world as though it were a damn great sheep farm, preparing everyone for the next world. You know what I think? I don't think there's a next world. No hell. No heaven. Nothing' (p. 112).

Griff's view of the Christian message, as focused on the afterlife, is a commonplace misinterpretation of the emphasis of Christianity. But it brings to the fore the way in which religion in twentieth-century Wales is haunted in a Derridean sense by the kind of pre-socialist aspirations voiced by *Llais Llafur*, as Robert Pope describes: '"The basis of the Christian faith", claimed *Llais Llafur*, should be "decent living conditions of life and labour here on earth"'.[14] There is an echo, too, in what Griff says of D. H. Lawrence's critique of Christianity's supposed over-emphasis on the crucifixion and on death. Griff's arguments reflect the way in which the First World War destroyed blind belief in the grand narratives of faith, patriotism and destiny. Pope describes how

> the war did not merely cause problems concerning religious teaching but widened the experience of many men who had never previously left the confines of their village. Apart from the horrors of trench warfare, their experiences gave them a new outlook on life and morality. Having won the war, they were encouraged to believe that they stood on the threshold of a new age.[15]

Outside the House of Baal demonstrates how what Pope calls 'the transition from Christianity to materialistic Socialism' was easier for some than for others.[16] Where it proved difficult, it was often because of the way in which a linear transition of the kind which Pope describes was conceptually too difficult. He acknowledges how at many levels Nonconformity and the labour movement in the early years of the twentieth century existed in a complex relationship with each other:

> In its early years the labour movement held similar ideals to the chapel on subjects such as temperance and coarse language, ideals which certainly had emanated from the chapel culture. The labour movement had ensured that its moral standards were similar to those of the chapel, thus rendering its existence acceptable to many working men in a culture so influenced and dominated by Nonconformist Puritanism.[17]

Griff's easy transition from Nonconformity to socialist materialism disrupts J.T.'s thinking. His response is to throw out phrases from a variety of sources: 'I am a stranger in this world' (p. 112) and 'He who says he owes nothing to the past is still a child' (ibid.). Griff's arguments are themselves subject to scrutiny in the novel, but, at this point in the narrative, they appear more logically developed than J.T.'s. Recalling the opening of *The Little Kingdom*, Griff optimistically declares:

> We are on the threshold of an absolutely new kind of world. I want to be part of that. Something that free men carve out for themselves, something new, something the world has never seen before. Think of what we shall be able to do soon – fly, go under the sea, move about at great speed, join up the ends of the earth ... (pp. 111–12)

What Griff does not recognize at this moment is how technology brings about war, death and unemployment as well as the benefits that he recognizes. Ironically, when he finishes speaking, his arms are outstretched. This image brings to mind both Christ as a preacher and the crucified Christ. It underscores the extent to which what he says is actually more rhetoric and vision than logic, reflecting the rhetorical achievements of the fascist leaders of the 1920s and 1930s. They were to sell their particular visions to millions of ordinary people and, of course, to take Europe into another war like that in which Griff is killed. This gesture is repeated later in the novel by Ronnie, listening to the ferocious argument between J.T. and Lydia in which he accuses her of lying about how she obtained the necklace he has found. In this position, with his arms stretched out between the walls on the stairs, Ronnie feels 'imprisoned' (p. 341). With his head lowered, he is redolent of the crucified Christ who was himself the victim of warring factions.

The dilemma in which J.T. finds himself is not simply one between Christianity and secularization but between J.T.'s version of Christianity and Nonconformity which in the second half of the novel comes down to a clash between the Old and the New Testaments. J.T. argues that 'the Gospel is wide enough and deep enough to provide mankind with a new way of living. A society that gives and not a society that takes. A society that creates, not a society that destroys' (p. 389). This is at the heart of his argument with T. Machno Jones over the Nonconformist creed of the sins of the fathers being visited on their sons, referred to earlier: 'the idea of total corruption flowing with the seed from father to son is primitive and barbaric and it leads in the end to making us morally impotent and unable to respond to the full challenge of the New Testament' (p. 299). For J.T., 'God is a God of love' and 'The New Testament is a testament of love' (p. 290).

Despite acknowledging the way in which Nonconformity and socialism interact, Robert Pope's study of the tension between them sees it primarily in linear terms, a movement away from Nonconformity, which eventually failed to meet the needs of the working class, to socialism:

Nonconformity had been perhaps the greatest single influence on Welsh life for half a century. The legacy of the industrial revolution was, for many communities, the constant threat to life and the stark reality of economic hardship ... While previously content with a religion that gave stability and hope in an unstable and precarious environment, the working class now sought a religion which would change their environment. Hardie and others had convinced them that religion should indeed do this. But the end result was that his use of religious language persuaded men to join a secular movement.[18]

Wynn Thomas argues:

> The core bourgeois society which late nineteenth-century Welsh Nonconformity had created and served was discredited after the First World war (which it publicly supported), not least because its religious, cultural and political beliefs were anathema to the new, cosmopolitan and increasingly radical inhabitants of the industrial valleys of the south, where the population of the country was overwhelmingly concentrated by 1900. There the reigning ideology soon came to be socialism in a variety of forms, and the realities of economic life as experienced by a proletariat partly comprised of immigrants meant that in the south there was little sense of connection, let alone of solidarity, with the Welsh-language culture that remained in the largely rural north and west.[19]

However, while this linear model effectively describes the way in which the differences between the north and the south in terms of political and religious allegiance arose, it does not capture the way in which Nonconformity remained an embedded part of life in north Wales. Pope describes how

> Nonconformity had enforced standards of morality, recognized individual responsibility and provided hope for a better life, albeit beyond the grave. Nonconformist zeal for temperance fostered 'the great trinity of religion, education and good living', and thus afforded the working class the opportunity and the training to develop the necessary skills for public life. Nonconformist influence extended beyond the spiritual needs of its members and adherents into social and political leadership in the mining, quarrying and agricultural communities.[20]

Thus, society in what Thomas identifies as the rural north and west remained, in Derrida's term, 'haunted' by the spectre of Nonconformity. Nonconformity continued to have such an impact upon the individual and cultural sensibility in these areas of Wales that Derrida's concept of a 'pluri-dimensional', rather than a linear model of history is closest to the experience in north Wales which Humphreys's novel captures and explores.

9

Land of the Living and Epic Theatre

The Land of the Living septet has a traditional plot in which a young girl who begins life as an orphan eventually becomes a lady of the manor. As an independently minded, highly motivated but somewhat self-centred character, Amy Parry is an example of a recurring female figure in Emyr Humphreys's work that includes Ada from *A Man's Estate* and Lydia from *Outside the House of Baal*. The septet allowed Humphreys further opportunities to develop his interest in assertive, dominant women. The saga is also indebted to the chronotopic fiction which preceded it, especially *Outside the House of Baal*, in which time and space are woven together in a largely episodic structure; to Humphreys's interest in narratives centred upon dilemma; and to the sense of social, moral and personal progress which he identified with 'dramatic' or 'Protestant' fiction, discussed in chapter 2.

However, what separates the septet from Humphreys's earlier work is the priority of social and cultural change over character. All Humphreys's texts reflect his interest in Welsh social and political history but, as he himself says, Amy 'was to be the main mirror walking down the twentieth-century street and her erratic progress would need to reflect the strains and stresses of a society no longer certain of itself, swept along on a tide of transition'.[1] Like Raymond Williams's trilogy – *Border Country* (1960), *Second Generation* (1964) and *The Fight for Manod* (1979) – to which I referred in chapter 1, Land of the Living traces social change in Wales over several generations. However, unlike Williams's trilogy, which focuses upon the lives of two men, Matthew Price and Peter Owen, Humphreys's septet is based on a group of characters, and in particular Amy Parry.

The first book to be published in Land of the Living, *National Winner* (1971), is actually the sixth in the chronology of the septet. In this novel, Amy, in late middle age, has obtained an estate and considerable wealth through her three marriages. She now lives with her husband John Cilydd, a solicitor-poet, but despairs of her marriage to him, and she has two sons by different fathers, Peredur and Gwydion, as well as her stepson, Bedwyr. The second novel, *Flesh and Blood*, is actually the first in terms of the chronology of the sequence. It depicts Amy's childhood and the social and familial factors which influenced her particular psychology, including the impact which the behaviour of older men had upon her, to which I will return later. Thereafter, the novels – *The Best of Friends* (1978), *Salt of the Earth* (1985), *An Absolute Hero* (1986), *Open Secrets* (1988) and *Bonds of Attachment* (1991) – follow a chronological narrative, into which *National Winner* has to be slotted. Thus, the sequence begins with Amy in a period which is contemporary to that in which the novel is written and, thereafter, takes us back in time, unravelling the forces that created the middle-aged Amy and the social milieu in which she now lives, before moving forwards in time with the last novel, *Bonds of Attachment*. According to a notebook in the Emyr Humphreys archive at the National Library of Wales, he originally thought of what he called Land of the Living as five novels of about 400,000 words each; a note in the margin in capital letters reads: 'Two millions words Don't say Too much.' The proposed titles for the novels are: 'Flesh and Blood'; 'Fame and Riches' or 'Bright Blue Sky' or 'The Best of Friends'; 'Lady Amy'; 'National Winner'; and 'Take Me Home'.[2]

THE INFLUENCE OF EPIC THEATRE

Raymond Williams's 'Border Country' trilogy may have had an influence upon Land of the Living. However, a more profound influence, and here we must remember that Humphreys had for a period been a director of drama for the BBC and a university lecturer in drama, was the German modernist playwright and theatre practitioner Bertolt Brecht's concept, which he first outlined in his essay 'The modern theatre is the epic theatre' (1930). Brecht's theatrical model is closely aligned to Humphreys's notion of 'dramatic fiction'. Both genres present the spectator/reader with dilemmas and choices and are as concerned with a wider world view as with the individual experience of particular characters.

In this chapter, I want to suggest, through detailed reference to several texts and wider reference to the saga as a whole, that, although Brecht's influence can be seen throughout Humphreys's fiction, it is most pronounced in the Land of the Living sequence. In thinking of the structure, Humphreys clearly invokes the central concept in Brechtian theatre that each scene is self-sufficient. In arguing that the turbulent nature of change in the twentieth century dictated the nature of his sequence, Humphreys maintained: 'The unit of construction would be the "dramatic episode": an event or occasion with something of the inner resilience of the short story speaking for itself with a minimum of decoration or authorial intervention.'[3] In 'The epic theatre and its difficulties', Brecht argues: 'the essential point of the epic theatre is perhaps that it appeals less to the feelings than to the spectator's reason. Instead of sharing an experience the spectator must come to grips with things.'[4] This is true also of the Land of the Living sequence which looks for meaning, as Ioan Williams says, 'not in individual experience but in the relationship between individual character and its environment' and where 'the action of [Humphrey's] novels is derived from social history'.[5]

Thus, in Humphreys's work, social history, or more specifically the social changes which are identified, and defined, by his characters, corresponds, as for Brecht, with the principal transformations in the mentality of his time.[6] This is evident in *The Best of Friends*, *Salt of the Earth* and *Open Secrets*, two of which were mentioned in chapter 5 for the importance of their exploration of the changing opportunities for feminism between the wars, upon which I will focus in this chapter.

Let us turn first to *Salt of the Earth*, one of the least discussed of Humphreys's novels. This book, in which Amy Parry has graduated and become a county secondary teacher, is important to the Land of the Living sequence because it is not simply set in the 1930s but defines this decade as an 'interim' period in which the country has emerged from the impact of the Great War. It now faces an uncertain future which has an evident impact upon Welsh nationalism and how Welsh socialists define themselves. The politically conceived Enid, referred to in chapter 5, tells her friend Amy, with considerable irony given how the 1930s were to end: 'In art and in life. The 1930s are a breathing space. Just time enough to breathe. To create rather than destroy.'[7]

Perhaps more than any of the other early Land of the Living novels, *Salt of the Earth*, to which I will return several times in this chapter, exemplifies how Humphreys see the potential of theatre and literature to form, in Brechtian terms, 'the "ideological superstructure" for a solid, practical rearrangement of our age's way of life'.[8] What this means for us as readers of Humphreys's fiction is that, while characters, events and 'scenes' in *Salt of the Earth* interest us, the novel is likely to be seen as primarily concerned with an engagement with the different ideologies competing in the Wales of the 1930s. In its various debates and conflicts it suggests how these are relevant to how we conceive of Wales, particularly the Wales of the interwar period, and how we conceive of Welsh identity.

Within this Brechtian framework, the reader of Humphreys's fiction, like the audience in Brechtian theatre, 'must come to grips with things' by means of engaging with the characters.[9] Ioan Williams argues: 'He does not present characters primarily as actors in a drama. The action of his novels is derived from social history rather than the emotional involvements of individuals.'[10] The point, however, is that Humphreys's characters *are* 'actors in a drama' but in a Brechtian drama. Williams is right in maintaining that the action of Humphreys's novels is 'derived from social history', but, through Brecht's influence, they aspire to more than this suggests in terms of their relationship to social context. What is at the heart of Land of the Living is not simply the personal experience of ideologically conscious characters but a larger project akin to the transformation which Brecht sought to enact in epic theatre and describes in 'The modern theatre is the epic theatre':

> Once the content becomes, technically speaking, an independent component, to which text, music and setting 'adopt attitudes', once illusion is sacrificed to free discussion, and once the spectator, instead of being enabled to have an experience, is forced as it were to cast his vote; then a change has been launched which goes far beyond formal matters and begins for the first time to affect the theatre's social function.[11]

Although Land of the Living is character based, the grand illusion of fiction, that we are privy to the consciousnesses of the characters about whom we read, is subservient to social and political points of view and to ideological debates which the reader as spectator is made to confront. Reading the sequence is rather like being in the audience at a theatre or cinema, observing a text moving between scenes and, in going 'beyond formal matters', affecting the novel's social, or specifically 'intellectual', function in ways parallel to Brecht's intention of affecting 'the theatre's social function'. Thus, Humphreys's Brechtian appreciation of the correspondence that should exist between art and what the German dramatist described as 'the whole radical transformation of the mentality of our time' is crucial to Land of the Living.[12] Such an approach renders particularly acute the intellectual dilemmas and choices facing modern Wales and highlights especially the extent to which the country seizes, or is able to seize, the historical moment.

THE PERSONAL AND POLITICAL

The argument that Humphreys's Land of the Living places a greater emphasis than even *Outside the House of Baal* upon 'the whole radical transformation of the mentality of our time' does not mean that the saga is without interest in character, character formation or emotion. Indeed, Brecht himself said that trying to deny emotion in epic theatre 'would be much the same thing as trying to deny emotions to modern science'.[13] Like Humphreys's fiction generally, Land of the Living is centred upon moral, intellectual and emotional dilemmas faced by its central protagonists and is structured around the possibilities of social, moral and personal progress. In regard to the latter, Humphreys sees Amy as exhibiting 'a path from poverty to affluence, from chapel discipline to free-thinking atheism, from red revolution to neo-royalism'.[14]

The title of the first novel, *National Winner*, is generally taken as referring to Amy's husband, the Eisteddfod-winning poet John Cilydd who commits suicide after the Second World War, over which he and his wife held different opinions and, as we saw in chapter 5, in which they became involved in different ways. While John supported conscientious objectors, Amy, an avowed Welsh socialist, became more directly involved with the war effort and also became anxious about the possible negative impact of her husband's actions on her public image. Stephen Knight, borrowing John Pikoulis's term 'the wounded bard' to describe Cilydd, argues that through him Humphreys suggests that 'Being a national winner … is also a way to become a national loser.'[15] However, the title of the novel could also refer to Amy who has suppressed her idealism and 'political' ambitions in favour of a more self-centred, materialist outlook. It is worth noting how, in her late middle age and as a widowed lady of the manor, she tries to pressure her sons into setting up a trust which would satisfy the altruistic ambitions that she once had and which have never been entirely vanquished. Moreover, the title, *National Winner*, may also refer ironically to Amy's sons. Peredur, named after the hero in the Welsh Arthurian romance, *Y Mabinogi* (the Mabinogion), wishes to turn his mother's mansion in north Wales into a monument to his father, which she resists. Gwydion, who Knight points out is named after 'the meretricious magician of the *Mabinogi* tale "Math fab Mathonwy"', supports the project as a potential tourist attraction linked to Arthurian romance.[16] The less colourful son Bedwyr, named after Arthur's loyal spear carrier, lends the project money and support.[17]

Whilst the twists, turns and uncertainties of twentieth-century Welsh social and cultural history determine the plot and structure of Land of the Living, the novels never lose sight of the complexities of Amy as an independent female developing in a century which saw new-found opportunities for women from which she was never able to benefit as fully as the generations of women who followed her. Her birth before the First World War also meant that her life was coterminous with the most turbulent years of the twentieth century. Humphreys himself explains that 'in the case of the world around her' she is faced with 'nothing less than the terrors of total war, of genocide, of the technology of nuclear destruction and ecological catastrophe'.[18]

In taking the reader, after *National Winner*, back to Amy's childhood, *Flesh and Blood* begins the narrative of social and technological change that occurred with the First World War. But it also unveils the influence that two older men in particular had upon her. First, her uncle, Lucas Parry, who is responsible for the material poverty of Amy's childhood and, through his impracticable moral idealism, causes her to reject Nonconformity. Secondly, the rector, who, in an episode in which he puts his hand down Amy's dress while she is having tea with him in the vicarage, leaves her with a lifelong suspicion of men and male sexuality even though she is attracted to older men such as Jack Pulford. In *The Best of Friends*, Amy receives a note from the rector delivered by his brother and her reaction is: 'I don't want to see him. It will just bring back things I want to forget.'[19] The influence of this childhood incident is implicit in subsequent novels through episodes which, as here, are Brechtian in that they cast the reader as a spectator trying to 'come to grips with things'.

The Best of Friends is the third novel, but the second in terms of the chronology of Land of the Living. It deals with Amy's college years at Aberystwyth and her early adulthood. Recognizing its significance in the sequence, Ioan Wiliams notes: 'it greatly expands our awareness of the meaning of *Flesh and Blood* – as life opens out around

Amy we become much more aware of what her character and reactions imply'.[20] More so than in the previous novels, in which Amy is an ageing woman and a child respectively, there is a strong sense in The Best of Friends not simply of social upheaval but of what Brecht termed 'the whole radical transformation of the mentality of our time'. The period during which Amy is a student is one which saw the development of Welsh nationalism and the emergence of the labour movement in south Wales.

Ioan Williams, not recognizing the Brechtian aesthetic behind Land of the Living, sees The Best of Friends as focused on individuals who are somewhat removed from the ideologies that constitute the different social realities with which they engage: 'The struggle between Communism and Nationalism, after all, is the conflict between two ideologies, neither of which were actually chosen by the people of South Wales, nor by Amy, the central character.'[21] In fact, the focus is on presenting the reader, as in Brechtian theatre, with dilemmas and debates about which they must make decisions.

Williams is nearer the mark in suggesting that the reconciliation of Amy's 'simple determination' and her friend Val's 'analytical idealism' is 'impossible in a patently sick society'.[22] However, while he is right to recognize this dialectic in The Best of Friends between 'idealism' and a 'sick society', the tension is distinctly Brechtian. Consciously or unconsciously, at the heart of this novel is one of Brecht's key perceptions of the radical transformation of the twentieth century as involving 'unhealthy changes stimulated by the operation of really new mental influences on our culture's aged body'.[23]

The relevance of this concept to mid-twentieth-century Wales is examined in Humphreys's novel in relation to points of view articulated and discussed through the relationships between four principal characters: Amy, who in the previous novel, Flesh and Blood, serves to focus a rejection of the ethos of Nonconformity and a penchant for materialist excess; Val Gwyn, Amy's first lover, who enables the text to explore the idealism of nationalism tied to traditional values of Nonconformity; Pen Lewis, who enables the juxtaposition of these intellectual positions and dispositions within the historical determinism of the mid-twentieth century; and Cilydd, who, in National Winner is a 'chaired' poet at the National Eisteddfod, married to an older Amy, and who in this text is a vehicle for an exploration of a Welsh-language poetic energized at its best by the traditions upon which it draws.

Whereas Humphreys does not consistently regard all changes as 'unhealthy', there is a strong sense in *The Best of Friends* of 'changes stimulated by the operation of really new mental influences on our culture's aged body'. The 'new mental influences' which enter this novel are especially evident in the public behaviour of young women. The cultural critic Homi Bhabha draws attention to how the representation of women as Woman in a culture often 'dramatizes' what is, in his view, a 'rather paradoxical boundary between the private and the public spheres'.[24] By this he means the way in which the 'private' and the 'public' are not as clearly separated in practice as we might wish to believe. The complex intermixing of the two which belies the concept of a boundary between them is demonstrated and 'dramatized' throughout *The Best of Friends* in the behaviour of Amy and Enid. In part one of the novel, the reader observes them, shortly after they have arrived at university, on a Sunday afternoon in Aberystwyth: 'Arm in arm they walked down the short street. They were both nervous, both conscious of being too easily observed.'[25] Walking with linked arms, the two women express their personal support of each other but are nervous in doing so and are also anxious because they are planning on visiting a man, Val Gwyn, in his lodgings on the afternoon of the Sabbath in a Nonconformist town. Thus, the dialectic here is between the public display of friendship and an emergent feminism and the Nonconformity which Amy, for personal as well as intellectual reasons, finds oppressive: 'I never thought I'd live to see a town with so many chapels in it, to be quite honest. It is the most awful dump on a Sunday. It really is.'[26]

For the personal reasons explored in *Flesh and Blood*, referred to earlier, Amy associates Nonconformity with, to employ Brecht's words, the 'culture's aged body'. But this is contrasted with Enid's assessment of the importance of Tasker Thomas in the next novel, *Salt of the Earth*. Believing 'it is time to lay the foundation for something new', she tells Amy that 'He is a sign of the times and a sign for the times. A special phenomenon. A spark of hope for Welsh non-conformity at the very moment when it seems to be dying on its feet.'[27] The interest in both these novels is not simply in Amy as a character but in the dialectic between what Amy and her friends perceive as 'new' and 'old' ideas. In *The Best of Friends*, despite Amy's rejection of Nonconformist Wales, she is dismayed to hear that Val Gwyn is in Paris and considering travelling to America: 'If he wants to make a new Wales he can do it right here. The old one is dead and dying.'[28] Indeed, at times in the novel Val Gwyn can appear to be a more uncompromising mouthpiece for the view that Wales is a sick and dying culture than even Amy: 'Fifty years ago there was growth here of a kind. Some kind of a hope. Some kind of a vision. Now there's nothing. It's worse than provincial. It's dead. It's riddled with a disease of the spirit.'[29] But, in a Brechtian sense, Humphreys is less concerned with presenting Val to the reader as a consistent character than with using him to articulate different perspectives about Wales's future. Thus, when Val walks with Amy at the end of part one, shortly after expressing this view, he appears to contradict himself: 'The old world is finished. And yet out of it we can make something new.'[30]

Bhabha's thesis that the cultural figure of the woman as Woman dramatizes the intermixing of the private and the public spheres provides a framework, as we have seen, to examine the complex space which Amy and Enid occupy in *The Best of Friends*. But, although they invariably find themselves in difficult and ambivalent locations, they often articulate confidence in the future of modern Wales and, more generally, the twentieth century. A case in point is Amy's expression of her Welsh feminism and nationalism: '"I think I fancy driving a tank," Amy said. 'Up and down and over hedges. With "Women For Ever" on the front, and "Wales For Ever" on the back.'"[31] I say 'appears' because, as in all the novels in Land of the Living, there is as much for the reader to observe in *The Best of Friends* as to listen to: 'Amy turned on her heel to study uneasily her own reflection in a shop window.'[32] As in a film or a play, it is a moment when a character's silent behaviour suggests more than what she actually says. Here, in her imagination, Amy presents herself to all intents and purposes as a 'woman terrorist' who, as Jacqueline Rose, drawing on the work of another feminist, psychoanalytical critic Julia Kristeva, says signifies 'the woman who, too brutally excluded from the socio-symbolic, counter-invests the violence she has experienced and takes arms against the State'.[33] But, 'uneasily' observing her own reflection, Amy demonstrates what Rose describes as the 'logic of fantasy in which violence can operate as a pole of attraction at the same time as … it is being denied'.[34]

Rose's observations provide an insightful framework within which to read aspects of Amy's behaviour in Land of the Living. It draws attention to the paradoxical boundary between 'protest' and 'terrorism' which the reader is invited to observe in a sequence which examines the boundaries of violence in regard to the turbulent war years through which Amy lives. In doing so, Humphreys shares Rose's interest in the fantasy of violence and how this proved a significant feature of fascism.

The interconnecting of the personal and the political in the novel is highlighted by its title *Salt of the Earth* because this is the expression which Tasker Thomas uses to describe the Glanrafon family.[35] But, at other levels, it refers to the fact that Cilydd, whose father drowned, is haunted by the sea and it also alludes to Amy's confession that she is 'salt dry' inside.[36] What she is referring to here is that although she desires Pen Lewis – 'So much sometimes I'm ashamed of it'[37] – she rejects him because she believes marrying him would bring her poverty. Indeed, the episode in which Amy and Pen make love for the first time is packed with symbols. The stable is said to be a site of 'ancient poverty';[38] the scythes and sickles on the wall are symbols of a rural pattern of life which remained unchanged for generations but are also symbols of the socialist revolution to which each of them, but especially Pen, is committed; the manger is an overt symbol of the birth of Christ and of the Christianity which Amy has rejected; the remnants of the hay harvested in earlier times has pagan connotations; Pen talks of Amy wrapping herself in 'a magic Celtic cloak';[39] and, in contrast to all of this, Amy's suspender belt signifies modern, female sexuality and the fetishization of the female.

SOCIAL, CULTURAL AND TECHNOLOGICAL CHANGE

If, as mentioned earlier, *Salt of the Earth* interpreted the 1930s as a period of contemplation and anxiety, the 1920s, despite occasional moments of nervousness, is characterized in *The Best of Friends* by various forms of fantasy, energy and a sense of urgency, exemplified by the arrival of the train at the beginning of the text: 'Compartment doors were flung open long before it came to a halt. Passengers in a hurry to make their connections plunged into the shadowed tide of those advancing urgently towards the opening doors.'[40] This highly visual opening is like a railway station scene from a film in the 1930s or 1940s. But, whereas the scene conjures up a sense of urgency, confusion and determination, the language connotes speed, recklessness and, even, a suggestion of violence. In part 2 of the novel, when Enid visits Cilydd at his home, and is introduced to his family and his past life, a local mole trapper observes that speed is 'the motto of the age'.[41]

In *The Best of Friends*, social, cultural and technological changes are interwoven. This is evident further in Amy's ride on the back of Cilydd's bike:

Amy sat on the pillion sideways and hung on to the belt of Cilydd's thick coat. The motor cycle shot forward down the empty street. Amy crouched behind him and cried with delight as the bike picked up speed. He drove first through the deserted side streets that led towards the college buildings and then out to the promenade so that Amy could enjoy the speed of the bike from one end of the bay to the other. Outside the granite mass of the women's Hall of Residence she jumped off, clapping her hands and laughing. Young women appeared in the windows, curious at hearing the rumble of a motor bike at the dead end of the prom on a Sunday afternoon.[42]

Once again, this is like a scene in a film which the reader is free to experience and interpret almost as they wish. The authorial intervention is minimal and we share what Amy is experiencing through external observation. Travelling pinion on a motorbike pushes back the boundaries defining and confining female behaviour. It redefines how women should behave in public, legitimizes the expression of exuberant emotions – Amy 'clapping her hands and laughing' – and makes public behaviour between men and women which has been generally private. But it also uses the figure of the woman, in this case Amy, to dramatize again the paradoxical boundary between the private and the public sphere. In this regard, Amy's exuberance may be compared with her reaction later in part one to Val's expression of his emotions: 'He put his hands on his hips, threw back his head and roared with laughter so loudly that Amy looked around her in alarm.'[43]

However, the figure of the woman straddling the boundary between the public and the private is developed in some of the subsequent novels, which also dramatize the boundary between public and private masculinity, in a more aggressive way than in *The Best of Friends*. When Pen brings Amy into a church to make love in *Salt of the Earth*, she turns on him: 'I know how men like you talk when they get together. I'm not a complete fool. I know what you're doing.'[44] In *Open Secrets*, Amy, no longer Miss Parry the school teacher, is a mother living at home with her children and husband, Cilydd, who was previously married to Enid. She tells Cilydd that his grandmother has emasculated his uncles by ruling them 'with a rod of iron'.[45] Her own relationship with Cilydd, as she tells him, is made difficult by the perceived relative unimportance of her social role compared with that of her solicitor-poet husband:

'Men have the remarkable gift for distancing themselves from the sordid trivialities of the domestic scene,' Amy said. 'It's wonderful really. The way

they can turn up at home from work like weary travellers from another
country arriving at the first convenient hotel and be quite put out when
the antics of squabbling children interfere with the service.'[46]

Although not pursued as far as it is in *Open Secrets*, Amy's social
role as wife and mother is the one that the vibrant, political Enid is
expected to assume in *Salt of the Earth* by giving up her protesting and
campaigning. The district nurse advises the expectant mother: 'Now
then I say to you, the time is coming to concentrate on being a wife and
a mother. Leave politics to the men, isn't it Mr More?'[47] The scenario
presents what Jacqueline Rose in another context has described as
'a femininity appealed to and denied, a masculinity parodied and
inflated'.[48] But, in Land of the Living, it is not so much Cilydd as Pen
Lewis who stands for 'masculinity parodied and inflated'. Knight
describes him as,

> a handsome and sexually aggressive man and Amy, herself very desir-
> able, is bowled over by him, on more than one occasion literally. Roaring
> about on his motorcycle, striding into meetings, vowing intransigence to
> the bosses and damnation to all half-hearted non-activists, Pen is himself
> almost a caricature of male power.[49]

However, the culturally, as well as biologically, determined gender relations to which Rose and also Knight refer works on a number of levels
in the text. In a Brechtian sense, Lewis encapsulates a forceful, politically dominant position within the overall ideological superstructure
of mid-twentieth-century Wales, and especially south Wales. Knight
shrewdly argues that,

> The name seems to refer to Lewis Jones: 'pen' means head, and Pen Lewis
> can be translated as Chief Lewis. But his full name, Penry Aneurin Lewis,
> refers more widely to the south, combining the Communist novelist's
> name with the first names of Rhys Davies's autobiographic hero from
> *Tomorrow to Fresh Woods* and the famous south Wales labour politician
> Aneurin Bevan.[50]

Cilydd's response to Amy's criticism of their respective social roles in
Open Secrets is in the form of activity which the reader, in a Brechtian
sense, is left to observe and interpret: 'He extracted a penknife and
began to ease a hole in the bowl of his pipe.'[51] The penknife and the
pipe are objects generally associated with men and masculinity and are
also phallic objects. The tightly packed tobacco might suggest the deep
discourse that legitimizes the male social position to which Amy refers.

But the image of the knife, in the hand of the somewhat disturbed Cilydd, creating a hole in the vulval bowl of the pipe is both sensual and slightly sinister. It also brings to mind one of the horrific images in Cilydd's dream which opens the novel – 'There was a corporal using his bayonet to punch holes in a bucket to turn it into a brazier'[52] – which similarly contrasts a phallic and violent object associated with men with a holding, vulvac object which it penetrates.

Salt of the Earth opens with a 'scene' in which an older man who takes too much physical interest in Amy appears to awaken memories that she would rather forget, about which the reader learned in *Flesh and Blood*. Amy has afternoon tea with her best friend Enid's aunt, Miss Sali Prydderch, a nationalist and somewhat overbearing school inspector, who disapproves of her niece's marriage to the poet Cilydd More. At one level, what is significant in this episode is the relationship between women and social change, an important subject throughout Land of the Living. Sali Prydderch's and Amy's smoking is a case in point. It is disapproved of by Professor Gwilym, whom Knight aptly describes as 'one of the many boring and self-centred professional men who damage good causes in Humphreys's novels'.[53] When he takes it upon himself to join them, he announces: 'I am entirely broad-minded in these matters. If ladies feel inclined to smoke, in public or in private, then by all means let them do so.'[54] The reader, cast as a spectator to watch the subsequent interaction, is given only limited access to Amy's and Miss Prydderch's consciousness: 'Amy held out her unlit cigarette so that Miss Prydderch could replace it in her case.'[55] This episode, in which Amy says relatively little, is dominated initially by Miss Prydderch and subsequently by the professor.

The reader is presented with behaviour, much of it involving an intrusion into Amy's personal space, which suggests that there are larger issues involved and which encourages the reader to conjure what Amy might be thinking. When Miss Prydderch first greets her, we are told: 'She clasped the young woman's hand in both her own and held on to it as she spoke.'[56] Amy's reaction, the reader is told, is to blush. When the professor sits close to her, his laughter allows him 'to lean over closer' to her. Rather than present the reader fully with what Amy thinks at this point, the sentence that immediately follows describes how she does not react, which is itself a reaction: 'She held on to her cigarette waiting for Miss Prydderch to light it.'[57] How Amy feels about the professor's intrusion into her private space, both physically and also mentally through increasingly intimate conversation, is made clear soon after this. Again it becomes apparent through what the reader, like a member of a theatre audience, observes: 'He was studying her legs appreciatively. When she became aware of this she tucked them as far as she could under her chair.'[58] Later, Gwilym reaches out 'to squeeze her forearm in order to press home his message of goodwill' but 'by moving closer to Miss Prydderch Amy placed herself out of his reach'.[59]

As a spectator, in Brecht's words, trying 'to get to grips with things', the reader, watching Professor Gwilym's behaviour, is faced with more than a rekindling of the rector's assault on Amy when she was a child. The episode conjures up the confusion of the early 1930s. By smoking and taking tea together in a seaside hotel, Amy and Miss Prydderch represent how the freedom in female behaviour associated with the metropolitan areas was now a feature of more diverse urban communities and, as is made clear in the previous novel *The Best of Friends*, in college towns, through the influence of American movies and popular magazines. In *The Best of Friends*, Gwenda represents the 'new woman' of the 1920s and 1930s:

> [Mrs Herbert] tried to extend her daughter a cautionary glance but Mabli was too absorbed in greeting Gwenda to see it. Gwenda's copper-coloured hair was cut in an Eton crop. Mrs. Herbert looked with ill-concealed disapproval at the white skin exposed at the nape of her neck. Gwenda's college blazer showed a year's use and seemed ill-matched with the striking green frock she was wearing and the flesh-tinted silk stockings. She wore conspicuous make-up and there were nicotine stains on her thin fingers.[60]

The influence of Hollywood on female behaviour is something which appears to disturb Professor Gwilym in *Salt of the Earth*:

> Only this morning you know I picked up a tabloid and reading between the lines I glimpsed something of the frightful power those Hollywood moguls exercise over impressionable young ladies who yearn to become film stars. Something between old fashioned prostitution and serfdom.[61]

Allowing Gwilym to speak as if he were a character in a play is effective because, depending on the level of the reader's engagement with the text, Gwilym says much more than he thinks he does. Appearing to regard tabloids with disdain, he, nevertheless, reads them. Eliding sexually liberated women with prostitution, he fails to recognize the extent to which he sees women as sexual objects:

Pendraw is a seaside gem attached to one of the strongholds of our native culture. Like a jewel on a beautiful woman's throat. That's the way I look at it. And now that you are there Miss Parry, that seaside gem sparkles even more brightly.[62]

Thus, attitudes and forms of behaviour are unveiled before the reader in ways which depend upon the reader's engagement not only with what is said but with the actions he or she observes, including meaningful juxtapositions and contradictions, as if they were part of a play or a film.

One of the key concerns in *The Best of Friends* is with the change stimulated by the operation of ideas associated with modernity on the traditional culture and outlook of Wales. In this novel, the motorbike changes the relationship between the individual and space – specifically it alters the means of travel from one end of a bay to another – and introduces the importance of the subjective enjoyment of technology in its own right. There is, too, a strong sense of disruption, especially on the Sabbath, as 'young women appeared in windows' at the roaring passage of the bike. It is as if it awakens the past, suggested here by the 'dead end of the prom' and 'the granite mass' of the women's hall of residence.

The architecture of the hall of residence and the college buildings brings a Gothic past into the text. The Irish cultural and literary critic Gerry Smyth, who emphasizes the importance of discourse to the creation of the nation state, maintains that the Gothic has a special relevance to Anglo-Celtic, postcolonial cultures as a manifestation of 'guilt and alienation, a fixation on the ways in which the past persists in the present'.[63] Within this context, the presence of the women students in the college signifies the encroachment of a transparent modernity: 'the gloomy Gothic precinct had been transformed into a temple of youth, alive with spontaneous student cordiality.'[64]

Images in one novel in Land of the Living are frequently revitalized and expanded in a later book in the sequence. An example in regard to modernity is Cilydd's four-seater, tourer car, which is introduced in *The Best of Friends* and reintroduced in *Salt of the Earth*. In *The Best of Friends* it is a sign of modernity:

A four-seater tourer with the hood up had been freshly polished that morning. The blue bodywork shone even in the sharp-edged shadow cast by the whitewashed stores across the dusty road that separated it from its associated buildings. The modernity of the machine was impressive and the mole-trapper was very ready to be impressed. He chewed ruminatively as he absorbed intriguing detail. The spare wheel sunk in the running-board was covered in a mysterious protective material of its own. Alongside it was anchored an oblong petrol can that contained more of the mysterious fluid which made the engine run. Robert Thomas squinted enquiringly at a chromium-plated figurine with outstretched arms that balanced with one foot on the radiator cap. This object, too, had something to do with an abnormal power of motion.[65]

Through the presence of the mole trapper, the reader is once again cast in the role of spectator who, like the former, is trying to 'get to grips' not simply with the car but with what it represents. Some of the words are significantly American – 'hood' and 'running-board' – and introduce the 'Americanization' of Wales which is taken up again in the subsequent novel, *Salt of the Earth*, when Professor Gwilym talks about Hollywood moguls and film stars. The car introduces a sense of mystery – the word 'mysterious' is actually used twice – and also intrigue in a part of Wales where a way of life, exemplified by the figure of the mole trapper, has gone on unchanged for some time. With its outstretched arms and one foot off the ground, signifying speed and flight, the figurine on the bonnet contrasts with the bucolic environment. Indeed, it is disruption which the 'new' brings about, and not simply the 'new' in itself, which defines the 'modern':

> There were tin signs advertising mustard and paraffin oil and cattlefood nailed to some of the half-doors of the extremities of the long white building. All the doors and the woodwork were painted in red ochre. A pony and trap in the shade beyond the motor car looked old-world.[66]

In Humphreys's use of American language, we see the English language, to employ Bhabha's words, 'confronted by its double, the untranslatable – alien and foreign'.[67] But, as Bhabha argues, when this happens the traditional discourse of the nation as an 'imagined community' is replaced by the circulation of alternative narratives of nationhood.[68]

The image of the tourer in Mrs Lloyd's Glanrafon Stores is echoed in *Open Secrets* where Cilydd leaves his car outside a deserted smithy up the road from the stores. It is an image that comes from the past but also, given the prospect of a German invasion, from the future:

> He turned off the engine. There was an abnormal silence about the place. The door and windows of the smithy had been painted recently in red lead. The absence of noise was unnatural. It was all too tidy. The bellows were cold and lifeless. Harrows and ploughshares leaned against a fallen wall gathering rust as they waited attention. Grass grew between the cobbles.[69]

Glanrafon Stores seems to belong to an older Wales which Cilydd in *Salt of the Earth* described as 'the fag-end of an exhausted culture'.[70] In this passage, both the new and the old 'engines' of Wales have been turned off. The tourer and smithy in juxtaposition reflect both the continuity and discontinuity in Welsh social history: ploughshares, bellows and the combustion engine. What becomes significant is not simply how one has given way to the other in a relentless march of 'progress' but how progress itself is a sequence of interruptions. The Land of the Living saga can be seen in the same terms, as each new novel 'interrupts' its predecessor(s).

The scene at the smithy, along with the sceptical views expressed (sometimes inconsistently) by Cilydd and Pen Lewis, interrupts the idealism of *The Best of Friends*. This is reinforced by the reintroduction of Mabli Herbert whose idealism in the 1920s has been undermined by the 'reality' in the 1930s of impending war: 'We were going to make a better world and it seemed such a straight forward task … Wales seemed ripe for remaking in those days.'[71] At the same time, she interrupts the scepticism of *Open Secrets* by challenging Cilydd with memories of the role that he and others had played during the 1920s: 'We had our heroes like John Cilydd More and Val Gwyn to show the way.'[72]

DILEMMAS AND DISRUPTION

The way in which men approach women, a recurring topic in *Salt of the Earth*, is itself linked to the theme of 'disruption'. In the school staff room, Eddie Meredith craves Amy's forgiveness for not having delivered the leaflets which he undertook to distribute. However, he uses the occasion to seek to hug her legs and feet, an incident which anticipates Pen Lewis with Amy in the church later in the novel: 'He sank to his knees on the stone floor so that he could embrace her thighs and rest his head in her lap.'[73] Eddie, on his hands and knees at Amy's feet, is a comic counterpoint to Amy's begging Val's forgiveness for having had sex with Pen Lewis. But there are examples of more aggressive approaches to women, such as the way in which Robert Thomas, the mole catcher, makes advances to Mrs Lloyd's granddaughter, Nanw, while he is drunk and the way Enid is verbally abused for distributing leaflets by a stockman who calls her a 'Welsh Nash female' and suggests that she will be selling herself on the streets next. These examples demonstrate the overarching ideological framework within which young women activists such as Amy and Enid have to work.

Salt of the Earth shares with *The Best of Friends* an interest in relating the personal to the political, but it does so through a much more tightly organized structure, based upon rooms and interiors and the dilemmas that occur in them. Thus, chapters of the novel open successively with Amy seated in Pendraw school staff room; Amy alone in a third-class train compartment; Val Gwyn's chalet in the sanatorium; Enid working in a back room of Glanrafon Stores on the history of Calvinistic Methodism by Cilydd's grandfather; Enid in a rocking chair in the bay window of her terrace house; Pen and Amy together in Mrs Rossetti's boarding house; the vestry of a chapel; the front office of the printing works; and Cilydd in the basement of their house, baling out water from the high tide. The effect of this sequence of interiors is to emphasize the way in which the novel is structured around what Humphreys, as noted earlier, referred to as 'dramatic units' and also around dilemmas. The latter include Cilydd's anxiety that he is not good enough for Enid, having been made to feel inadequate by her commitment to political protest; Amy's divided feelings for Pen and Cilydd; and the way in which Val is caught between his political ideals and the possibility of marrying Amy.

Salt of the Earth is framed by two episodes involving the presence and influence of Enid. At the beginning of the novel, Amy and Cilydd discuss the latter's feelings of political inadequacy in his relationship with Enid. In this episode, he admits to being jealous of her but whilst the reader may take this to refer initially to his envy of Enid as a grassroots activist, he is about to say more when they are interrupted. What he appears to have been about to say is that he is jealous of her relationship with Amy. The novel closes with Enid's impending funeral and Amy's insistence that they keep their ideological aspirations alive after her death: 'We mustn't drown in our private sorrows.'[74]

The association of the 'disruptive' figure with a 'modern' perspective is developed differently from the previous novels in *Open Secrets* through a greater emphasis, inevitable given the period in which it is set, upon war. Like *A Toy Epic*, *Open Secrets* is as concerned with the psychology of a nation heading towards war as with the individual consciousnesses of its characters. The movement towards armed conflict in both novels is associated with masculinity, as in Virginia Woolf's *The Waves* which influenced *A Toy Epic*. However, *Open Secrets* differs from *A Toy Epic* in its emphasis on the impact of the Great War, exemplified by Cilydd who served in it, and on the greater prominence given to the female voice, in this case that of Amy. Cilydd occupies a paradoxical role: he is an *enfant terrible* and 'an accredited correspondent from the outside world bringing back reports on an increasingly incomprehensible situation'.[75] Although the novel stresses how he has been personally affected by the First World War, his role is determined by the dialectic in the text between various discourses about war that emerged during the 1930s. Knight points out that shortly before his death, Cilydd is working on a poem about Myrddin Wyllt [Wild Myrddin, usually known in English as Merlin], 'a poetic exile haunted by horrors'.[76] The arguments between Cilydd and Eddie are, in a Brechtian sense, the clash between alternative ideologies. Cilydd argues 'And I certainly don't want the protection of an alien state. I don't want to be overwhelmed by it and I don't want to be absorbed by it. I'll stand on my own feet, until I drop.'[77]

Cilydd's attempt to interpret his nightmare at the outset of the novel suggests that *Open Secrets* is a text in which the reader will be cast as an observer and interpreter of visual signs. Indeed, at the heart of the representation of Cilydd's opposition to some of the dominant discourses of the 1930s is a piece of visual 'theatre' which he seeks to establish in the Pendraw school hall. This is based on the juxtaposition of two visual 'scenes' which, as Brecht said of epic theatre, goes 'beyond formal matters' and affects art's social, or specifically 'intellectual', function.

The first 'scene' features the school's memorial window to pupils killed in the First World War:

> The lead was more conspicuous than the stained glass, the *dulce et decorum* inscription barely visible around the outlined feet of the angel of victory. A north-west wind driving sleet in gusts against the windows obliged Cilydd to raise his voice.[78]

Like the school roll of honour in the school in *A Toy Epic*, the window is intended to induct young people into a particular culture in which war is valorized. The memorial window exists in opposition to an absent presence invoked by the phrase *dulce et decorum*: Wilfred Owen's well-known war poem revealing as a lie the old maxim: *dulce et decorum est pro patria mori*. The horror of trench warfare in the realist writings of poets such as Owen is juxtaposed in Cilydd's installation art with Cilydd's revelation of another level of horror which had been kept secret in official discourses about the war: 'A boy stripped to the waist. Little more than a boy. A sacrificial figure lashed to the wheel of a gun-carriage. Field punishment number one. In cruciform. Can you imagine a more powerful image?'[79] Cilydd's piece is not only visual but based around figures: the angel of victory; Cilydd alone on the dais with his arms outstretched; and the cruciform of the boy lashed to the gun-carriage wheel. Each of these details invokes an image of Christ: the risen Christ (through the angel at the empty tomb); the messianic Christ and the crucified Christ. They also signify transubstantiation, power and suffering. Moreover, with the exception of the asexual angel, which is nevertheless associated with masculinity through victory in war, the images are masculine. It is ironic that Amy, observing Cilydd, acknowledges supportively that he appears 'masterful and confident'.[80]

In Land of the Living, Humphreys returns to a trope which first entered his writing with A Toy Epic: the interconnection of technology, machinery, war and death. It is an idea that is articulated in Open Secrets by Cilydd but which transcends his particular subjective perspective: 'We've constructed a vast industrial complex and it's grown of its own momentum into a monstrous machine with an appetite that will devour the world.'[81] This is a concept which is expressed in visual terms that recall the train imagery which opens The Best of Friends: 'The train was moving and no one could stop it. That was the meaning. It's coming and no one can stop it.'[82] As in A Toy Epic, the machinery of war is a product not simply of industrial revolution but of a particular rhetoric and discourse: 'Angels of chaos. You can see them quite plainly. Elevated by the collective delusions of the masses into the seats of unlimited power.'[83] The phrase 'angels of chaos' appears to stand in contradistinction to the 'Angel of Victory', invoked later in the novel, but in Cilydd's world view the boundaries between them are permeable. In fact, Cilydd is caught with Amy in a dilemma which he only partly recognizes. At one point, she implores him not to keep talking about the war machine for reasons that he does not immediately understand. Ultimately, as Amy reveals, it is a discourse that brings about 'intellectual' and 'political' paralysis as does the linking of the end of the Spanish Republic to the demise of Wales as a national entity.

Amy recognizes that in Cilydd's configuration of the war machine as a hyperreality, he risks implicating himself in what he denounces, as is suggested when he stands before the memorial window in the Pendraw school hall, 'masterful and confident', in a vision that he has created. Nevertheless, he creates an image of, and for, those in Wales who position themselves as national pacifists. The potential link between Welsh nationalism and pacifism, which is examined through the character of

J. T. Miles in *Outside the House of Baal*, is developed in *Open Secrets* as part of a wider ideological debate about the position of Wales in relation to England in a forthcoming war. Cilydd and Tasker Thomas, each deeply affected by their own experiences of carnage, dream of turning Cae Golau, 'Field of Light', into a self-sufficient retreat for conscientious objectors.[84] The way in which Tasker conceives of this 'retreat' is redolent of the way writers and visionaries such as Ralph Waldo Emerson envisaged transcendental communities in nineteenth-century America: 'A community of conscientious objectors, not cut off from the world but bonded together more effectively to save the world.'[85] However, in a novel that, following Brechtian theatre, juxtaposes different political and ideological points of view, Tasker's idealism contrasts with what Amy notices. Her observation brings to the fore another aspect of nineteenth-century American history: 'The conscientious objectors ... They look just like white slaves, don't they?'[86]

The Welsh master, Samwell, a former colleague of Amy's, who approaches Cilydd in the Pendraw school hall, has two functions in the text: to demonstrate the rekindling of a former radical spirit in Wales and to underscore the way in which Cilydd and the school's new head-master, ap Vychan, are opposites of each other. In some respects, ap Vychan represents 'modern' Wales as understood by Cilydd and Amy and faced with the prospect of war. Samwell says of him: 'He's very go-ahead. Full of new ideas ... A bit unlucky perhaps with everything so unsettled.'[87] The head teacher's name identifies him as the son of a Welsh family, as one of generations of Welsh people, but he is also threatened by complacency. He declares to Cilydd: 'As we celebrate our golden jubilee we want to show that we are not content to rest on our laurels. We want to be modern and go-ahead in the arts.'[88] However, he unwittingly betrays what, in addition to war, threatens Wales: a nation resting on its laurels and afraid to embrace the modern. He comments on the visual display that Cilydd has in mind: 'I can see the dramatic force ... I have doubt whether this is the appropriate occasion.'[89] Amy presents the modernist's argument:

> 'If it gives offence,' she said, 'well, modern art always does, doesn't it? If we want to be up-to-date it's a risk we have to take. And in any case the whole point of the thing is to make people think, isn't it? To think deeply, and feel it deeply. That's what I think anyway.'[90]

Complacency is a recurring threat to nationalist progress in Land of the Living. When Enid and Cilydd in *The Best of Friends* find themselves in a hotel in the heart of Welsh-speaking Wales where the proprietors are content not to learn to speak Welsh, Enid despairs: 'In our own country. Just exactly where else in the whole wide world …'[91]

The Land of the Living novels present the reader with alternative arguments about nation and nationhood in Wales. The subject of alternative narratives and histories comes to the fore in *Bonds of Attachment*. Amy's son Peredur, referred to earlier, a graduate from an English university who has failed to obtain an academic post at what was then the University College of Wales, Aberystwyth, embarks upon researching his father's life and death. Through Peredur's reading of Cilydd's diaries and notebooks, the novel offers different versions of events which we have witnessed as readers in the earlier novels. The title of the novel is ambiguous. The word 'bonds' can refer to positive, loving relationships but it can also mean servitude, and 'attachments' can be both positive, in the sense of supporting, but also negative in the sense of confining.

At the heart of both the earlier novels, which are in many ways rewritten in the course of this one, and also a central preoccupation of Cilydd's diaries, are questions about the encroachment of modernity onto the past in Wales and about the language in which the 'modern' in Wales, including the experiences of war, is to be articulated. The 'modern' narrative (informing the search through Cilydd's books; the focus upon the reality of the First World War; the period between the wars; violence and strained domestic relationships) contrasts with the mythical framework of the novel. And, as mentioned earlier, the names, Peredur, Bedwyr and Gwydion, suggest not only Welsh but specifically Arthurian myth. It is a literary device that a number of contemporary writers, including the national poet of Wales Gillian Clarke, have used to suggest a 'Welshness' that transcends the individual and which constitutes a larger sense of identity. Peredur, or Percival as in Virginia Woolf's *The Waves*, was an outsider, described by Knight as 'a classic "holy fool" figure', who found himself having to undertake the quest for the Holy Grail.[92]

There is a sense in Land of the Living that Welsh mythology encapsulates what may be exploited for commercial rather than nationalistic purposes, as in the case of Gwydion's ambitions for his mother's mansion as a tourist attraction focused on Arthurian romance. But, for a writer like Humphreys who chose to learn Welsh as an adult, Welsh myth can embody the 'foreignness' of Wales, an understanding of which is essential in order to become 'Welsh'. Through its symbolism,

Land of the Living interweaves the 'realist' and the 'mythological' while interrogating the ways in which myth and realism function on many different levels. In *Open Secrets*, for example, Peredur is baptized by water from a bowl which is part of family history and compared to the Holy Grail.[93] Here, the bowl is an object configured by its special place within the family and that family's history (known and unknown), but it is also tied to Arthurian and Christian myth, through the comparison with the Holy Grail, and to concepts of ancestry and destiny. As the Land of the Living saga progresses, it becomes increasingly interrogative of 'realism' and what is 'known', and in its style more mythical and symbolic.

There are many dimensions to Land of the Living but among the most important of the different readings of the sequence is the intermixing of a 'realist' history, aspects of which have not been fully explored, with a sense of another Welsh-language history which is more closely imbricated in Welsh mythology and is not as fully present. A sense of the latter continuously interrupts Land of the Living, in regard to, say, its representation of the social and cultural history of Wales, war, gender and sexuality. But, in doing so, it gives Humphreys's work an important role in reclaiming the partially written, or even the unwritten, histories of Wales.

10

Warring Families: *Unconditional Surrender* and *The Gift of a Daughter*

Unconditional Surrender and *The Gift of a Daughter* were published within two years of each other, five and seven years respectively after *Bonds of Attachment*, the last novel in the Land of the Living sequence. Neither novel has the sweep of time of Land of the Living as a whole or of *Outside the House of Baal*, but, in their focus upon a concentrated period within the life of a particular family, both works conform to the pattern of the series as a whole. *Unconditional Surrender*, as mentioned in chapter 1, shares with *Bonds of Attachment* alternating first-person narrators. But *The Gift of a Daughter* is a more traditional first-person narrative.

Both novels concern a father who finds himself challenged by developments within and outside his family and comes to see his wife and daughter as strangers to him. The difficulty of knowing fully even those with whom we have intimate relations is a theme in two subsequent collections of short stories, *Ghosts and Strangers* and *Old People are a Problem*, as in the twenty-first-century novel, *The Shop*, which will be discussed in chapters 11 and 12 respectively.

Both novels are also examples of dissident fiction, as Humphreys defined it. They are each concerned with the moral and spiritual progress of their central protagonists: Edwin Pritchard, a rector in a north Wales rural parish, and his wife Olwen in *Unconditional Surrender*; and Aled Morgan, an academic authority on ancient history, and his wife Marian in *The Gift of a Daughter*. Each novel is focused upon family dilemmas as well as dilemmas in the wider world. At the end of each novel, the knowledge of self which the father achieves is painful and he is left bereft of his family.

Like *Bonds of Attachment*, both *Unconditional Surrender* and *The Gift of a Daughter* combine two approaches to the dilemma-centred narrative of social and moral progress which, as already noted in chapter 2, may appear to be contradictory. The first, and perhaps key, approach of the dissident narrative, as Humphreys conceived it, stresses the need for individuals to resolve the social and moral dilemmas with which they are faced. The central protagonists achieve moral development primarily through the analysis of the situations in which they find themselves as well as by focused self-analysis. The second approach, which is post-Freudian, recognizes that individuals are as much products of the unconscious as the conscious mind; they may be unaware, or only partly aware, of some of the drives and desires that motivate them. Thus, within this paradigm, as discussed in chapter 4, individual moral progress is inseparable from psychoanalytic self-analysis.

CONSCIOUS AND UNCONSCIOUS DILEMMAS

The rational, conscious modelling and the psychoanalytical configuration of the fathers are effectively intertwined in *Unconditional Surrender* and *The Gift of a Daughter* because of the part which their relationships with their daughters play in their personal narratives and tragedies. In *Unconditional Surrender*, which has the same title as the third novel in Evelyn Waugh's *Sword of Honour* trilogy,[1] Edwin's seventeen-year-old daughter, Megan, who has a relationship with a local boy who has not gone to war because he is a conscientious objector, worries her father by becoming involved with a young German prisoner of war. At the end of the novel, Meg is pregnant by him and she and her mother, Olwen, are working as unpaid volunteers in a refugee centre. Olwen is preparing to run off with the English colonel who is responsible for the prisoners of war. In *The Gift of a Daughter*, Aled and Marian are distressed by their daughter's relationship with an Englishman, Buddy Thwaite, whom they despise. Their hostilities come to a head and Rhiannon runs off with him. However, on returning home, pregnant by him, she is killed in an accident. Both fathers are forced to revisit their relationship with their daughters and to consider the responsibility that they must assume in losing them.

Obviously, the sense of loss is greater in *The Gift of a Daughter*, in which Rhiannon is killed, than in *Unconditional Surrender*.

In both novels, the ongoing self-analysis in each father's first-person narrative is interwoven with a psychoanalytic focus because of the two contexts in which the texts place the father and daughter relationship. At one level, the daughter exists within a socio-symbolic network that can be oppressive, but in psychoanalytic terms she is also an object within the domain of her father's unconscious.

The place which Meg has in her father's consciousness is disturbed by the way in which she becomes the object of the attention of the two men mentioned earlier. Their attraction to Meg unsettles Edwin's ambitions for his daughter and causes him to think more deeply about the nature of his feelings for her. In his mind, there is a clear distinction between the two suitors, one a north Walian and the other a northern European, and the alternation between them reflects the way in which his thinking about Meg shifts between the social and psycho-symbolic and is also based upon duality in his own mind.

On his way to visit the German prisoner of war who is in a hospital after being wounded by the conscientious objector in a fight, Edwin ponders: 'Unless we can keep our instincts and desires firmly under control we are nothing better than an inferior species of animals ourselves.'[2] In thinking in this way, Edwin betrays the influence of Freud, modelling the mind in terms of an *Id* – 'desires and instincts' – and an *Ego* which provides the control necessary for social relationships to exist. The dualism reflected here informs further distinctions that he makes between the conscious and unconscious, the human and animal, and the civilized and uncivilized.

On the journey to the hospital, Edwin's thoughts move, with growing intensity, from the two suitors to the subject of love itself: 'This business of falling in love: what is it except the excuse we need to unleash our animal desires?' (p. 117). Eliding love with the psycho-symbolic rather than the socio-symbolic, Edwin's particular focus betrays his own repressed emotions: 'The affairs of the young disturb the settled order of things. They force us against our will to re-examine our own emotional record' (ibid.). The phrase 'the young' refers, of course, to Griff and Klaus, but, without naming her, also includes his daughter. The word 'affairs' is ambivalent, suggesting their social and political concerns but also their sexual liaisons. The phrase 'settled order of things' seems enigmatic, referring, at one level, to the custom and conventions of the community which the radical and rebellious behaviour of the young disturbs. But the word 'order' implies a Symbolic Order that includes more than tradition and convention. Like the way the unconscious can disrupt the conscious, the young disrupt overarching structures. But the next line traces Edwin's line of thought from 'young people' per se to the nature and origins of our 'emotional' life. Again, Edwin's choice of words is enigmatic and unusual. The shifting nature of his thoughts suggest to the reader the extent to which he confronts but fails to acknowledge fully his own desires and instincts. Meg's affairs, in more than one sense, cause her father to recognize not only his own instincts generally, but his feelings towards her and the fragility of his own dualistic way of looking at things. When Edwin discovers his daughter waiting for Klaus, it becomes clear that his protectiveness toward her embraces jealousy of her lovers and that his feelings for her are more complex than he has previously admitted to himself.

The complex, unacknowledged feelings that Edwin has for his daughter are echoed in the enigmatic interest that the other narrator, the Countess, shows in Meg, often manipulating her mother so that she can influence the young woman's thoughts. The Countess is a development of Humphreys's interest in an elderly, female member of the European aristocracy in *The Anchor Tree*, in which one of the key protagonists is Cornelia von Kalwitz, described by the narrator as a 'confident' and 'assertive' woman, 'beyond the reproductive phase', a widow of a German general, and a product of 'organisations for peace and war' (p. 186).

Following the failure to elect a Welsh Nationalist MP, the Countess discovers a bitterly disappointed and disillusioned Meg waiting for Klaus. On this occasion, the route which the Countess takes to the rectory is overly symbolic. It is not her 'preferred route' and the path is overgrown with wild brambles and flowers. The overgrown path suggests what lies outside the 'norm' and the social order. The boundary between the path and brambles, between order and disorder, becomes blurred. When she first sees Meg, she is in 'a pool of sunlight', an image which in religious iconography suggests serenity and purity, but the Countess soon realizes that she is angry and does not really want to see her. It is as if Meg, as configured in the Countess's idealized view of her, has displaced the frustrations and constraints of living in north Wales onto her. Because she has chosen to live in that region of Wales, the Countess finds she has become Meg's scapegoat: 'I could see the ray of her displeasure already shifting in my direction' (p. 134).

However, Meg's new-found enthusiasm for Klaus is based not only on the new political opportunities but on the sexual possibilities that he offers her. Although, like Edwin, the Countess barely admits this to herself, she seems jealous of Meg, observing of her that 'She had been sexually roused as she had never been roused before' (p. 135). Ironically, the depth of the Countess's ambivalent feelings for the girl is paralleled by the extent of the anger which she projects onto Klaus, 'The grinning sewer rat' (p. 134). At one level, the Countess associates the young German with the invasion of her country and her life by the Nazis but clearly he is also cast as an object of hate because of the way in which he comes between her and Meg. In each case, Meg and Klaus cease to be individuals in their own right and become a phantasy object, or 'imago', within the Countess's psyche.

The tension between the daughter as part of a socio-symbolic network and as a phantasy object in her father's unconscious is explored most explicitly in *The Gift of a Daughter*. This is a novel in which the central protagonists are surprised by the expression of emotions and desires relating to their daughter's death, such as Rhiannon's mother's momentarily considering driving her vehicle into the man she blames for her daughter's death and Aled's becoming obsessed with a young woman in Tuscany whom he believes resembles Rhiannon.

In chapter 4, we discussed the way in which psychoanalytic themes are explored in Humphreys's work through 'implication'. It is possible to see this novel as a reworking of Ovid's myth of Proserpina, particularly through its examination of the conflation of father/uncle and rapist. However, while Ovid is invoked, as an example of the way in which this dark psychoanalytic theme has been explored in myth, it has to be admitted that, of all Humphreys's novels, *The Gift of a Daughter* is the most explicitly psychoanalytic text. After her death, Rhiannon becomes the central protagonist in her father's psyche, especially when he and his wife are in Tuscany, trying to get away from their family tragedy. The dilemma with which Aled is faced, when he finds himself obsessively attracted to an Italian teenager who reminds him of his daughter, causes all his preconceptions about himself to unravel. Indeed, in coming face to face with a kind of 'ghost' from his unconscious, Aled finds that not only is his relationship with Rhiannon and the way he has thought about her turned upside down, but so has the very nature of thought itself. According to contemporary psychology, this is not unusual in mourning, as Jacqueline Rose has pointed out: 'So if mourning initiates thinking, it also severs us once and for all from any certainty of thought.'[3] Thus, not surprisingly, Aled finds himself confused about his feelings towards Rhiannon. The terms of the socio-symbolic structure in which he had always thought about her are displaced by the drives and fantasies of his unconscious. The young Italian for whom he develops sexual desires is both a young woman in her own right and the emergence from his psyche of his own daughter, freed from the socially sanctioned terms in which he had consciously thought of her, and present as the unconscious phantasy object which he repressed.

Aled's infatuation with a young woman who is young enough to be his daughter, and whom he elides with his daughter, is a development of the scenario from *The Anchor Tree* in which the narrator, a professor of history, falls in love with a young woman who is half his age. In the build-up to the scene in which Aled kisses Grazia, he increasingly draws comparisons between her and Rhiannon. Both Aled and Marian, who teaches Grazia English and literature, come to regard her as a substitute for their deceased daughter. Aled even comes to resent her boyfriend Giorgio as he had resented his own daughter's lover: 'The truth was at the moment I found him more objectionable than Buddy Thwaite.'[4] In Aled's case, Rhiannon becomes the main point of reference almost every time he speaks with Grazia: 'Like Rhiannon she was determined not to take herself too seriously and this added to her enchantment' (pp. 117–18); 'Rhiannon was like this: wide-eyed, smiling, asking questions like musical phrases' (p. 118). He comes to occupy a state between love-sick youth and father figure: 'In my mind I would go over every word she uttered for the rest of the day' (p. 119). In his description of himself as 'a green youth', the word 'green' suggests both the innocence of youth and the envy of the father. Thus, what Aled is trying to cope with is a personal tragedy but also something that, in psychoanalytic terms, involves the archetype of the jealous father who is protective of the daughter he cherishes but unconsciously desires.

The Etruscan context is significant not only for the comparisons which may be made between the ancient Etruscan and Welsh societies, but also because it allows Aled to enter tombs and chambers which signify the depths of the unconscious mind. However, references to the Etruscans create a semi-mythical ambience which underlines the way in which we are encouraged to see the relationship between Aled and Rhiannon/Grazia in terms of psychic myths. The descent into the caves can be seen as an allusion to the Orpheus and Eurydice myth, especially in terms of a descent into the underworld/hell, which is one way of viewing Aled's growing infatuation with Grazia/Rhiannon. Although *The Gift of a Daughter* has a more traditional narrative structure than *Unconditional Surrender*, it develops Humphreys's long-standing interests in time, memory and myth and in the boundary between 'reality' and fiction. Thus, Grazia, as a 'real' young Italian woman and as Aled's phantasy object, linked to his dead daughter, is on the boundary between fact and fantasy, the conscious and uncon-scious, and the past and the present. The reader can never be certain how much of Aled's account of Grazia is a product of his imagination/ unconscious.

In the scene in which he kisses Grazia, Aled's conception of his daughter is not the realist one of her before her death but one that comes from his unconscious. However, as a historian more used to analysis and rational thought, Aled finds it difficult to understand what is happening: 'I could hardly account for my own behaviour. I could not begin to provide her with an alibi for hers. What fantasy in her mind coincided with mine to produce this dangerous reality?' (p. 147). In their different ways, Aled and Grazia have each crossed the boundary between the two symbolic orders in which the daughter acquires meaning. He crosses over from the socio-symbolic order to kiss, in a sexual way, another man's youthful daughter. But, in terms of his own psychic archetypes, he gives expression to his repressed desires for his own daughter. Grazia, too, traverses the boundary between the socio-symbolic and the psycho-symbolic in kissing another young woman's father, releasing her unconscious desires for the 'ideal' father. Thus, the setting of the lake is both significant and ominous. It is an archetypal symbol of the unconscious but, in myths and legends, it is often a site of transition, too, between bodily states and different realms of 'reality'.

Almost from the moment in which Aled first sees Grazia, he distances her, and himself, from the socio-symbolic by shrouding her in religious iconography. When she first comes to speak with him, he says: 'Her face was as serious and as perfect as an angel of annunciation' (p. 117). This association of Grazia with Gabriel, the archangel of the annun-ciation who brings Mary news of her miracle pregnancy, emphasizes how, in his mind, she is associated with purity, grace (hence her name) and, of course, virginity. In Christian, and particularly in Catholic Marian, art, the annunciation is a key image in promoting constancy and the ideal of the virgin. Aled's perceiving Grazia in this way is both ironic and, since unconsciously he desires her, contradictory. However, the father who thinks of his daughter in terms of purity not only denies her sexuality but protects himself, and his daughter, from his unconscious drives.

After Grazia has been struck by her father, Aled follows her to the lake, telling himself that: 'I couldn't leave her wandering alone in the darkness along the shore of the lake. She was out there beyond the reach of the outside lights of the *trattoria*, nursing her sorrow' (p. 145). It is significant that she is beyond the lights of her father's restaurant because they suggest his control over her but also the conscious, socio-symbolic order which defines her. The image of her 'wandering alone in the darkness' invokes Eve after she is expelled from Eden. However, it also connotes the isolation and uncertainty which comes with moving outside conventional social structures and in surrendering to the unconscious, signified by the lake and the darkness. It is signifi-cant that Grazia is at the 'shore of the lake'. This in-between location emphasizes that she stands at the boundary between the social and the psychic, between constraint and freedom, and between her father and Aled as substitute father/lover.

Whereas the language in which the *trattoria* is described places Aled, Grazia, Grazia's father and Giorgio within the socio-symbolic, the language of the lake scene is psycho-symbolic as is the descrip-tion of the 'lake water lapping the roots of the cane reeds that grew at the water's edge' (p. 145). The reference to the water's edge repeats the symbol of the boundary; the water signifies the unconscious; and the canes – a phallic image – suggest desires that originate in the unconscious or at the boundary between the socio-symbolic and the psycho-symbolic. When Aled finds Grazia, he sees her 'clinging with arms outstretched to the high wire fence protecting one of the narrow strips of land reaching from the old Via Cassa to the lake' (p. 146). Once again, it is difficult for the reader to distinguish between what Aled sees in an objective sense and what he projects onto the scene from his own unconscious. The language is overly symbolic and Grazia is config-ured in the image of the crucified Christ and/or of sexually suggestive surrender. She clings to 'a high wire fence' which, in protecting land that runs from the 'old Via Cassa', suggests both the protection and constraint of the Symbolic Order.

Aled also notices 'intensely cultivated gardens' that are 'jealously guarded by their owners' (ibid.). These gardens signify daughters who are 'intensely cultivated' but also 'jealously guarded' by their fathers.

Significantly, Grazia is 'locked out' of these gardens, suggesting the plight of the daughter – Grazia through refusing Giorgio and Rhiannon in choosing Buddy Thwaite over her parents – who steps outside the socio-symbolic. Aled's detailed description of Grazia brings to mind a number of traditional images from art: 'Her head, her hair, her body hung down with the erotic desperation of a crucified figure' (ibid.). This view of her combines two archetypal images: the vulnerable maiden and the crucified Christ. The traditional sexual image of loose hair is elided with the coyly lowered head and the limp, accessible body. With her hair, head and body lowered, Grazia invokes the fallen women of a genre of Victorian art known as 'dilemma painting', which depicted women in situations that viewers were encouraged to interpret. Like a Victorian damsel beside a mythical lake, Grazia, in need of support and affection, is vulnerable, and desirable to Aled. Positioned, as it were, against a background of traditional erotic imagery and beside a lake, a traditional site of transformation, Aled finds himself drawn to her and she to him. As mentioned earlier, this is a dissident narrative and the moral progress that Aled makes in the novel is dependent upon his gaining self-knowledge. What emerges here is the way in which Aled becomes increasingly aware of how the daughter figure is eroticized in terms of religious iconography within his unconscious.

It is significant that Aled arrives at a fuller state of self-knowledge when he speaks with Grazia in his daughter's bedroom. Ironically, Grazia is to repeat history by running off with Buddy. This scene, in which Aled finds Grazia in his torch beam, recalls the one earlier in the novel when Aled's torch lit up Rhiannon sneaking into Buddy's bedroom. Aled would prefer Grazia to meet her father part-way, an arrangement which he has helped make possible through the influence which his friends can bring to bear upon Grazia's father. Again the irony in the text is compounded when Aled laments: 'To defy her father? To act as if the future was her exclusive domain?' (p. 230). While Grazia had once substituted for Rhiannon as the psychic object of Aled's unconscious fantasies, in Rhiannon's bedroom she replicates Rhiannon's determination and self-will.

The title *The Gift of a Daughter* is an ambivalent one. It suggests that, in one regard, a daughter is a gift from God but that, in another respect, in both traditional Welsh Nonconformist and in Italian culture, she is passed as a gift from her father to a 'stranger' who will become her husband. But Humphreys's text complicates this feminist critique of marriage within patriarchal cultures in two ways. First, in the second half of the novel, Grazia becomes literally an agent of exchange. If she marries Georgio then her father, whom Aled begins to see as a tyrant, will become allied with Luca Pri, who will have Grazia as part of his collection, and through Luca Pri's influence will become the most powerful man in his part of the Lido. But Humphreys also examines how, while the daughter is determined and constrained by the expectations of the Symbolic Order, she may also rebel against that order. When Grazia explains to Aled why her father wants her to marry Giorgio, he realizes the parallels between the behaviour of Grazia's father's towards her and his attitude towards his own daughter: 'What better way to encourage young love than to put obstacles in its path? That was something I knew about' (p. 148). In the final part of the novel, when Grazia becomes involved with Buddy Thwaite, the focus of the text shifts once more from the psycho-symbolic to the socio-symbolic and the capacity of the daughter, as in *Unconditional Surrender*, to define herself in her own terms.

POLITICAL DILEMMAS

Unconditional Surrender and *The Gift of a Daughter*, as noted earlier, develop the trope of national identity which recurs in Humphreys's novels and anticipates the concern with the impossibility of even getting to know others which is a central theme of his subsequent work. However, another important concern is the ambivalence of civilization. In one of his narratives in *Unconditional Surrender*, Edwin observes that 'we are marooned on this earth to feed our lives on a perpetual diet of alternating hope and despair'.[5] This conviction is embodied in the individual narratives in the text as they alternate between optimism and bitter realism. The use of the two narrators, one located in a lifetime's experience in north Wales and the other providing a particular kind of European perspective, further enhances the alternating structure by juxtaposing Welsh and European perspectives which eventually come together when Edwin reflects on the pictures coming out of mainland Europe:

> There are endless pictures of devastated cities ... I can absolve nobody and nothing. Bremen is a waste land licked by a black river. The ruins of Nürnberg stretch over two pages like a bloated corpse being eaten by blind worms. There is no noise of explosions, but the centre of Cologne has become a black and white catastrophe. (p. 93)

The photographs, as interpreted by the rector, like Vernon's drawing in *Outside the House of Baal*, offer no compensatory symbolism and convey a stark sense of the abjection of death and dissolution. In standing, in Edwin's view, outside absolution, their content belies the sense of a 'black and white catastrophe', which is 'black and white' in terms not simply of the photographic media but, more significantly, of their ideological content. As a priest, Edwin finds it difficult to think in terms of the binaries which are employed to justify war and vindicate its consequences. As was suggested in *Salt of the Earth*, discussed in chapter 9, nationalism and pacifism are linked in a singularly Welsh perspective.

From one perspective, Germany is seen as the defeated, evil enemy but, from another, it is conceived as a civilization brought to an end. In the graveyard, confessing to Olwen, the Countess reflects to herself: 'A whole civilization has collapsed while this lichen under my finger expanded its modest space on this stone' (p. 102). The image underlines the contrast between what has happened in continental Europe with the relative protection of rural north Wales.

Within the socio-symbolic network of the north Wales community in which Meg comes to maturity, she is caught between two competing perspectives which mirror what her father says about being 'marooned on … a perpetual diet of alternating hope and despair'. Campaigning with her father for the Welsh Nationalist candidate who loses the election, Meg loses her convictions. She tells the Countess that north Wales is 'nothing but a refuge for the second-rate. That's all. I can't for the life of me see what you see in it' (p. 133). Meg alternates between the despair which she experiences on losing the electoral campaign and the sense of becoming involved in rebuilding Europe to which Klaus introduces her.

Feeling unable to continue in a country which appears to have lost its sense of direction, and attracted by the promise of being able to make an important contribution to the development of post-war Europe, Meg is caught in a dilemma. *Unconditional Surrender* explores what has always been a central subject of Humphreys's work, the need to look away from the English and Welsh binary and to think more in terms of a European Welsh identity. In this regard, Meg signifies a further dilemma in Welsh politics. At one level, the text is concerned with a rural parish rector's daughter and her infatuation with a German prisoner of war but, at another level, their relationship signifies the possibility of an alignment between northern Europe

(Klaus) and north Wales (Meg). Moreover, what Meg is unaware of at this point is that her mother had voted for the Labour candidate, later confiding to her disappointed husband that she felt it was important to give Labour a chance to rejuvenate north Wales. Her personal political, and to some extent family, dilemma mirrors the dilemma in which the people of the community find themselves.

First published at a time when Wales was on the verge of having its own Assembly and concerned with a Wales which was half a century from this achievement, however incomplete, *Unconditional Surrender* identifies the rhythm of nationalist politics in Wales. Edwin's point about alternating 'hope and despair' reflects the experience of nationalist politicians and those supporting them as elections and referenda are alternately won and lost. This rhythm is evident in the experience of the election where Edwin, impressed by the candidate's dignity and philosophical acceptance of defeat, is inspired to renew his efforts. In this regard, he contrasts with his daughter, who is not so easily rallied to the Welsh nationalist cause.

Unconditional Surrender, set in the last years of the Second World War, concludes with the central dilemma that faced the allies at that juncture: whether or not to use their devastating new technology to end the war quickly. When the rector delivers the news of Hiroshima to the German Countess, she is raking out the cinders in the old kitchen range and, ironically, appears like 'a scarecrow come to life in order to clear up the ashes under the fire' (p. 153). At this point, the novel that has been concerned with a present that has been shaped by the war years brings into view a future of uncertainty created by the oncoming nuclear age.

Unlike *Unconditional Surrender*, war does not enter directly into *The Gift of a Daughter*. However, Jacqueline Rose points out that 'the familiar destructiveness of war represents not, as is commonly supposed, finality but uncertainty, a hovering on the edge of what, like death, can never be totally known'.[6] This, of course, is the conclusion of *Unconditional Surrender*: 'The genie is out of the bottle, Countess. Mankind has found the means to destroy itself' (p. 156). In fact, both Humphreys's novels conclude, to use Rose's words, 'on the edge of what, like death, can never be totally known'. At the end of *The Gift of a Daughter*, the principal male protagonist, Aled Morgan, is photographed by a family. Like Aled, emerging from the tomb, the photograph is literally on the edge of what cannot be known because it is impossible to know how it will be interpreted in the future. In both novels, albeit in different contexts, the note of uncertainty is connected with the death of civilizations and also, in *The Gift of a Daughter*, with the death of an individual.

'Uncertainty' is a recurring feature of *The Gift of a Daughter*. Aled arrives to meet his wife Marian at the *Stazione Centralle* because 'my uncertainty compelled me to be precise'.[7] There is uncertainty as to what the farmer who now owns the chapel intends to do with it, whether to sell it as a site for Country Bingo or as a convalescent home. And Rhiannon's postcards are written cryptically. Then there is also the uncertainty of the situation into which Aled gets himself with the teenage Grazia in Tuscany. The reason why these novels dwell on the indeterminable is that they are each concerned not simply with the fear of death and dissolution, but with the way in which they place us on the edge of the known.

11

Strangers in a Strange Land: *Natives, Ghosts and Strangers* and *Old People are a Problem*

This chapter is concerned with three collections of short stories: *Natives* (1968), *Ghosts and Strangers* (2001) and *Old People are a Problem* (2003). The short story has been an important genre in the literature of Wales, as of Ireland, and Humphreys is an author who has continued to write both long and short fiction. Indeed, he has himself admitted that he has drawn 'much on the special characteristics of the short story for use in the novels I've written, particularly from the 1960s onwards'.[1]

NATIVES

The stories in *Natives* have the concise content and carefully inte-grated detail which characterize Humphreys's novels of the 1950s and 1960s and may be regarded as 'modernist' rather than 'traditional' in character. Ann Charters points out that 'Literary critics distinguish between two types of stories ... "traditional stories", descending from Poe and Maupassant, which are plotted and closed ... and "modern stories", descending from Chekhov and Joyce, which are less plotted and more open'.[2] The modernist story, as written by authors as diverse as Elizabeth Bowen, James Joyce, Katharine Mansfield, Kate Roberts,

Dorothy Richardson and Jean Rhys, are often a slice through life at a particular moment in time.

Humphreys has said that he chose the title, *Natives*, because of the Latin root of the word: 'the root of "native" in the Latin *natus* – meaning, of course, a person born in that particular place'.[3] It is a word that is double-edged, as Wynn Thomas says, 'being so evidently the pejorative term used by the colonizers of the colonized'.[4] The term suggested the primitiveness of the colonized peoples in the eyes of their conquerors which in turn implied childlike simplicity in terms of intellect, emotions and experiences. However, the Latin root of the word highlights the trope of 'place' and 'rootedness' in *Natives* as well as the complexity of individual lives within that sense of place, which stands in mocking contradiction of the pejorative connotations of the title.

Natives is primarily concerned with the 'respectable' Wales, of the Welsh middle class: wealthy landowners, clergy, head teachers, town councillors, local government officers, lawyers and secretaries. Pursuing the pejorative colonial connotations of the title, these figures may be seen as members of the class that most assimilated the values of the anglicizing colonizers. Humphreys has explained that 'A great deal of the post-colonial situation – that is, the consolidation of colonial "occupation" into a settled state of affairs – depended on the willing subservience of the natives'.[5] However, *Natives*, through its focus on the middle class, complicates the phrase 'willing subservience' by showing that colonization depended, as Stephen Slemon has argued, upon 'the constitutive power of professional fields of knowledge' and 'colonialist relations'.[6] The middle class is connected in *Natives*, through recurring tropes and images, with a power system which is dependent upon knowledge and a particular kind of relationship to others. What Slemon calls 'colonialist relations' are evident in *Natives* in many public and private situations and across diverse workplaces from schools to solicitors' offices and to farms. But what makes *Natives* especially interesting is the way in which it deconstructs this term in regard to Wales from a twin perspective on 'power' and place', and does so at a moment in time when those who have held power find themselves faced with change. This echoes the decolonization that took place in the decades following the Second World War and, within Wales itself, the politicization of the Welsh-language movement.

Several of the stories in *Natives* involve elderly people who, although they have known change, have previously not been touched by the kind of transformation now taking place around them. Major Dafydd in

'The Hero' is embittered by what he perceives as the shallowness of
the emergent mass-media celebrity culture influenced by America and
epitomized by the young north Wales lawyer, Gwilym Tist. The eighty-
five-year-old owner of the large farm in 'Dinas' is unable to pass his
life's work onto his son who is not interested in maintaining it as a
farm. Instead, like the plans that Dan Llew has for Argoed in *Outside
the House of Baal*, he plans to turn it into a caravan and chalet park.
The elderly professor in 'With All My Heart', who is a head of depart-
ment and dean of the faculty, is conscious that, as a philologist, he
is no longer the type of academic that some of his colleagues, with
a more 'modern' outlook, would ideally wish to see in that position.
The head teacher in 'The Rigours of Inspection' is threatened by what
might be called, to adapt the term from 'With All My Heart', 'progres-
sives': 'What you're telling me is just pure commonsense dressed up in
the latest psychological jargon.'[7]

In several of the stories, the changes which are taking place at a
local, community level are analogous to larger dilemmas within Wales
in the middle of the twentieth century. Robert Cyffin describes his
farm, Dinas: 'The old home. In the family for nearly three centuries. A
sacred trust' (p. 191). The farm represents what has been up until now
part of the rural, and also the religious, heart of north Wales: in order
to resolve the dilemma of who shall inherit the farm he turns to scrip-
ture. The nurse who, through an inheritance from her father, is to take
over the farm is clear as to the importance of maintaining a line of
inheritance for Dinas: 'This is the only real foundation for me. That's
how the best things are carried on anyway. From generation to generation' (p.229). But not all those whom she implores to help her are
interested. Ifan Huw, who has worked on the farm for years, declares
that he is leaving to start his own business: 'A milk round in the village.
This is my chance. I've got the goodwill. And the smallholding. The
bank will help me. It's what I've always wanted' (ibid.).

While Nurse Jones advocates the importance of 'generations', Ifan,
in reply, stresses what *he* wants and what is good for *him*. Whereas
Dinas has been anchored in one family over many generations, Ifan's
smallholding is based on a much more narrowly focused personal
ambition. This is a feature of the 'new' in rural mid-twentieth-century
Wales which is shared also by Old Robert's son whose caravan park,
signifying a rootless, English-language tourist culture, is the antithesis
of what Dinas, at the heart of a long-standing, and one may presume
Welsh-language, community, represents.

The HMI in 'The Rigours of Inspection', associated by the school's head teacher with the 'latest psychological jargon', arrives at the school in a striking car. In fact, the story is framed by the arrival and the departure of the car. On its arrival we learn that it is a Volkswagen, signifying the new global economy, and on the HMI's departure that it is yellow, reinforcing not simply the way in which the old is being challenged by the new but also the clash between them. The reader's discovery at the end of the story of what would be perceived, at that time and in that small community, as the car's garishness should encourage him or her to revisit the hostility between the HMI and the head teacher. The Volkswagen's brashness is at odds with the latter's sobriety: 'The rain-spots landed on the dark material of his Sunday suit and plated soft patches on his stiff white collar' (p. 31).

For the most part, the stories in *Natives* explore what lies behind the seemingly staid and traditional. The opening of 'The Suspect' stresses suburban respectability. However, the reader soon discovers that John and Phoebe are far from the stereotypical, happily married, middle-class couple. She is having an affair with a bachelor optician and she and her husband have agreed to continue to live together for the sake of the children. Mel in 'Mel's Secret Love' has a relationship with her married boss who, in the end, refuses to leave his wife and family for her, while Jess in 'A List of Good People', who is now married to Vince, was originally his secretary. The diversity of sexual relationships in *Natives* highlights the way in which relationships develop across genders, classes and ages and this, in turn, becomes a vehicle for exploring the fluid nature of mid-twentieth-century Wales.

In other words, in post-industrial society, the relationship between words, signs and meanings becomes increasingly arbitrary and elusive. Thus, 'optician' in 'The Suspect' becomes a very slippery concept. In the story, the term acquires one set of meanings through its association with the sign's professional connotations, linking it to a dentist, doctor or a district nurse, for example, and another through its association with a self-employed shopkeeper. This confusion of signs establishes an enigmatic framework within which Max himself is situated: Jewish, handsome ladies' man, respectable professional, fashion-conscious bachelor, rootless flat-dweller, town councillor, adulterer, potential rapist and victim of prejudice.

The fluidity explored in *Natives* with regard to private and public relationships is extended to different accounts of masculinity, as in the description of Max's fastidiousness where the boundary between traditional 'masculinity' and 'femininity' is slightly blurred:

> In contrast to his surroundings, Max was very clean. He was a short man with curly hair, merry eyes and unusually broad shoulders. Twice a day he had a shave and a shower and he used an expensive after-shave lotion. His clothes, including his shirts, were specially made for him. Gold cuff-links and a generous display of cuffs drew attention to his hands of which he was very proud. They were broad, soft and beautifully manicured. (p. 69)

In this description of Max, as in the account of the HMI's brash Volkswagen in 'Rigours of Inspection', Humphreys is interested in how professional, middle-class men are becoming more flamboyant. But he is also interested in how in this process traditional signifiers of masculinity and femininity are changing, for example, the association of 'beautifully manicured' fingernails, expensive jewellery and bright colours with femininity. Within a wider context, related to this, Humphreys explores the increasing importance of the relationship between objects and cultural meanings in what, towards the end of the twentieth century, became known as postmodern society.

Indeed, both traditional and new meanings attached to objects become an increasing focus in Humphreys's fiction. The 'gothic entrance' to the school in 'The Rigours of Inspection' suggests its history but it is also a piece of architecture in which power and negotiations of social relations are rendered in concrete form. It would obviously dwarf the pupils and fill them with a sense of awe if not dread. It is about indoctrinating pupils in a particular set of power relations rather than welcoming them and it obviously stands in the community as a signifier of particular educational ideologies. While the HMI, his latest ideas and his flashy German car signify the present, the Gothic entrance to the school suggests the past and an almost Victorian educational ideology.

In *Natives*, the fluidity of meanings, where once singular and fixed referents become plural and unstable, resonates with a wider sense of instability in terms of the power relationships on which society is based. Signifiers of the latter range from an exercise book grudgingly tossed to a school pupil in 'The Rigours of Inspection', to the sale of Dinas to the district nurse and some of its contents to a scrap merchant, to the demolition of property in 'Mel's Secret Love' and the purchase of derelict property in 'A List of Good People'. Within many of the stories, what seems under threat is the exchange that passes between men and includes objects, as in 'Dinas', the female body as in 'Mel's Secret Love' and 'The Suspect' and, as in 'A List of Good People', property.

GHOSTS AND STRANGERS

The stories in *Ghosts and Strangers* are more obviously novellas than even the longer stories in *Natives*. The collection was originally to be subtitled 'Four Love Stories'.[8] The title brings to the fore some key twentieth-century ideas about self knowledge, knowledge (or perhaps lack of knowledge) of others and the nature of intimacy. In a discussion of mourning, Jacqueline Rose argues, drawing on Freud, that 'Death is a problem, not because we cannot surmount its loss or imagine our own death, but because it forces us to acknowledge that what belongs to us most intimately is also a stranger or enemy, a type of foreign body in the mind'.[9] Ruth Parkin-Gounelas points out that, according to Nicolas Abraham, the phantom which haunts all human subjects is 'not the content of repression Freud called a familiar stranger' but a 'bizarre foreign body within us'.[10] Humphreys's title juxtaposes two spectralities, 'Ghosts' and 'Strangers', which, as post-Freudians Rose and Parkin-Gounelas suggest, do not stand in contradistinction to each other as 'ghosts *and* strangers', but are elided with each other.

Parkin-Gounelas maintains that 'Ghosts and spectrality in a wider sense, have become popular in recent post-structuralist theory'. In this regard, Derrida's *Specters de Marx* (1994) is 'characteristic in its use of spectrality to represent deconstruction's challenge to metaphysical distinctions – between presence and absence, past and present, life and death'.[11] This is precisely what Humphreys does in his collection of short fiction, *Ghosts and Strangers*. There may be an 'and' in the title but in the text there is no conjunction between these spectralities. In this regard, it is no coincidence that the cover of the first edition is illustrated with a death mask from Karen Ingham's *Death's Witness* exhibition. The back cover also bears a reproduction from the same exhibition so that the text is sandwiched between two death masks which, as we ponder them, demonstrate Rose and Parkin-Gounelas's arguments whilst erasing the conjunction between the terms of the title. Indeed, on the cover, 'and' is denoted by '&', reducing the space between them.

Parkin-Gounelas points out: 'It is their disruption of temporal and spatial boundaries which makes ghosts such effective figures of psychic and semantic disturbance.'[12] In Humphreys's text, 'strangers' are equally effective as 'figures of psychic and semantic disturbance'. In the titular story, Gwion Roberts, a gardener who has inherited considerable wealth and is travelling alone through Europe, catches sight of Simon Huff, a poet from Yorkshire, on a railway station platform. Simon enters Gwion's mind as a 'foreign body' and a site of disruption. It is not clear at first whether Simon is 'uneasy' or whether he makes Gwion 'uneasy'.

The title of this story may be interpreted in different ways. It may be seen as referring to the way in which spectralities, such as 'ghosts' and 'strangers', as throughout this story, disrupt 'metaphysical distinctions – between presence and absence, past and present, life and death'.[13] However, it may also refer to the way in which characters in an author's mind are ghosts and strangers to him or her. One of the protagonists in 'Ghosts and Strangers', Lillian Trenova, with whom Simon appears to be obsessed, is planning a film about D. H. Lawrence in Fiasherino. To her, 'they are ghosts' and the title for the film that she considers is 'Ghosts and Lovers'.[14] The story is told by a narrator whom we do not get to know. This may parallel the way in which Gwion may be something of a stranger to the author. He is somewhat detached from people and, at one point, admits that he became a gardener because plants, unlike animals, do not answer back. He is more naturally an observer than a participant. There is something cold and detached about him, which makes one think of him as having some of the traits of a psychopath.

In fact, Gwion is haunted by three deaths: those of his employers, Lord and then Lady Pescant, and, more recently, of their nurse Rowena whom he married. This plot is itself 'ghostly', haunted as it is by familiar inheritance murder narratives in which elderly wealthy people are killed by the nurse who looks after them. Certainly, there is gossip in the village that Rowena could have murdered them. Indeed, Simon glibly suggests that Gwion could be a murderer on the run in Europe. We do not really discover why he is wandering around the Continent. His explanation is that, after Rowena's death, he is visiting the great gardens of Europe but Simon may be right in his suspicions. Rowena haunts the story and we get some sense of her through her aphorisms which interrupt the narrative. The constant reference to her suggests that she and Gwion were very close but throughout the narrative he appears as someone who has difficulty with intimate relationships.

Moreover, it is difficult for us to know, too, how much Simon supposedly remembers is memory and how much is a product of his imagination. He can be dependent upon Lillian one moment but assert his independence of her the next. In the narrative, the boundary between 'reality' and fantasy is a major theme. Simon is configured by Gwion as a volatile personality who can withdraw into his own writings and imaginings. He can be depressed one moment but exuberantly embroiled in a fantasy project the next. Indeed, there is something dangerous about both male protagonists: Gwion has some of the traits of a psychopath, unable to sympathize fully with the sufferings of others, while Simon suffers from violent mood swings and dark bouts of depression. But, of course, we are witnessing Simon through Gwion's eyes.

Names are very important in this story. Simon calls Gwion 'Welshy', making him a bit part in his life narrative whilst imposing a narrative upon him. When Lillian calls Simon 'Si', Gwion realizes there is intimacy between them. Gwion refuses to take his full name Gwion Lloyd Roberts because he believes that it would be too pretentious a name for a gardener. Sylvia Hoffman-Egle shortens her name to Sylvia Hoffman. By contrast, the names of Lord and Lady Pascant and Rowena are never shortened. This gives the text a slippery, enigmatic sense of identity which is aligned with the way in which actions are never fully explained. Why does Gwion allow Simon to latch on to him for so long, even going back to him at one point after he has dumped him? As noted earlier, Gwion could be a murderer and, maybe through guilt, he clings to the one man who has suggested this to his face. Why does Lilian, having been warned off Simon and his family maintenance problems, suddenly decide to meet him? All of this recalls the point made by Jacqueline Rose that even 'what belongs to us most intimately is also a stranger or enemy, a type of foreign body in the mind'.

In 'Ghosts and Strangers', Gwion remembers his employer Lord Pascant's saying that 'we clutch at each other for comfort in this world' and that all of us know 'in our heart of hearts that we are lost' (p. 67). Like 'Ghosts and Strangers', 'Menna' is focused on a relationship, this time between a married couple, and also involves a journey through Europe, in this instance France. Once again, there is a protagonist who is haunted by a female figure. In this story, Lisa is haunted by her husband's mother who is not dead but constantly interrupts her life and, even when she is not there, affects her thinking processes. Menna is the daughter of a Welsh-speaking farmer, Dafydd Cyffin, who has earned himself a reputation as a skilled castrator of animals. With this protagonist, a Freudian dimension enters the story as, according to Freud, young girls come to view their mothers as 'castrated', envying their fathers their penises, and Dafydd's reputation suggests he is a symbolic triumph over the male fear of castration.

To her husband Arnot, Lisa represents the beautiful, desirable female which he can support in his large muscular body. This is the role that she seems happy to play at times but at other times she transforms herself into a 'bitch', another fetishized version of womanhood but one which allows her to explore a lexicon of violence, domination, submission and victimization. In seeing herself in this role, she does not wish to resist and destroy Arnot's romanticization of her but presents herself masochistically as the object deserving of, and desiring, punishment: 'You spoil me. You ought to beat me sometimes. Make me suffer' (p. 86). It is significant that Lisa is interested in Menna as someone caught between a tyrannical father and a bullying husband. It is as if these men represent her fetishism of masculine domination, transforming the way she thinks of her relationship with Arnot. In this regard, she moves in her imagination from the stable way in which Arnot thinks of their relationship to one which involves an imagined absent presence of a dominating male.

Although Menna's haunting of Lisa is not an actual haunting there are a number of ghosts in this story. Arnot's twin brother, Idris, who was killed by a lorry when Menna was distracted, haunts his mother and his brother. The Count, with whom Lisa for a while wishes to become involved in an arts and culture project, has a twin brother who commits suicide because he is accused of photographing naked children and Menna conflates Arnot, who helps push a car about to burst into flames from a petrol station, with her husband who once entered a burning building.

OLD PEOPLE ARE A PROBLEM

The stories in *Old People are a Problem* are much more integrated than even those in *Ghosts and Strangers*. The work is 'framed' by two stories – 'Old People are a Problem' and 'Glasshouses' – which cryptically echo each other. Within this frame, there are a number of stories that 'mirror' each other in some way. 'The Man in the Mist' is a story told by Gwyn(daf) Ronald, an academic, about his relationship with

Glyn(dwr) Brace, a television personality and producer. This story is echoed by the structure of 'Sisters' in which one sister, who is a painter, tells of her relationship with the other who is also a painter, albeit in a different style, and lives on the same street.

The titular story *Old People are a Problem* suggests that old people can be a problem. Alderman and businessman Mihangel Parry-Palin complains that old people are a problem during the course of thinking about his ninety-three-year-old aunt, Mary Keturah Parry. She will not move from what he perceives as unsuitable accommodation in Soar chapel to the Cartref Residential Home. In 'The Arrest', a Nonconformist minister is regarded as a problem by his wife and the police because, like Humphreys himself who received a prison sentence in 1973, he refuses to pay for his television licence in protest over the dearth of Welsh-language programmes. However, talking with Mary about his own daughter, Iola, who has billeted a single mother and her son on him, Mihangel in 'Old People are a Problem' suggests: 'It becomes clear that the young are a problem, too.'[15]

The rebellious daughter invokes the Freudian concept of the ego and the superego which seeks to curtail its drives. At one level, the daughters in 'Old People are a Problem' and 'Glasshouses' might be seen as demonstrating how, as Jacqueline Rose points out, 'the superego inherits the aggression of the drives it curtails ... Subjects introject their own aggressiveness, sending it back, so to speak, to where it originally belonged'.[16] In psychoanalysis, there is a close link between the superego and the law of the father. Rose maintains that 'the model for the superego is therefore a drama of torture which takes place between father and child'.[17]

In 'Old People are a Problem' and 'Glasshouses', the daughter has lost her mother, leaving her more exposed in her relation to the law of the father and embroiled more nakedly in a struggle between ego and superego of which the father–daughter relationship is an analogy. In both stories, the daughter refuses to pursue or finish a degree course, which her father thinks she ought to complete, and behaves in radical but unselfish ways which leaves her father baffled. In both of these two stories, the daughter challenges her father's values. Mihangel asks: 'Did the girl do anything these days except protest, and when she could spare the time, call the whole purpose of his way of life into question?' (p. 12). From their points of view, the fathers in both stories have ostensibly achieved much in their lives. In 'Old People are a Problem', Iola's father is a successful businessman and member of the council, who has also been the mayor, and in 'Glasshouses', Ceri's father is a well-known architect. But, following the death of his wife, each man lives a lonely life removed to some extent from the world and, in both stories, their homes are referred to as 'retreats'.

In 'Glasshouses', Ceri Melor works in a market garden and the rehabilitation centre for convicts which it supports. This retreat is run by an ex-convict, 'Father' Ambrose, who had a conversion to Christianity while in prison and has a criminal record dating back to his youth, but has recently served a long sentence for an offence for which he was allegedly framed by the police. In psychoanalytic terms, the rebellious daughter and the criminal in this story are linked. Rose points out that according to one branch of psychoanalysis, the object relations theory, the child is a potential criminal because 'the child is warding off, through socially unacceptable behaviour, the edicts of an internal persecutor compared with which the chastisement of an external authority is a positive relief'.[18] In other words, it is the overpowering strictures of the superego that lead to what is perceived as antisocial or criminal behaviour. Anticipating Ceri's involvement with an ex-convict, Iola, in the opening story refers to the single mother whom she has befriended as her 'partner in crime'. This link emphasizes how both women are involved with what is outside the 'respectable' boundaries of society, unmarried mothers and convicts, and so challenge the boundaries of ' insider' and 'outsider'.

Following his conversion, Ambrose wears a clerical collar and refers to himself as Father Ambrose. Ceri, who is referred to as 'The Spirit of the Place' (p. 229), at times wears a grey cloak and walks around like a nun. The retreat fetishizes discipline: Ambrose wants Ceri 'to keep an eye on him' and 'be as stern' as she can in order to prevent him from being 'lax and lazy' (ibid.). In other words, through the cloak, mimicking a nun's habit, and a stern disposition, Ceri is to remould any soft femininity she may have. Significantly, in converting the housekeeper's sitting room into a cell for meditation, the elaborate flower pattern, which might be seen as feminine, is removed for being 'too distracting' and is replaced by grim, 'battleship grey' (ibid.). This does not necessarily mean that Ambrose is a masochist but that he is 'warding off … the edicts of an internal persecutor' who has become more prominent following his conversion to Christianity. This psychoanalytic approach is appropriate to *Old People are a Problem* because it seems to be concerned not with obedience to the 'law', interpreted broadly, but with *how* to obey it.

In the opening and concluding stories, the independent and radical behaviour of the rebellious daughters contrasts with their fathers' bewilderment but is linked to that of their mothers. In the final story, 'Glasshouses', Ceri inherits Janet's idealism and, like Bethan Mair Nichols in the subsequent novel *The Shop*, seeks to understand her mother. At the latter's grave, anticipating Bethan, Ceri announces: 'I have to go over every moment of her existence before the end. And the end is the beginning. That is what we have to make out. The meaning' (p. 228). Iola's strength and will in the opening story 'Old People are a Problem', however, are inherited from her aunt Mary Ketruah Parry's great-great-great-grandmother, Jane Amelia Parry, who used to walk thirty miles to a preaching meeting. Iola's baking a cake at Penllwyn echoes Mary Ketruah Parry's peppermint cake making.

However, the relationship between Mary and Iola in the text is complicated, not least because Mary is, like Ceri in her cloak, both a figure of authority and a psychic fantasy. She is a stern figure who, with her uncompromising glare, has dominated her nephew Mihangel all his life and, in many respects, is the strict, dominating figure into which Ambrose, in 'Glasshouses', would seem to want to turn Ceri. In Mihangel's imagination, Mary combines two psychic fantasies. One is making peppermint cake in a dirty saucepan over a fire at Soar Chapel. The elderly woman is a witch but she is also in his eyes 'an emaciated simulacrum of the stern deacon and Sunday School teacher who had tyrannised his childhood' (p. 16). The comparison between Mary and a witch – significantly she meets her death, like many witches, in a fire, albeit one for which she is responsible – reminds us of the way in which women who have represented alternative discourses have been demonized throughout history. However, she is not supportive of Iola's globetrotting participation in protest marches and thinks that she should have been bought up more strictly.

'Old People are a Problem' is an opening story in which history seems destined to repeat itself. Mihangel was relieved when his wife moved the stern portrait of her grandfather, who had had Penllwyn built, to the attic. He is perturbed when his young daughter Iola returns home with Maristella, the young unmarried mother and active protester against globalism, and moves his photographs, including the one of him in mayor's robes, to the drawers. It is an act that disrupts Mihangel's view of himself and, since she says that one of the reasons she moved them was that they were too 'English', rewrites colonial discourse. By this, I mean that here the way in which Wales has historically looked subserviently towards its Anglocentric colonizer, as Humphreys believed, is replaced by a viewpoint that is more centred on Welsh concerns. Although Iola has inherited her mother's idealism, she has also inherited some of her great-aunt Mary's qualities and she becomes a stern presence in her widowed father's home. Representing an uncompromising Welsh nationalism that might wish to drive the English out of Wales, Iola has come between him and women he might have married, including one whom she considered too 'English'. Despite her father's initial displeasure over having Maristella and her child foisted upon him, they reawaken in him the pleasures of family life. At the end of the story, at Mary's funeral, he proposes to her, as Iola walks formidably towards them, his action anticipating the way in which Gareth Pengry tries to propose to Ceri over her mother's grave in 'Glasshouses'.

The principal theme of *Ghosts and Strangers*, that we do not know completely even those with whom we are most intimate, is developed in *Old People are a Problem*. In the two stories that have so far been considered and which frame *Old People are a Problem*, the fathers suddenly discover not only that they do not know their daughters but also that they do not necessarily know themselves. In the title story, Mihangel awakes in bed to see in his wardrobe mirror 'a white ghost that was nothing more than his own dishevelled image' (p. 29). In an echo of Charles Dickens's *A Christmas Carol*, the spectre that confronts him is a reminder to Mihangel of how he has lost sight of his true human side. When watching Maristella pushing her little boy Nino on a swing, Mihangel observes a scene in the present which, in the Derridean sense, discussed in chapter 3, brings the past and the future before him: the past in which he participated in family life and the future in which he fears he will be increasingly bereft of this kind of warmth.

The female relationships in *Old People are a Problem* are a 'problem', too. In the story 'Before the War', which like 'An Artistic Mission' in *Natives* involves the capturing of the memories of an elderly person, Elsie Probert, who is being recorded by her great niece, Non, for a Ph.D. thesis, concludes by advising her: 'We are related, aren't we?' (p. 78). In some respects, Non is at the end of a continuum of social change for women which can be traced back through the twentieth century to the Second World War, a period examined in *Unconditional Surrender*, and then on beyond the 1930s and 1920s to the First World War, the period explored in the Land of the Living sequence. In this regard,

there are many Welsh women who are 'related' in their shared struggles. However, Non's life as a young woman, echoing aspects of the
lives of female characters from earlier novels such as Amy Parry, Enid
Prydderch, Meg Pritchard and Rhiannon Morgan, is very different
in terms of the opportunities available to Elsie Probert as a young
woman. Her access to education and a career is on a par with that
of the young woman Bethan Mair Nichols in post-Assembly Wales in
The Shop. As Non explains to her great-aunt about her relationship
with an ambitious young man who works for an American publisher in
London: 'And when the thesis was well and truly finished and she had
her Ph.D. she could tread with Master Gilbert on a more or less equal
footing' (p. 56).

The kind of life which Elsie lived in her parents' house was closer
to that of Kate and Lydia in *Outside the House of Baal* except that her
family was church rather than chapel. The intellectual and emotional
escape from this life was provided by a young woman, Prydwen Parry,
who came to play the organ in their church. Like a number of women
characters in Humphreys's fiction, Prydwen acts as a kind of 'trickster'
figure making the community face up to its structures and strictures.
As mentioned, in 'Old People are a Problem' Mary is conceived by
Mihangel as a kind of wicked witch in a fairy story. In 'Before the
War', Elsie remembers how she thought of Prydwen as having 'a fairy
tale quality' about her (p. 62). She persuaded Elsie's parents to allow
her to attend a girls' weekend camp and, in a move which brought her
much criticism from the church, blurred the boundary between church
and chapel by establishing a branch of the Urdd (the Welsh League of
Youth). At the weekend girls' camp, Elsie experiences an emotional
closeness with girls from different backgrounds in the community,
which made it difficult for her to 'return to the house of long silences
governed by a climate of likes and dislikes impossible for a young girl
to identify' (p. 64).

The image of the stallion, and all that it represents, divides the two
halves of the story: the pre- and the post-lapsarian. In the second half
of the text, Prydwen undergoes a transformation in Elsie's eyes: 'She
wasn't a fairy princess, only a pantomime demon in disguise intent on
awakening a sleepy but contented village with a poisoned kiss' (p. 73).
She is seen by Elsie's brother Tom kissing the rector and is thought to
be complicit in making alcohol available to his wife so that she humili-
ates herself by stripping and dancing on the altar steps in a drunken
stupor and has a serious accident. Prydwen's and the rector's kissing is

described as something that 'verged on forbidden fruit', which underscores the comparison between Llannerch and Eden. In the second half of the story, she is cast as Eve after the Fall. But the 'forbidden' knowledge is as much Elsie's as it is Prydwen's as she now sees Llannerch, and life generally, in different terms.

12

Intimate Strangers: *The Shop*

As suggested in the previous chapter, Humphreys's short fiction collection *Ghosts and Strangers* and the novel *The Shop* may be seen as belonging to the same wider project in which Humphreys examines key twentieth-century ideas about self-knowledge, knowledge of others (or perhaps the lack of it) and the nature of intimacy. As we have seen, *Ghosts and Strangers* may be read within a framework that has been developed by the psychoanalytic critic Jacqueline Rose, drawing on Freud. Of particular relevance to *Ghosts and Strangers*, it has been argued, is her thesis that 'what belongs to us most intimately is also a stranger or enemy, a type of foreign body in the mind'.[1] Concerned with intimate relations, as are many of the stories in *Ghosts and Strangers*, *The Shop* also bears out Ruth Parkin-Gounelas's reiteration of Nicolas Abraham's point that the phantom which haunts all human subjects is 'not the content of repression Freud called a familiar stranger' but a 'bizarre foreign body within us'.[2] We have already seen how Humphreys's title, *Ghosts and Strangers*, juxtaposes two spectralities ('Ghosts' and 'Strangers') which Rose and Parkin-Gounelas suggest do not stand in contradistinction to each other, but are elided one with another. This is a theme which Humphreys further explores in *The Shop* which, like the stories in *Ghosts and Strangers*, is concerned with the way in which the 'personalities' of different couples are constructed in relation to each other.

The novel is narrated by a Welshman working in Italy, Eddie Lloyd, who has fallen in love with a Welsh photographer Bethan Mair Nichols, whom he meets on the Continent. However, there are two other voices in the narrative that are not filtered through Eddie. The voice of Bethan is heard speaking in her letters to him and another voice is heard in a letter which has been left to Bethan by one of her family. In some respects, *The Shop* is an inversion of the traditional female romance in which the woman's life revolves around finding the right man with whom to settle down. The novella presents us with a very ambitious young woman and a man who wishes to settle down. Eddie observes at an early stage in their relationship that though 'I couldn't say it in the face of [Bethan's] tumultuous and unconventional ambition – I would like to be married and even starting a family'.[3]

Bethan's enigmatic and edgy qualities are stressed even before Eddie and the reader encounter her: 'Welsh. Very keyed up sometimes. Very touchy. Something to do with her background' (p. 11). The reader of *The Shop* observes a relationship between a man and a woman which grows in intimacy throughout the text. However, at the same time, there are tensions between them which stress the extent to which they remain strangers to each other. In contrast to Amy Parry in the Land of the Living sequence, Bethan's mother and stepmother grew up during the second wave of feminism and she lives in a period which some critics describe as 'post-feminist'. Sarah Gamble distinguishes between these two phases in a way which is appropriate to Humphreys's fiction: 'Whereas the [former] was the *women's* liberation movement, postfeminism aims to liberate the *daughters*; a view of itself which is reinforced through its consistent appeal to youth.'[4] Bethan is one of a generation of women for whom feminism, in Gamble's words, is 'an incontrovertible part of their cultural landscape'.[5]

Thus, it is not surprising that Bethan shares characteristics with the key protagonists of the mass-produced, popular genre known as 'chicklit', although there are many differences, too, to which I shall come in a moment. Like the 'heroines' of chicklit, Humphreys's Bethan focuses a concern, albeit in a specific Euro-Welsh context, with what Gamble maintains is central to the popular contemporary genre: 'defining the aims and aspirations of the modern young woman who has grown to maturity in a world inescapably influenced by second-wave feminism'.[6] But a further parallel between *The Shop* and chicklit, as far as the principal female protagonist is concerned, is the central importance they both attach to addressing a dilemma. Gamble argues that the chicklit protagonist 'sees herself as facing dilemmas which lie outside the experience of previous generations of women' and this is certainly true of Bethan although the novel seeks to find lines of continuity between her and her foremothers.[7] But although she shares these characteristics with chicklit heroines, and provides us with an interesting example of the post-feminist heroine in serious literature written by a man, there is one area in which they are very different. Gamble points out that, although the aspirations of the chicklit heroine arise from having grown up in a world influenced by second-wave feminism, she 'can be regarded as a lamentable kind of heroine for whom happiness depends upon the most limited and hackneyed of objectives: romantic fulfilment'.[8] This is not true of Bethan in *The Shop*, which makes Humphreys's novella much more complex than a chicklit novel.

As is true of Lisa in her relationship with Arnot in 'Ghosts and Strangers', Bethan is intellectually more lively than Eddie. Linguistically, she seems to dance around him at first, playfully using his ancestral name and calling him 'Eddie Cynddylan, Eddie C.'. She also suggests somewhat mockingly that he might be her adviser, 'Socrates-Cynddylan'. Bethan's wisecracking, at times flippant, attitude is again something that she has in common with the chicklit heroine. But there is one important difference between them in this regard, too. Gamble argues that the wisecracking attitude of the chicklit protagonist 'conceals deep anxieties concerning her relationships (or lack of them), her body image, and what she considers to be her advancing age'.[9] However, Bethan is concerned about her identity as a young, professional Welsh woman, her relationship with, and obligations to, her foremothers, her creative aspirations and the future of the projects which she initiates or with which she becomes involved.

Although Bethan can be flippant, her wit generally has a serious purpose. At one level, it protects her from the shock of inheriting Pentregwyn and her consequent re-linking of herself with her female ancestry. But it also serves an emancipatory function, freeing her from the resistance paradigm of second-wave feminism, and allowing her to define her own aims and aspirations as a young, Welsh woman in a post-feminist world. In this regard, her irreverent humour is not so much a reaction against conventional social discourse, as it is in many Euro-American feminist novels of the 1970s and 1980s, but the product of how she is defining her own discourse as a woman who has grown up with social structures and expectations created by feminism. Thus, getting to know Bethan is not simply an issue for Eddie, it is a challenge for the reader throughout the whole of the novella which, through exploring her attitudes, examines aspects of postmodern and post-feminist Wales.

THE PHOTOGRAPHER AND HER PHOTOGRAPHS

The subject of discoveries and rediscoveries made by people in relationships and friendships in *Ghosts and Strangers*, as they each seek to understand each other, is developed in *The Shop* from a wider perspective which includes relations with one's family and with Wales. Like all of Humphreys's 'dramatic fiction', the novella is based around a series of dilemmas, the most important of which involves Pentregwyn General Stores which Bethan inherits. She finds herself caught between her career as a photographer and, as she begins to work on her project for the store, the way in which the centre of her life becomes defined by a letter from her Aunt Sulwen about her female relatives.

The fact that Bethan is a photographer is important to understanding the way in which she thinks and the way in which the narrative is structured. Indeed, the narrative itself turns on photographs, including Bethan's photographing of the standing stones at the beginning of the novel, her photographing of the Pentregwyn General Stores and the photograph which she is handed showing her birth mother on her release from a prison sentence for a Welsh-language protest. The photographs encapsulate the 'hauntology' in the narrative, to use Derrida's term, which is glossed by Susan Sontag in *On Photography*: 'In its simplest form, we have in a photograph surrogate possession of a cherished person or thing, a possession which gives photographs some of the character of unique objects.'[10] Thus, family photographs are not simply constant reminders of the past, they are spectres that inhabit our present and, as Jacqueline Rose has argued, they become foreign bodies in our own minds.

Eddie expresses his surprise, in a photographic metaphor, when Bethan reveals the purpose of their journey to Pentregwyn to him. Convincing himself that Bethan cannot really value his opinion, he argues: 'If she really wanted to know she would have put me in the picture at the very start of our journey. Plainly she was more intent on astonishing me' (p. 61). Eddie's phrase 'put me in the picture' is ambivalent. It can mean 'include me in a photograph' or, as Eddie means it here, 'inform me of what is going on'. Although ostensibly very different, both interpretations are based on a transition from 'outsider', outside the photograph or outside knowledge of what is happening, to 'insider', being inside the photograph, presumably with others, or party to what is happening. However, as we have suggested, a photograph renders the subject as a stranger, reminding us how little we really know of them, and knowledge of anything is always partial. Thus, the text complicates the conventional binary between insider/outsider and known/unknown.

Initially, both Eddie and Bethan see the world as photographs generally present it to us. Sontag maintains: 'Through photographs, the world becomes a series of unrelated, freestanding particles; and history, past and present, a set of anecdotes and *faits divers*.'[11] This is the way in which Humphreys's fiction, as discussed in chapter 3, tends to present 'history'. His episodic, longer fiction, as argued, constantly interrupts itself. This is a quality of all narratives created by those who are excluded from official histories and is also a feature of Humphreys's dual concern with a history which has unfolded and, to use Derrida's concept, with 'a past that has never been present'.[12] In many respects, this is how Bethan initially conceives of her maternal ancestry. Bethan does not simply trace her family ancestry, she 'interrupts' it; and what she recreates in her own mind, as Humphreys does in his fiction, is a past that has never been present.

The way in which the camera makes reality 'atomic',[13] to use Sontag's word, is reflected in the headings which Aunt Sulwen includes in her long letter to Bethan about the family: 'My father, Henry Bowen' (p. 83), 'My sister Megan' (p. 88), 'Ffion Locksley, your mother' (p. 91), and 'Myself alone' (p. 98). However, the contents of the letter present the reader with what the subheadings and photographs deny: 'interconnectedness' and 'continuity'.[14] Sulwen's letter is instrumental in Bethan's creation of a family past that has never been present. This is why it becomes a 'text' which Bethan reads over and over again and which is also annotated. In reading and re-reading the letter, Bethan finds herself in a dilemma. Whilst trying to make Sulwen's narrative of the past, intended as passing knowledge from one female generation to another, her present, Bethan encounters the paradox to which Jacqueline Rose draws attention; that those of whom we feel we have intimate knowledge, inevitably become all the more of a stranger to us.

Rose's point is made in the title of the section about Sulwen which concludes the letter to Bethan, 'Myself alone'. It is partly her realization of the essential solitariness and unknowability of any individual that makes Bethan's hand tremble when Dr Seth ap Thomas, the Pentregwyn executor, hands her a curling photograph of her birth mother, taken outside Pucklechurch Prison in the early 1970s (p. 77). But the photograph makes an impression on Bethan for other reasons, too. There is a sense in which such a visual image, as Sontag says, conveys the message that 'everything exists to end in a photograph'.[15] At one level, the photograph which Bethan takes of Pentregwyn Stores suggests all that the shop with its 'grimy plate-glass' and 'mournful blinds' has become (p. 61). It is as if it was destined to end in this photograph. But in this novel, photographs, to employ Sontag's words, 'cannot themselves explain anything, are inexhaustible invitations to deduction, speculation, and fantasy'.[16]

At a crucial moment in the narrative, Bethan's and Eddie's differing responses as they peer into the shop distinguish them. Through a photographer's eyes, albeit still thinking 'atomically', Bethan sees the sense of mystery and fantasy which photographs can convey: 'Isn't that just something?' (p. 61); 'just look at that' (p. 62). This sense of mystery and imagination is important because only through them can Bethan realize what is motivating her: the past which has never been present. Eddie, on the other hand, can see only 'dispiriting shapes and shadows' and a 'bucket dangling forlornly' (ibid.). In many respects, the 'shadow' is himself and it is ironic that previously in the churchyard he had recognized his 'shadow' was 'falling across her shot' (p. 58). When Bethan later remains at the store and Eddie returns to Rome, her letters to him suggest how she is coming to terms with his absence as a shadow across her visions and discoveries at Pentregwyn.

As mentioned above, photographs play a major role in maintaining the way in which the past always haunts the present. But they also demonstrate how the present is haunted, as Derrida suggested, by the spectres from the future.[17] Photographs, especially family photographs, are taken, as books are written, with future audiences in mind. Like all photographs, the picture Bethan takes of Eddie entering Pentregwyn General Stores freezes a moment which later viewers might scrutinize as Bethan scrutinizes the photograph of her mother and her fellow protestors outside the prison. The frozen moment of Eddie entering the store suggests how, in becoming involved with Bethan, he is entering her family and familial past. The general store is caught at the end of something but is also captured in an 'in-between' moment, between what the store had been and what it may become. Thus, Eddie, who thinks of himself as a ghost, is entering a family and community to which he is a 'ghost' in the sense of a foreigner or stranger. But he is also entering one of Bethan's projects. In this latter respect, he is not so much a subject in his own narrative but an object in someone else's. In passing through the Pentregwyn Stores doorway, Eddie moves from one condition of being, in which he has been largely concerned with himself, to another in which he finds himself caring more for other people, not only Bethan but the badly injured Curig for whom he initially had little regard. The difficulty of this transition is underscored by the way in which it is represented in the novel as the 'unspeakable'. When he is first told by Lowri that Bethan and Curig have been attacked and injured, the Welsh that he has learned in order to embed himself in the community breaks down and he begins to stutter.

The store in Bethan's photograph is caught at the beginning of its regeneration. Thus, *The Shop*, like the novels in Land of the Living, casts the reader as a spectator in the Brechtian sense, discussed in chapter 9. The regeneration of the shop represents the social, moral and cultural progress which, along with a concern with dilemmas, has, as has been argued throughout this book, always been a feature of Humphreys's dramatic fiction. Cast in the role of observer, the reader is left to come to an understanding of what this regeneration means. It anchors a wider concern with rejuvenation in the text which includes the references to numerous regeneration projects being undertaken in post-National Assembly Wales.

However, Bethan's project also serves to measure the spiritual, personal and social 'progress' made by herself and Eddie as the novel's central protagonists. Above all, it underscores the intimacy which they develop, or fail to develop, as a couple. At the end of the novel, this, too, is expressed in terms of a photograph: 'She comes behind my chair, puts her hands around my neck and places her face alongside mine as though we were having our photographs taken. An image in any case to develop in her parents' minds' (p. 207). If this were a photograph, it would be the first in which they have been photographed together. It would also be the first that would not have been taken by Bethan although, ironically, it is she who initiates the 'photograph'. The suggestion that this is a photograph which Bethan's parents, who are present, might develop signifies how the future lives of Eddie and Bethan, as a couple, will be interpreted within a family narrative, as part of a family album. After this expression of intimacy, Bethan and Eddie sleep in Sulwen's bed where Bethan symbolically places not simply herself but herself and Eddie within Sulwen's family narrative. But this scene also suggests how family narratives are cyclical rather than linear.

What makes the narrative in *The Shop* different from that in Land of the Living is that it is based on the dilemma invoked by photography's freezing of moments. Sontag points out:

This freezing of time – the insolent, poignant stasis of each photograph – has produced new and more inclusive canons of beauty. But the truths that can be rendered in a dissociated moment, however significant or decisive, have a very narrow relation to the needs of understanding.[18]

Thus, the last chapter but two ends with an image of Bethan returning to bed: 'She snuggles into my shape and murmurs how nice it is to be together again' (p. 209). It is for both of them a moment of transcendental peace which the prose captures as if it were a photograph. But it has, to adapt Sontag's words, 'a very narrow' relation to the narrative not least because the moment is 'captured' by Eddie – 'an entrancing image of delicate submission' (ibid.) – and reflects the way in which he wants her to submit to his aspirations for them as a couple. The narrative cannot end here any more than a photograph can continue to be held outside the flow of time. Bethan in the subsequent chapters resumes her place within her narrative of movement, accepting Barry Parrott's documentary film project 'on the present state of racial and class relations in seven major English inner cities' (p. 223).

TWENTY-FIRST-CENTURY WALES AND EUROPE

In *The Shop*, the European travel element in 'Ghosts and Strangers' and 'Menna' has been expanded, providing a more substantial global context in which the concept of 'Welshness' in the twenty-first century is explored. The condition of 'exile' is handled very differently in this novel from its treatment in Humphreys's early work. Acknowledging the relevance of the concept of exile to 'The Modern Movement, that lasted really in all the arts from about 1880 to after the Second World War', Humphreys has admitted that what was once a '*sine qua non*' has 'become meaningless in a world that has shrunk to a parish'.[19] The Europe of *The Shop* is very different from that in which Humphreys set his earlier work. It is a Europe where the economic realignment of global capitalism raises questions about the future of micro units, global aspirations and shadowy global institutions. Eddie Lloyd works for the United Nations Food and Agricultural Organization. At one point, he describes himself as 'International' rather than British or Welsh. Initially, Bethan has a love-hate relationship with Wales through her ambivalent relationship with her birth mother, Ffion Locksley and her stepmother, whom she calls her 'moulding mother' (p. 136), Lowri Philip: 'I had Welsh and Welshness shoved down my throat ever since I can remember. I took this job to get away from it all' (p. 15).However, Bethan lives in a Wales where globalization and internet technology are restructuring the country's relation to other parts of the world. She takes Eddie to task for not thinking in this way himself: 'Hardly part of the modern world, Eddie darling, with satellites and e-mails and the world-wide web making the whole world just one big village from China to Peru!' (p. 216). Whereas Eddie looks inward, to a sense of place, Bethan, demonstrating the distinction between place and space, discussed in chapter 3, looks outward, to see the stores in Wales within a global economy.

However, this is not to say that Eddie, who has spent much of his working life in Europe, has no sense of spatial 'politics'. In *The Shop*, Wales is presented much more in terms of cultural difference and sites of social tension. Eddie describes the local pub:

> There is an area of English-speaking newcomers. 'Settlers' as they are known locally. At the other extreme the Cymraeg speakers; divided between the young and vociferous and the middle-aged who don't have much to say to each other. In between are the casuals and visitors. (pp. 184–5)

The problem with Eddie is that his spatial awareness is based on binaries: monoglot English-speaking settlers/indigenous Welsh-language locals; young and vociferous/middle-aged; inhabitants/visitors. The reader does not know whether this is how things are in the local pub or whether this is how Eddie perceives them. Whichever interpretation is correct, there is a risk that a community locked inside binaries set in place by custom and practice, in their own way powerful discourses, cannot progress. Not that far from the rural Pentregwyn is a reminder, in the figure of the Indian doctor who treats Bethan in hospital, that Wales is a country where the traditional binaries are no longer applicable. Existing and new ethnic communities, bringing about a greater range of languages in Wales, are complicating the English/Welsh binary on which Welsh identity has been traditionally based.

The attack upon Bethan and Curig when they are alone at night in the shop is a reminder of a negative geography based around crime. Viewed from this perspective, parts of Wales are no longer rural idylls but vulnerable 'outlands' where there is no regular policing:

> The shop became a treasure house loaded with gold. There are gangs you see that operate up and down the North Wales coast. It's hard to believe, in such a quiet innocent place as this. The word gets around the criminal

network. And there's the drug culture too you see. Both worlds touch each
other. Co-operated you could say. Like a cancer in a sick society you could
say. (p. 178)

One might ask whether the individuals who inhabit the political
worlds of Humphreys's earlier novels could be cast only as ghosts and
spectres in his later work which is set in a more confidently nationalist Wales. Up to a point, the Wales represented in *The Shop* is one
in which older people might be made to feel a stranger: a Wales of
regeneration projects and people chasing posts in the new Welsh
Assembly. Alwyn Nichols, suddenly called back to Cardiff 'to attend
some critical piece of devolved government' (p. 191), represents this
new Wales of boards, trusts and committees, but also a Wales where
the centre of socio-economic gravity remains in the south rather than
the north. Lowri, who seeks to stand for the Assembly, has political
views which are ostensibly different from those articulated in the older,
pre-Assembly Wales of Land of the Living: 'What is needed is a social
and economic regeneration led from the front by a genuinely patriotic
government' (p. 193). But post-Assembly Wales is perceived as existing
on a precarious boundary between the institutionalization necessary
for Welsh development and the need for vision. Thus, the political
discourse in *The Shop* is not a departure from that seen in, for example,
Land of the Living. It simply adds new terms to the debates with which
Humphreys's fiction has always been concerned.

At one level, *The Shop* is 'haunted' by Francis Fukuyama's concept
of the end of history.[20] Fukuyama coined this concept to refer to the
way in which capitalism would eventually achieve a future that was
beyond historical change, based on the repression of dissent and opposition. It is this which makes Bethan's return to Wales, and decision to
regenerate Pentregwyn's General Stores, significant. In Fukuyma's
kind of post-capitalist utopia, Bethan can only be a stranger. Each of
the photographic projects in which she becomes involved engages her
in debate and dissent, sometimes, as at the beginning of the novel, with
her own directors.

Thus, Bethan's move to Pentregwyn is inevitable because it is a
movement out of a 'present' which, in Fukuyama's terms, is a kind of
stasis. This stasis is evident through the narrative's focus on the condition of being 'in-between'. Examples of this include Eddie's long wait
for Bethan to finish at Pentregwyn; Eddie's alternative, temporary relationships; and Bethan's dilemma as to what she should do. In making

this transition, Bethan does not simply return to her home country or even family, she enters a present which, as throughout Humphreys's fiction, offers further transition and possibilities. The novel suggests that personal relationships have to be constantly reinvented and revised and aligns this concept to the need to recognize that nation states, and the 'reality' presented by concepts of nation, similarly require revision and redevelopment.

13

Independence, Globalism and Nonconformity: *The Woman at the Window*

The Woman at the Window (2009) is a collection of twelve stories, assembled by Wynn Thomas in consultation with the author, some of which – 'The Grudge', 'Rendezvous', 'Luigi', 'Vennenberg's Ghost' and 'Nomen' – had already been published in the Welsh periodical *Planet*. They pick up themes and subjects from Humphreys's previous fiction, including the relationship between the present and the past; the 'stranger' and the difficulty of knowing even those with whom we are most intimate; the 'intruder' who brings 'disruption'; the contrast between the Nonconformist past and mid- or late twentieth-century globalism; war and pacifism; betrayal; and the permeability of national boundaries.

We have already noted Humphreys's interest in strong, independent female characters, such as Ada in *A Man's Estate*, Lydia in *Outside the House of Baal*, Amy in *Land of the Living* and Bethan in *The Shop*. There are equally independent women in *The Woman at the Window*, but a distinctive feature of the book is the number of strong, older women. These include widows, such as Dilys in 'Home' and Mrs Picton in 'The Woman at the Window', who demonstrate considerable personal strength as well as a number of women who were once teachers, such as Catrin Dodd in 'The Grudge' and Mrs Roberts in 'A Little History'.

The stories include numerous women characters at significant moments in their lives: for example, Rhian Mai in 'The Grudge' and

Heather and Katica in 'Home' who have been left by their husbands, and Mrs Picton in 'The Woman at the Window' and Dilys Mifanwy in 'Home' who are recently widowed. There is a recurring concern also with women who have been unable to fulfil their careers through marriage or having to assume the role of a carer. These include Catrin Dodd, who has had to give up a career as a lecturer in religious studies in 'The Grudge'; the harpist, Heather, who has had to concentrate on teaching rather than performance in 'Home', and Mrs Roberts who has given up a school teaching career in 'A Little History'.

The concept of 'performative' identity in Humphreys's work, discussed in chapters 5 and 6, is developed somewhat disturbingly in regard to war in two of the stories. 'Nomen', which will be discussed in more detail later, includes the punishment and humiliation of female collaborators, who clearly had to assume roles to impress enemy soldiers, and, in 'Luigi', Sylvana, who belongs to one of the wealthiest families in Castiglione, and is said to be 'style incarnate' (95) in her black uniform.[1] At the end of the story, Sylvana dances with an English officer, 'As elegant as ever. So gay. So charming. Enslaving another admirer. Giggling out her bits of English and the officer so plainly entranced' (p. 102).

Continental Europe is a significant trope in *The Woman at the Window*. The centre of the book consists of stories ('Luigi', 'Vennenberg's Ghost' and 'Nomen') set on the Continent and several of the stories set in Wales also have a European dimension. The latter is developed through Continental Europeans marrying into Welsh families and/or living in the country (such as Zofia Worowski in 'A Little History', Claus in 'The Grudge' and Axel in 'Home') or Welsh or English people living overseas for a while (such as Daniel and Owain in 'Home', living in the Greek islands and America respectively; Elwyn Anwyl, who has lived most of his life in Italy, in 'The Woman at the Window'; and Dennis and Dilys in 'Home'). Often globalism is contrasted in the stories with the Welsh-language, Nonconformist past, another key theme in Humphreys's work, typified by Ifan's grandfather in 'A Little House', Huw Picton's great-grandfather in 'The Woman at the Window', and, to a lesser extent, Gwilym as a crowned and chaired poet in 'The Grudge'.

NONCONFORMITY AND RADICAL THOUGHT

The Woman at the Window is 'framed' by 'The Grudge' and 'A Little History'. The title of the latter story refers to the particular, localized, family history with which it is concerned but it is ironic because the family history described involves much larger world events, including the rise of fascism in twentieth-century Europe and anxiety about the prospect of nuclear warfare. The story is introduced and concluded by a daughter from the relationship between the two main protagonists, the son of a local farmer and a young Polish woman whose family has been dispersed because of the Second World War. The daughter's narrative, in which she recalls being taken by her mother to Greenham Common, is more contemporary than the rest of the story which concerns her parents' relationship as young people themselves in post-war Wales.

'The Grudge' is a more contemporary story than 'A Little History', but it, too, is based around a family with roots in Welsh-language Wales which is 'disturbed' by the arrival of an 'outsider'. Gwilym Hesgyn, a Welsh-language poet, is already enraged by the destruction of the trad-itional landscape, the settlement of people he regards as 'intruders' and by his daughter's marriage to a feckless Dane in the early 1980s, when his cousin, Lord Parry of Penhesgyn, whom he hates, retires to Hesgyn. Both storylines – Lord Parry's arrival and the break-up of the marriage of Gwilym's daughter – concern reconciliation. Gwilym is encour-aged to make up with his cousin and it is suggested that his daughter is considering some kind of reconciliation with her estranged husband.

Each of these two stories invokes the Welsh-language Nonconformist past without embarking upon a detailed examination of it. In 'The Grudge', the leading protagonist, as mentioned earlier, is a crowned and chaired Eisteddfod poet and 'A Little History' features an elderly Nonconformist minister who, befriended by his grandson, represents the radical, progressive Nonconformity which promoted pacifism. As we have seen, daughters figure predominately in Humphreys's most recent three novels and collections of short stories, and in each of these stories, a daughter, albeit unwittingly, suggests the reawak-ening or continuance of the cultural legacy of Nonconformity. In 'The Grudge', Rhian Mai takes a copy of her father's poems to the hospital, where he is suffering from a stroke brought on by his anger at discov-ering that she has been receiving letters from her estranged husband.

She hopes that her father will recognize his work and that this will help his recovery.

In 'A Little History', Ifan and Zofia's daughter, whose voice, as we noted, introduces and concludes the narrative, appears to have inherited her mother's conviction that 'History comes to an end when you can't do anything about it' (p. 221), and promises to be a radical thinker like her Nonconformist paternal grandfather. Both stories contrast the cultural and intellectual life of Nonconformity with a more pragmatic political outlook, typfied by the politician Lord Parry in 'The Grudge' and by the way in which Ifan is forced to abandon his poetic ambitions to run the family's farm and caravan park in 'A Little History'.

It is impossible to reduce *The Woman at the Window*, or indeed individual stories, to a single theme. Through the intermixing of different generations and nationalities, the stories juxtapose different possibilities, some of which lead to success but others to failure. Despite his early achievements at the Eisteddfod, Gwilym in 'The Grudge' fails to fulfil his initial promise as a bard. Although the Reverend Hughes in 'A Little History' seeks to nurture the poetic talents of his grandson, the boy's literary ambitions become only a hobby when, as a married man, he has to devote himself to his farm work. Ironically, the caravan park, which supplements his income from farming, is a disused quarry. As noted in chapter 1, slate mining in north Wales was a local industry which provided a forum for political, cultural and religious discussion which, in turn, contributed to the Welsh-language Nonconformist life and culture of the region, including local eisteddfodau. The disused quarry suggests the demise of Welsh-language Nonconformity as well as the end of a particular industry upon which local communities were dependent. But a further irony is that the caravan park is part of the tourist industry which, at that time, was replacing slate and, increasingly, farming as the principal economic activity, encouraging holidaymakers who, unlike those who worked in the slate quarries, had no roots in the area.

Nonconformity enters into further stories also. Mrs Picton, in 'The Woman at the Window', left with her would-be novelist husband's manuscripts which he failed to get published, wants his ashes buried with the remains of his grandfather who was a Nonconformist minister. This returns him to his past but also implies the end of something. Dilys in 'The Home' returns to her childhood Nonconformist home to find a boarded, almost derelict, house. However, in some stories, Nonconformity is perceived as a progressive, intellectual force which has relevance for the present day. This is suggested by the outcome of the argument over pacifism in 'A Little History' between Reverend Hughes, who may be compared with the real life George M. Ll. Davies whom Wynn Thomas has suggested was the model for J.T. in *Outside the House of Baal*,[2] and his grandson's Polish girlfriend, Zofia Worowski. That is not to say that the story encourages us to accept the viewpoints of Reverend Hughes, who typifies the pacifist movement within Nonconformity, discussed in chapter 8. In chapter 9, it was noted that Humphreys's work, certainly from *Outside the House of Baal* onwards, tends, in Brechtian fashion, to weave different perspectives for the reader to consider. As 'a pacifist, Hughes is critical of Britain's refusal to ban aerial bombing, but Zofia, whose family and people suffered during the war, initially under the Russians and then, for a longer period, under the Germans, believes her father when he says, 'if the Nazis got here we would be the first to be hanged from the nearest lamp post' (p. 230). However, their eventual agreement, that the destruction of whole cities, as occurred in the Second World War, coud not be allowed to happen again and that the pressing issue was the 'struggle ahead to survive' (p. 233), constitutes a new critical force, in which history will continue to be questioned. Ifan, impressed that 'the two wisest people he knew were in sufficient agreement', now believes that 'there would be a way ahead' (ibid.).

At one level, the discovery of common ground between Nonconformity and European anti-fascism, suggests the relevance and energy of the former's pacifist thinking. At another level, it exemplifies the importance of the way in which Nonconformity, especially where it promoted pacifism, provided space for discussion and debate. The importance of this intellectual culture is suggested by the contrast between the impassioned argument between Mr Hughes, the minister, and Zofia and Ifan's father's response to them, reflecting the poverty of his own intellectual life: 'These things go too deep for me. It takes me all my time to keep this farm going' (p. 230).

Protest has always been an important theme for Humphreys, who himself became involved in the Welsh-language campaigns of the 1970s. We have already considered examples of his treatment of protest in a number of works, including *Outside the House of Baal*, the Land of the Living sequence and *Ghosts and Strangers*. The stories in *The Woman at the Window* involve different types of protest. A number of them contrast a level of anger, linked to an almost obsessive narrowing of focus, with wider perspectives. This is true of the stories which open and close the book. Thus, Gwilym's unrelenting anger over what he alleges was his cousin's betrayal (at one point, he calls him a 'traitor' (p. 10), a word which conflates family and national disloyalty) is contrasted with the attempts of the local doctor and his wife, along with his own daughter, to bring them together. 'A Little History' opens with the women's peace protest at Greenham Common. Zofia, who becomes almost a professional protester, a figure we have noted previously in *Old People are a Problem*, and who is also typified in this book by Gabriel in 'Home', is said by her daughter to have 'dragged' her there, to spend 'even weeks on end' against that 'ghastly fence' (p. 221). The 'ghastly fence' is a boundary which signifies the limits of protest, but it also suggests how the cause has become an obsession that is not shared by her daughter, who, at this stage in her life, has not recognized the importance of not simply accepting how history unfolds. Of course, it was this perspective on history of not accepting things as they are which fuelled the Welsh nationalist protests of the late twentieth century.

Although none of the stories in *The Woman at the Window* constitutes historical fiction, the emphasis upon a radical, pacifist Nonconformity in 'A Little History' and 'Home' exemplifies the interest throughout Humphreys's work in historiography. In this regard, *The Woman at the Window* picks up on the contribution of his previous work to revising the way in which modern Welsh history, as discusssed in chapter 3, has tended to be seen from the perspective of south, rather than north, Wales with a greater emphasis upon the intellectual and cultural relevance of Nonconformity to Wales and a reassessment of its 'conservative' nature.

'HOME'

One of the most significant stories in *The Woman at the Window* is 'Home', which includes many of the themes and debates that occur throughout the book as a whole. But its principal concern is with the way in which a widow's attempts to reclaim her Nonconformist, Welsh-language past, after a life of globetrotting, helps energize the reconstruction of her home village. It is a first-person narrative in which Dilys Myfanwy, who has spent her life accompanying her husband, Dennis, on his global, 'erratic career to nowhere in the end' and still feels guilty at having put her father in a 'Minister's Retiring Home' in a part of the country he did not know (p. 147), wishes to 'Find a still centre in my confused world' (p. 146).

At one level, 'Home' is a 'return of the native' narrative, in which a linear biography – the principal protagonist leaves his or her 'home' to find fulfilment – is eventually replaced by a cyclical one, in which he or she realizes that, after all their time away, self-fulfilment is to be found in returning to the past that has been left behind. But, as argued in chapter 8, Humphreys tends to favour, in Jacques Derrida's term, a 'pluri-dimensional' concept of history rather than a linear cyclical binary. He values what Dilys discovers in reading her father's papers, the 'long correspondence, to and fro, from the new world to the old' (p. 155). 'Correspondence' here refers to her father's letters and writings. But it may suggest also the parallels between one period and another or the way in which one age seems to 'communicate' with another. It is significant, given what has been said about the reclamation of the radical nature of Nonconformity in Humphreys's work, that Dilys refers to the 'correspondence' between the past and the present as a two-way process.

How one period may be said to communicate with another is typified by the interest for Dilys's grandson Gabriel of her father's papers. They might have revealed debates and subjects of limited relevance to the present. But the way in which Gabriel, who admittedly knows more about Nicaragua than Nonconformist Wales, views his grandfather as a radical thinker and protester suggests that Nonconformity can be seen as part of wider radical thought, anticipating the outcome of the final story, 'A Little History'. How far Dilys's family has become removed from their Welsh-language ancestry is evident when her son, Daniel, who now lives with a male lover in the Greek islands, observes, 'I don't really remember [my grandfather], I was in that school in Sevenoaks when he died' (p. 147) . Looking forward to exploring her father's past with her grandson, Gabriel (although he does not go through with it), Dilys is excited that 'the things my father cherished were more than dust in a Pharoah's tomb' (p. 162).

'Home' reflects Humphreys's interest in his previous novel, *The Shop*, in the way in which local communities can be re-energized through reclaiming the radical spirit of the past. In developing this theme, both works feature the reopening of a village shop and suggest that the community is an analogue for the wider Welsh nation. Both stories ask a fundamental question, which has been posed by the postcolonial critic James Donald: what is it that the notion of a nation provides? Drawing on the Palestinian critic Edward Said's writings on 'place' and Benedict Anderson's view of a nation as an 'imagined community', Donald argues:

A nation does not express itself through its culture: it is culture that produces 'the nation'. What is produced is not an identity or a single consciousness – nor necessarily a representation at all – but hierarchically organized values, dispositions, and differences. This cultural and social heterogeneity is given a certain fixity by the articulating principle of 'the nation'.[3]

In 'Home', the community provides the kind of 'fixity' which Donald argues a nation represents. It is exemplified by 'Ffair y Borth' – the local hiring fair – which, up to a point, exemplifies the cyclical nature of history and community. For the young, a Welsh-language band is the big attraction as music, albeit of a different kind, must have been to previous generations. However, although the Welsh-language band has a traditional role at the fair, it has a further layer of relevance to modern Wales. It suggests that things can happen in Wales which have correspondence with English-speaking cultures, challenging Gabriel's conclusion, which disappoints his grandmother, that 'Wales wasn't a place where anything meaningful could happen' (p. 162).

Despite the acknowledgement that history is cyclical in 'Home', its narrative is based on numerous 'correspondences' between different historical periods and events which brings to mind Derrida's concept of the plural dimension of history, a recurring theme in Humphreys's novels. Cledwyn Price's insistence that the electronic Welsh-language band will be an education for Cyril, the son of Dilys's daily help, echoes what Gabriel's Indian friend, Vidya, says to him about the Ashram to which she takes him. When Cledwyn flees from a street fight, leaving Cyril to be stabbed by a gang from Bangor, Dilys finds herself assuming the role of 'healer', or 'peacemaker', which makes her think about the way in which her father sought to resolve disputes between deacons.

MYTHS OF RETURN

'Home' is 'central' to this collection of stories because it raises questions about the concepts of 'home' and of 'centre' which are posed in a number of the other stories. In this story, despite Dilys's nomadic life-style with her husband, the emphasis falls upon the 'return' and upon the 'reclamation' of home. But, as in many of the stories in this collection, the point of 'fixity' is itself the subject of change. As we have noted, Dilys's home is boarded up and derelict. In other stories, the erosion of what was once a symbol of continuity is a source of disappointment and despair. In 'The Grudge', the bard Gwilym is angered by the way in which ancient farms and fields are being built on, and in 'The Garden Cottage', Idris and Anna Adams, a married, middle-aged couple returning to where they first met, remember full, uneven hedges that have subsequently been transformed so that they now resemble neat, suburban boundaries, suggesting how suburbia is encroaching on the countryside. In 'The Woman at the Window', the widowed Mrs Picton looks out on a landscape which she feels has been destroyed by the erection of wind turbines.

In 'The Garden Cottage', Idris and Anna Adams are encouraged by the most prominent man in the district, Sir Robin Wiiliams Price, himself now elderly, to summarize how they met and how their lives together have turned out. Eventually, Sir Robin tells them about his life when one of the main contrasts between them is underlined; that they have three children, two of whom are sons, while he is the last of his male line. The cottage, in which they share memories and local knowledge, provides the story with some sense of 'fixity', to employ James Donald's term, while also focusing on how things have changed. This is a story concerned with mobility, dispersion and diversity. Anna and Idris have returned to Wales to live in Cardiff after some time away; their daughter Alice has a Continental European partner, Hans, and one of their sons, Alwyn, is studying at Oxford. Sir Robin's wife, Lady Marcia, was a Czech national and his daughters, whom he encouraged to marry well, eventually married, he tells them with some contempt, 'a property developer from Banbury and an Argentinian polo player who claimed he had a ranch near Cordoba which he couldn't touch because of political difficulties' (pp. 197–8).

The way in which Sir Robin refers to his sons-in-law suggests his contempt for those who come from another part of the world. This is typified, too, by the way in which he is less polite to Anna's husband, Idris, than he is to Anna who is Welsh: 'But you weren't a local boy were you? A young city gent enjoying his hols in the country?' (p. 190). Exploring how Continental Europeans, 'outsiders' more generally, are 'othered' is a recurring theme in *The Woman at the Window*. Many of the stories, as noted earlier, feature Europeans who have come into the country. In two of them, 'Home', where Katica, the daily help is from Bulgaria, and 'A Little History', where a local farmer marries a young Polish woman, they have an important role in the story in raising issues of prejudice. This subject is more fully developed in 'A Little History' than in 'Home'. Mrs Roberts disapproves of her son's girlfriend, Zofia, concluding, 'Surely there were better-looking girls around with authentic Cymric connections?' (p. 229).

The 'othering' of Continental Europe and Europeans is contrasted throughout the book with European-centred accounts of the impact of the Second World War. Thus, Zofia is introduced with a biographical sketch that includes how her family fled from Poland when she was four or five; how her father had been imprisoned and tortured in Moscow; how her little brother had died in in Siberia and how her father joined the Polish element in the British army. Her family's experiences exemplify Humphreys's reflections on the Second World War and also what he sees happening in post-war Europe in *The Taliesin Tradition*: 'All over the world there are tribes and nations and inconvenient categories of peoples being shunted about, transferred, incarcerated, liquidated to suit the convenience of one kind of state machine or other fuelled by a noxious mixture of lethal ideologies.'[4] Although Zofia is seen as 'other', she goes out of her way not to regard her new home in this way. She intends to learn Welsh and, when she visits her boyfriend's farm, she takes an interest in modern Welsh history and in buildings.

In *A Toy Epic*, as we have seen, a barber expresses attitudes and prejudices which he does not see contain the seeds of fascism. A number of events from different stories in *The Woman at the Window* 'correspond' with each other in their concern with the way in which dictatorial states deem certain categories of people 'inconvenient', subjecting them to violence, intimidation and expatriation. In 'A Little History', Zofia brings her family's experiences of this into a small, rural Welsh community. But there is a link between her family's story and the street battle between a gang from Bangor and the inhabitants of the small community of Henefial in 'Home'. The latter disturbingly reminds us that prejudice within and between communities, constituting the seeds of what happened on a much larger scale in Continental Europe in the decade preceding, as well as during, the Second World War, is as much a Welsh as a European problem. Indeed, what emerges here is a sense of a nation, even at the most localized level, as consisting of emergent as well as embedded rivalries.

However, it is with regard to Europe, rather than Wales, that *The Woman at the Window* develops Humphreys's reflections on how whole peoples are 'shunted about' and subjected to violence. The violence which can result from prejudice and partisanship is depicted most graphically in 'Luigi' and 'Nomen'. Watching Sylvana, upon whom he has a crush, dance with the young partisans, Luigi almost crosses a boundary which many of the partisans must have crossed:

> He refused to be sent away. I've got a grenade in my hand under my coat. You come with me or I'll blow us up. He struggled to stop his voice trembling. She was so close. You would never do it. Don't be so sure. You don't know what I've been through. You have no idea. (p. 102)

The principal protagonist in 'Nomen' tries to take the war's survivors back to a pre-war innocence where the world may once again appear 'fresh'. This is exemplified by the journey upon which he takes them through headless statues among 'blasted trees' to the 'tranquil lakes' (p. 132). The story has a mythical, symbolic dimension, evident here in the statues and the lake, which is reinforced by the name 'Nomen', which the others give him. Nomen appears to be a combination of two figures which Humphreys has identified: the sacrificial figure, such as Christ, and what he calls the 'necessary figure', 'one who has the courage and vision to lead at a certain given, and crucial, time in the life of a certain society'.[5] The name itself suggests that, like Christ, he is, up to a point, a man like his friends, but ultimately he is not a man. And there are further correspondences with Christ in that his fellow soldiers are too scared to go to his defence when he is killed while trying to persuade partisans to release women they are punishing and humiliating for collaborating with the enemy. And, like Christ, his magnetism increases after his death: 'Would we ever find again a person so intent on sharing the freshness of the world with the people living in it, every newborn child inheriting the newborn day?' (p. 137). But this ideal, bordering on romantic dream, is contrasted with the graphic violence of Nomen's death at the hands of partisans. The partisans have clearly crossed the boundary which Luigi almost crosses: 'They shouted that these women had consorted with the Tyrant's storm troops. They were treacherous whores and due for retribution' (p. 136). Ironically, after the war, they display behaviour which is not so dissimilar from that which gave rise to the fascism with which they have just gone to war.

The Woman at the Window provides an interesting lens through which to reassess Humphreys's previous fiction. It typifies his interest in narrative perspective, but, also, the major concerns and preoccupations of his work, including modern European as well as Welsh history, upon which his contribution to Welsh literature and culture is based. Many of his subjects and themes, such as war, gender, identity and nationhood, are to be found in modern literature generally.

But Humphreys's work provides particular perspectives from his own complexity as a Welsh writer whose fiction, written mainly in English, interweaves Welsh and European tropes. Thus, Humphreys's work makes an important contribution to wider contemporary cultural and literary debates. This contribution is summarized in the next chapter which is called an 'Afterword', not a 'Conclusion', in the hope that this book will stimulate further discussion of Humphreys's fiction.

14

Afterword

Although the majority of Emyr Humphreys's fiction is written in English, it is characterized by an increasing confidence in the Welsh national future that chimes with developing nationalist and Welsh-language aspirations over the last half of the twentieth century and the beginning of the twenty-first century. Spanning more than fifty years, his fiction, which examines key periods, movements, ideas and dilemmas in Welsh history, is itself written from a variety of historical contexts.

It is not surprising that the grand sweep of history represented in Humphreys's fiction, especially given its acknowledgement of European and global contexts, has led some critics to see his writing as 'historical' and 'realist'. However, neither term is entirely accurate. From a historical perspective, Humphreys is interested in the presence of a history of Wales that has hardly ever been fully present. This may seem like one of those philosophical conundrums that belie common-sense knowledge. How can a history never have been present? Yet, read through the lens of one of the late twentieth-century's leading European philosophers, Jacques Derrida, and his concept of 'haunt-ology', it provides an appropriate framework within which to read Humphreys's work. It highlights the importance to his writing, evident in *The Taliesin Tradition*, of the Welsh-language literature and culture in which Humphreys was immersed. One could argue that the irony is that much of Humphreys's work is written in English, the language of Welsh accommodation to what he regarded as the culture of the colonizer, but this irony is belied by the fact that all Humphreys's work is haunted, in a Derridean sense, by a Welsh-language past which has never been fully realized.

The stress which Humphreys's fiction places on a Welsh-language past that has never been present is not common within Welsh literature in English and it therefore makes an original contribution to it. The English-language literary criticism of late twentieth-century Wales is marked by greater recognition, than in the 1960s and 1970s, of the permeable boundary between the nation's two principal languages and Humphreys's fiction underscores the point that much English-language writing in Wales is about Welsh-language Wales. One of the reasons for the emphasis in Humphreys's work upon the absent presence of a Welsh-language nation is that, unlike many of the English-language prose writers of Wales, Humphreys is a product of north Wales where he has lived most of his life. His writing is rooted in north Wales as an epicentre of Welsh-language culture in the nineteenth and twentieth centuries as well as a territory in which the Welsh and English cultures met along a fault line between the two languages, even within families.

Humphreys's fiction presents us with an alternative version of the history of modern Wales to those that have been written by historians and novelists from south Wales, especially as far as the influence of Nonconformity is concerned. There is a recurring interest in his fiction not only with history but with 'historiography', history as a narrative based upon its own preconceptions, prejudices, emphases and silences, and with time. Although the two principal movements of time through a narrative feature in nearly all Humphreys's fiction, his most ambitious works explore a plural-dimensional sense of time, as of history, which means that his novels and short stories constitute themes, images and tropes that are constantly recalled, juxtaposed and revised. His novels, in particular, repay successive reading and, as one might expect of a writer educated at a time when critical practice was based on close reading and recognition of ambiguity and ambivalence, close analysis.

Humphreys's interest in the way in which an unrealized Welsh-language past is an absent presence in north Wales, particularly, suggests philosophical and political dimensions to his work which belie not only descriptions of it as 'historical' but also 'realist'. Emyr Humphreys's initial description of himself as a 'Protestant' author underscored certain features of his writing, especially the emphasis on individual, moral and social progress and on dilemma. But it has not done as much justice to his work as other terms such as 'dissident' and 'dramatic', which Humphreys has himself used, that better befit the intellectual depth of his writing.

One of the keys to Emyr Humphreys's fiction is modernism. The term 'modernist' most obviously brings to mind novels such as *A Man's Estate*, *A Toy Epic*, *Outside the House of Baal*, *Bonds of Attachment* and *Unconditional Surrender*, which experiment with narrative, time and perspective. But describing Humphreys as a modernist underscores other characteristics that his work shares with modernists such as Virginia Woolf, William Faulkner and Kate Roberts, particularly the way in which subjectivity is determined by cultural discourse. Humphreys, like Woolf, recognizes the determining and constrictive nature of cultural discourse. But it is not contested in his work in the same way as it is in Woolf's fiction, based on an analysis of how discourses are codified in everyday life and environments. In Humphreys's work, the determining nature of cultural discourses stands in contradistinction to its emphasis upon individual social and moral progress enacted through a series of linked dilemmas.

As far as the representation of individuality is concerned, it is not surprising that Humphreys's work anticipates late twentieth-century ideas about performative gender identity. His initial representation of independent women in his novels of the 1950s and 1960s was influenced by Elizabethan drama, especially the configuration of the illegitimate character on the Renaissance stage. In Humphreys's representation of contested gender identities, including masculinities, peformativity is rooted in tensions between resistance and conformity. This provides a vehicle through which Humphreys explores the effectiveness of performativity as a self-liberating modus operandi when it is based primarily upon resistance. The dialectic between resistance and proactive radicalism is explored principally in the representation of independent women through the dilemmas in which they find themselves which are, in turn, aligned with first- and second-wave feminism. The representation of this recurring figure develops in subtlety and complexity throughout Humphreys's work, from Ada Cwm in *A Man's Estate* to Lydia in *Outside the House of Baal*, Amy Parry in the Land of the Living sequence and Bethan Nichols in *The Shop*.

Humphreys's own life has involved significant dissidence and protest, for example, learning Welsh and becoming a Welsh nationalist when the movement was embroiled in controversy and declaring himself a conscientious objector in the Second World War. Thus, it is not surprising that protest and dissidence are recurring tropes in his work, particularly the exploration of how protest is linked to the way in which identity is constituted, not simply expressed, through behaviour. This culminates in the focus of his later work on the proactive articulation of dissidence.

Humphreys's fiction explores the close alignment of English-language and Welsh-language Wales but also the extent to which each is a stranger to the other. How far one can really know an/Other is a recurring trope in his work. As if to retain the enigmatic quality of characters as they emerge from the writer's subconscious, many of Humphreys's protagonists have a shadowy side, making them impossible to know fully. This is explored in the later work, sometimes quite cryptically, in father–daughter relationships. These novels and short stories are the most subtle and also the most disturbing of his psycho-analytical work. The daughter is part of a socio-symbolic structure that includes the discourses, as well as the preconceptions in even everyday language usage, which determine and define her gender identity. But she is also, often unknowingly, part of a psycho-symbolic field in which she is the object of her father's phantasies and anxieties which are projected onto her, sometimes without him being fully aware of what he is doing.

Another principal psychoanalytic theme which recurs throughout his work, and emerges more strongly in the later writings, is Humphreys's preoccupation with 'ghosts', 'spectres' and 'hauntings', not least the way in which even those with whom we live and are most intimate may, in mourning, be revealed as strangers to us. This is an aspect of Humphreys's work which is illuminated by the work of contemporary theorists such as Jacqueline Rose and Jacques Derrida.

As one would expect of a writer who, in the 1950s, thought of himself as a Protestant writer, there is an overt interest in Christianity in Humphreys's work which may appear to be at odds with its interest in psychoanalysis. But the modernist perspective on theology and psychology, to which Richard Sheppard has drawn attention, is that the two are linked. The self-confident progress of the modern individual, aligned with modernity itself, is disrupted by theories from psychology and theology in which the individual is the subject of forces over which he or she has less conscious control than they think they have.

Humphreys's fiction is informed by a probing as well as creative sensibility, interested in what lies beyond the immediate in terms of the individual and of history.

Although Humphreys's work has been written over half a century, its themes may be aligned with late twentieth-century and early twenty-first century critical and cultural agendas. Despite his prolific output as a novelist, his work embraces a variety of genres. But it is his fiction in English which constitutes the majority of his output. This study has suggested some of the critical frameworks and contexts in which his work may be read in the twenty-first century. It is not an exhaustive or definitive reading of Humphreys's work, as such a task would be impossible even if it were desirable, but it is intended to stimulate further critical readings and assessments of a writer who has made a significant contribution to Welsh literature and culture.

Notes

Notes to Chapter 1

1. Stephen Knight, *A Hundred Years of Fiction* (Cardiff: University of Wales Press, 2004), p. 131.
2. Ibid.
3. Murray Watts, 'The dissident condition: Emyr Humphreys interviewed', *Planet*, 71 (October/November 1988), 23–9.
4. Emyr Humphreys, *The Shop* (Bridgend: Seren, 2005).
5. Emyr Humphreys, 'The road to Rhyl', *Planet*, 52 (August/September 1985), 81.
6. Emyr Humphreys, *A Change of Heart: A Comedy* (London: Eyre & Spottiswoode, 1951).
7. M.Wynn Thomas (ed.), *Emyr Humphreys: Conversations and Reflections* (Cardiff: University of Wales Press, 2002), p. 8.
8. Humphreys is referring here to the arson attack on RAF Penyberth on the Llŷn peninsula by Saunders Lewis, poet and playwright, Lewis Valentine, poet and Baptist minister, and D. J. Williams, school teacher and writer.
9. Thomas (ed.), *Emyr Humphreys: Conversations and Reflections*, pp. 4–5.
10. M. Wynn Thomas, 'Emyr Humphreys: regional novelist?', in K. D. M. Snell (ed.), *The Regional Novel in Britain and Ireland 1800–1990* (Cambridge: Cambridge University Press, 1998), p. 206.
11. Emyr Humphreys, *Outside the House of Baal* (London: Eyre & Spottiswoode, 1965), p. 344.
12. Emyr Humphreys, *Open Secrets* (London: Dent, 1988).
13. Humphreys, 'The dissident condition', 25.
14. Emyr Humphreys, *Unconditional Surrender* (Bridgend: Seren, 1996).
15. Emyr Humphreys, *A Toy Epic* (London: Eyre & Spottiswoode, 1958).
16. Emyr Humphreys, *The Voice of a Stranger* (London: Eyre & Spottiswoode, 1949).

[17] Robert Pope, *Building Jerusalem: Nonconformity, Labour and the Social Question in Wales, 1906–1939* (Cardiff: University of Wales Press, 1998), p. 165.

[18] Watts, 'The dissident condition', 25.

[19] These exercise books are part of the Emyr Humphreys archive: Papurau Emyr Humphreys (Emyr Humphreys's Papers), National Library of Wales, Aberystwyth.

[20] Gerwyn Wiliams, 'Options and allegiances', *Planet*, 71 (October/November 1988), 31.

[21] Emyr Humphreys, *Hear and Forgive* (London: Gollancz, 1952).

[22] Emyr Humphreys, *The Little Kingdom* (London: Eyre & Spottiswoode, 1946).

[23] Dylan Thomas, *Under Milk Wood* (London: Dent, 1954).

[24] George Orwell, *Animal Farm* (London: Secker and Warburg, 1945); *Nineteen Eighty Four* (London: Secker and Warburg, 1949).

[25] William Empson, *Seven Types of Ambiguity* (London: Chatto and Windus, 1930).

[26] F. R. Leavis, *Revaluation, Tradition and Development in English Poetry* (London: Chatto and Windus, 1936); *The Great Tradition* (London: Chatto and Windus, 1948); *The Common Pursuit* (London: Chatto and Windus, 1952).

[27] Emyr Humphreys, *A Man's Estate* (London: Eyre & Spottiswoode, 1955); *Etifedd y Glyn* (Llandysul: Gwasg Gomer, 1981); *The Italian Wife* (London: Eyre & Spottiswoode, 1957).

[28] *The Triple Net: A Portrait of the Writer Kate Roberts* (London: Channel 4 Television, 1988).

[29] Jago Morrison, *Contemporary Fiction* (London: Routledge, 2003), p. 4.

[30] Ibid., p. 3.

[31] Ibid., p. 9.

[32] Ibid., p. 13.

[33] Emyr Humphreys, *Y Tri Llais: Nofel* (Llandybïe: Llyfrau'r Dryw, 1958).

[34] Emyr Humphreys with W. S. Jones, *Dinas: Drama Gyfoes* (Llandybie: Llyfrau'r Dryw, 1970),

[35] Emyr Humphreys, *Bwrdd Datblygu Teledu Cymraeg* (Aberystwyth: Cymdeithas Yr Iaith Gymraeg, 1979).

[36] Emyr Humphreys, *Darn O Dir* (translation of *The Little Kingdom*) (Pen-y-Groes, Caernarfon: Gwasg Dwyfor, 1986).

[37] R. Arwel Jones (ed.), *Dal Pen Rheswm: Cyfweliadau Gydag Emyr Humphreys* (Caerdydd: University of Wales Press, 1999).

[38] Emyr Humphreys, *Ancestor Worship: A Cycle of Eighteen Poems* (Denbigh: Gwasg Gee, 1970).

[39] Emyr Humphreys, *Landscapes: A Sequence of Songs* (Beckenham, Kent: Chimaera Press, 1979).

[40] Emyr Humphreys, *The Kingdom of Brân* (London: Holmes 1979).

[41] Emyr Humphreys, *Pwyll a Rhiannon* (Llafur Gwlad, Rhif 87, Ionawr, 2005).

[42] Emyr Humphreys with John Ormond and John Tripp, *Penguin Modern Poets* (Harmondsworth: Penguin, 1979).

43 Emyr Humphreys, *Miscellany Two* (Bridgend: Poetry Wales Press, 1981).
44 Emyr Humphreys, *Collected Poems* (Cardiff: University of Wales Press, 1999).
45 Emyr Humphreys, *Theatr Saunders Lewis* (Cymdeithas Theatr Cymru, 1979).
46 Emyr Humphreys, *The Gift* (London: Eyre & Spottiswoode, 1963); *Natives* (London: Secker & Warburg, 1968).
47 D. H. Lawrence, *Lady Chatterley's Lover* (Harmondsworth: Penguin, 1960).
48 Germaine Greer, *The Female Eunuch* (London: MacGibbon & Kee, 1970).
49 Raymond Williams, *Border Country* (London: Chatto and Windus, 1960).
50 Raymond Williams, *Second Generation* (London: Chatto and Windus, 1964).
51 Katie Gramich, 'Both in and out of the game: Welsh writers and the British dimension', in M. Wynn Thomas (ed.), *Welsh Writing in English* (Cardiff: University of Wales Press, 2003), p. 272.
52 Ibid.
53 Emyr Humphreys, *National Winner* (London: Macdonald & Co., 1971).
54 Emyr Humphreys, *Flesh and Blood* (London: Hodder & Stoughton, 1978).
55 Emyr Humphreys, *The Best of Friends* (London: Hodder & Stoughton, 1978).
56 Emyr Humphreys, *Salt of the Earth* (London: Dent 1985).
57 Emyr Humphreys, *An Absolute Hero* (London: Dent, 1986).
58 Emyr Humphreys, *Bonds of Attachment* (London: Macdonald, 1991).
59 Emyr Humphreys, *The Anchor Tree* (London: Hodder & Stoughton, 1980).
60 Emyr Humphreys, *Jones: a Novel* (London: Dent, 1984).
61 Emyr Humphreys, *The Gift of a Daughter* (Bridgend: Seren, 1998).
62 Emyr Humphreys, *Ghosts and Strangers* (Bridgend: Seren, 2001); *Old People are a Problem* (Bridgend: Seren, 2003).
63 Emyr Humphreys, *The Rigours of Inspection: Poems and Stories* (Llanrwst: Carreg Gwalch Cyf., 2005).
64 M. Wynn Thomas, '*Outside the House of Baal*: the evolution of a major novel', in Sam Adams (ed.), *Seeing Wales Whole* (Cardiff: University of Wales Press, 1998), p. 121.
65 Stephen Knight, '"A new enormous music": industrial fiction in Wales', in Thomas (ed.), *Welsh Writing in English*, p. 86.
66 Ibid., p. 78.
67 Kate Roberts, *Traed Mewn Cyffion* (Aberystwyth: Gwasg Aberystwyth, 1936).

Notes to Chapter 2

1 M. Wynn Thomas (ed.), *Emyr Humphreys: Conversations and Reflections* (Cardiff: University of Wales Press, 2002), p. 60.
2 Emyr Humphreys, 'A Protestant view of the modern novel', in Thomas (ed.), *Emyr Humphreys: Conversations and Reflections*, p.75.
3 Ibid., pp. 59–60.
4 Ibid., p. 71.
5 Ibid., p.59.

6 Ibid., p. 60.
7 Papurau Emyr Humphreys, National Library of Wales, CH 5/3. Some of the notes are written on University College of North Wales Bangor letter-headed paper, on the back of a Bangor summer school programme, and on the back of a letter dated 15 February 1966.
8 'Comment in the novel', handwritten MSS dated 9April 1951, Papurau Emyr Humphreys, CH2/13, notes.
9 Papurau Emyr Humphreys, CH/5/3.
10 Ibid.
11 Meic Stephens (ed.), *The New Companion to Literature of Wales* (Cardiff: University of Wales Press, 1998).
12 Jago Morrison, *Contemporary Fiction* (London: Routledge, 2003), p. 35.
13 Ibid.
14 'Comment in the novel', Papurau Emyr Humphreys, CH2/13, 2–3.
15 Ibid., 1.
16 Ibid., 3.
17 Thomas (ed.), *Emyr Humphreys: Conversations and Reflections*, p. 59.
18 Ioan Williams, *Emyr Humphreys* (Cardiff: University of Wales Press, 1980), p. 27.
19 *New Companion to the Literature of Wales*.
20 'Comment in the novel', notes.
21 Williams, *Emyr Humphreys*, p. 48.
22 Ibid., p. 19.
23 'Samuel Beckett: a silent lecture', Papurau Emyr Humphreys, CH2/9, 3.
24 Ibid., 2.
25 Robin Majundar and Allen McLaurin (eds), *Virginia Woolf: The Critical Heritage* (London and Boston: Routledge and Kegan Paul, 1975), pp. 321–2.
26 'Samuel Beckett: a silent lecture', 3.
27 Thomas (ed.), *Emyr Humphreys: Conversations and Reflections*, p. 66.
28 Ibid.
29 Emyr Humphreys, 'Under the yoke', Papurau Emyr Humphreys, DIII/40/II, 1.
30 Ibid., 5–6.
31 Richard Sheppard, 'The problematics of European modernism', in Steve Giles (ed.), *Theorizing Modernism: Essays in Critical Theory* (London and New York: Routledge, 1993), p. 9.
32 Ibid., p. 8.
33 Gerwyn Wiliams, 'Options and allegiances', *Planet*, 71 (October/November 1988), 31.
34 Ibid.
35 Humphreys, 'Under the yoke', 1.
36 Emyr Humphreys, 'The Hidden Spring', Papurau Emyr Humphreys, DIII/40/11, 2.
37 Ibid., 2–3.
38 Ibid., 2.
39 Ibid., 1.
40 Ibid.

41   Humphreys, 'Under the yoke', 5.
42   R. Arwel Jones (ed.), *Dal Pen Rheswm: Cyfweliadau Gydag Emyr Humphreys* (Caerdydd: University of Wales Press, 1999), pp. 85–6. I am grateful to M. Wynn Thomas for supplying me with this translation. This was originally quoted in Linden Peach, 'The Woolf at Faulkner's door: modernism and the body in Emyr Humphreys's 1950s fiction', in Tony Brown (ed.), *Welsh Writing in English: A Yearbook of Critical Essays*, 6 (Cardiff: University of Wales Press, 2000), p. 146.
43   Papurau Emyr Humphreys, CH/5/2.
44   David Barnes, 'A question of history', *Planet*, 139 (February/March 2000), 33.
45   Humphreys, 'The road to Rhyl', *Planet*, 52 (August/September 1985), 82.
46   A full textual history of *A Toy Epic* is given in the introduction to Emyr Humphreys, *A Toy Epic*, ed. M.Wynn Thomas (Bridgend: Seren Books, 1989), pp. 8–13.
47   Ibid., p. 12.
48   Louis Althusser, *For Marx* (1965), cited by Sheppard, 'The problematics of European modernism', p. 11.
49   Ibid., p. 13.
50   Papurau Emyr Humphreys, CH5/3.
51   Ibid.
52   Ibid.
53   Ibid.
54   Ibid.
55   Ibid.

Notes to Chapter 3

1   Gerwyn Wiliams, 'Options and allegiances', *Planet*, 71 (October/November 1988), 35–6.
2   Emyr Humphreys, *The Anchor Tree* (London: Hodder & Stoughton, 1980), p. 7.
3   Emyr Humphreys, 'The Hidden Spring', Papurau Emyr Humphreys, DIII/40/11, 2.
4   M. Wynn Thomas, 'Emyr Humphreys: mythic realist', in J. J. Simon and Alain Sinner (eds), *English Studies 111* (Luxembourg: Centre Universitaire de Luxembourg, 1991), p. 266.
5   M. Wynn Thomas, 'Emyr Humphreys: regional novelist?', in K. D. M. Snell (ed.), *The Regional Novel in Britain and Ireland 1800–1990* (Cambridge: Cambridge University Press, 1998), p. 206.
6   David Jones, *The Anathémata* (London: Faber and Faber, 1952).
7   John Powell Ward, 'Borderers and borderline cases', in M. Wynn Thomas (ed.), *Welsh Writing in English* (Cardiff: University of Wales Press, 2000), p. 113.

8   Wiliams, 'Options and allegiances', 32–3.
9   Hayden White, *Tropics of Discourse: Essays on Cultural Criticism* (Baltimore, MD: The John Hopkins University Press, 1978).
10   Friedrich Nietzsche, *On the Genealogy of Morals*, trans. Walter Kaufmann (New York: Vintage, 1969).
11   Michel Foucault, *Power/Knowledge: Selected Interviews and Other Writings 1927–1977*, ed. Colin Gordon (London: Harvester, 1980).
12   Kirsti Bohata, *Postcolonialism Revisited* (Cardiff: University of Wales Press, 2004), p. 108.
13   Papurau Emyr Humphreys, CH/5/7.
14   Bohata, *Postcolonialism Revisited*, p. 108.
15   The most recent study of Emyr Humphreys from this perspective is Diane Green, *Emyr Humphreys: A Postcolonial Novelist* (Cardiff: University of Wales Press, 2009). Green argues that Humphreys's fiction makes use of two particular techniques which she suggests might in themselves be seen as 'postcolonial': his use of Welsh history and of Celtic myth.
16   Ibid., pp. 8–9.
17   Janet Davies, *The Welsh Language* (Cardiff: University of Wales Press, 1993), p. 117.
18   Emyr Humphreys, *Bonds of Attachment* (London: Macdonald, 1991), p. 207.
19   Ned Thomas, 'Parallels and paradigms', in Thomas (ed.), *Welsh Writing in English*, pp. 321–2.
20   Ibid., p. 322.
21   Humphreys, *The Taliesin Tradition: A Quest for the Welsh Identity* (Bridgend: Seren, 1983), p. 2.
22   Humphreys, 'The Hidden Spring', 1.
23   Ibid., 234.
24   Jacques Derrida, *Of Grammatology*, trans. Gayatri Chakravorty Spivak (Baltimore and London: John Hopkins University Press, 1976), p. 85.
25   Emyr Humphreys, 'This World of Wales – The Hidden Spring (?)', 1.
26   Derrida, *Of Grammatology*, p. 86.
27   M. Wynn Thomas, 'Afterword', Emyr Humphreys, *A Toy Epic*, p. 143.
28   Diane Green, 'Narrative patterning in the novels of Emyr Humphreys', (Ph.D. thesis, University of Wales Swansea, 2000), 107–8.
29   Jacques Derrida, *Specters of Marx: the State of the Debt, the Work of Mourning and the New International*, trans. Peggy Kamuf (London and New York: Routledge, 1994), p. 99.
30   Ibid.
31   Ibid.
32   Antonio Gramsci, *Selections from the Prison Notebooks*, trans. Quintin Hoare and Geoffrey Nowell-Smith (London: Lawrence and Wishart, 1971), p. 55.
33   Tony Brown and M. Wynn Thomas, 'The problems of belonging', in Thomas (ed.), *Welsh Writing in English*, p. 192.
34   Ibid.
35   Ned Thomas, 'Parallels and paradigms', p. 318.

36 Ibid.
37 Brown and Thomas, 'The problems of belonging', p. 193.
38 Bill Ashcroft, 'Is that the Congo? Language as metonymy in the postcolonial text', *World Literature in English*, 29, 2 (1989), 3–10.
39 Bohata, *Postcolonialism Revisited*, p. 108.
40 Brown and Thomas, 'The problems of belonging', pp. 194–5.
41 Erica Carter, James Donald and Judith Squires (eds), *Space and Place: Theories of Identity and Location* (London: Lawrence and Wishart, 1993), Introduction, pp. viii–ix.
42 M. Wynn Thomas (ed.), *Emyr Humphreys: Conversations and Reflections* (Cardiff: University of Wales Press, 2002), p. 11.
43 Ibid., p. 8.
44 Emyr Humphreys, *The Little Kingdom*, p. 5. Further page references in this section to this novel will be included in the text.
45 The significance of the titles of Humphreys's novels is discussed in Diane Green, 'Narrative patterning in the novels of Emyr Humphreys', 9–21.
46 M. Wynn Thomas, '*Outside the House of Baal*: the evolution of a major novel', in Sam Adams (ed.), *Seeing Wales Whole* (Cardiff: University of Wales Press, 1998), p. 136.
47 Ibid.
48 M .M. Bakhtin, 'Forms of time and of the chronotope in the novel: notes towards a historical poetics', in *The Dialogic Imagination: Four Essays*, ed. Michael Holquist, trans. Caryl Emerson and Michael Holquist (Austin: University of Texas Press, 1981), p. 84.
49 Deborah Mutnick, 'Time and space in composition studies: "through the gates of the chronotope"', *Rhetoric Review*, 25, 1 (2006), 42.
50 Charles E. May (ed.), *The New Short Story Theorists* (Athens, OH: Ohio University Press, 1994), p. 26, cited by Rachel Falconer, 'Bakhtin's chronotope and the contemporary short story', *The South Atlantic Quarterly*, 97, 3/4 (1998), 703.
51 Mutnick, 'Time and space in composition studies', 43.
52 Michel de Certeau, *The Practice of Everyday Life*, trans. Steven Rendall (Berkeley: University of California Press, 1984), p. 119.
53 Emyr Humphreys, 'The road to Rhyl', *Planet*, 52 (August/September 1985), 82.
54 Emyr Humphreys, *A Toy Epic*, p. 24. Further references to this novel in this section will be included in the text.
55 Bakhtin, 'Forms of time and of the chronotope in the novel', p. 230.
56 Ibid.
57 Ibid.
58 Watts, 'The dissident condition', 81.
59 Leena Kore Schröder, '"Reflections in a Motor Car": Virginia Woolf's phenomenological relations of time and space', in Anna Snaith and Michael H. Whitworth (eds), *Locating Woolf: The Politics of Space and Place* (Basingstoke: Palgrave Macmillan, 2007), p. 131.

60 Ibid., p. 132.
61 Ibid., p. 133.
62 Ibid., pp. 133–4.
63 Emyr Humphreys, *Salt of the Earth*, p. 12.
64 Ibid.
65 Emyr Humphreys, *The Shop* (Bridgend: Seren, 2005), p. 9.

Notes to Chapter 4

1   Richard Sheppard, 'The problematics of European modernism', Steve Giles
    (ed.), *Theorizing Modernism: Essays in Critical Theory* (London and New
    York: Routledge, 1993), p. 22.
2   Sue Vice (ed.), *Psychoanalytic Criticism: A Reader* (London: Polity Press,
    1996), p. 6.
3   Ibid., p. 7.
4   Ibid.
5   Papurau Emyr Humphreys, B11/18/4.
6   Ibid.
7   Vice (ed.), *Psychoanalytic Criticism*, p. 7.
8   Papurau Emyr Humphreys, B11/18/4.
9   Ibid.
10 Vice (ed.), *Psychoanalytic Criticism*, p. 7.
11 Papurau Emyr Humphreys, B2/18/11.
12 Emyr Humphreys, *Outside the House of Baal* (London: Eyre & Spottiswoode,
    1965), p. 279.
13 Papurau Emyr Humphreys, B11/18/Inserts.
14 Vice (ed.), *Psychoanalytic Criticism*, p. 116.
15 Humphreys, *Outside the House of Baal* (London: Eyre & Spottiswoode,
    1965), p. 278. Further references to this novel in this section will be included
    in the text.
16 Barbara Johnson, 'The frame of reference: Poe, Lacan, Derrida', in Vice
    (ed.), *Psychoanalytic Criticism*, pp. 92 and 93.
17 Ibid., p. 95.
18 Papurau Emyr Humphreys, B2/18/11, 270.
19 Joan Rivière (ed.), *Developments in Psycho-Analysis* (London: Hogarth,
    1952), p. 29.
20 Papurau Emyr Humphreys, B2/18/11, 271.
21 Anthony Giddens, *The Transformation of Intimacy: Sexuality, Love and
    Eroticism in Modern Societies* (Stanford, CA: Stanford University Press,
    1992), pp. 113 and 114.
22 Papurau Emyr Humphreys, B1/3/8, 448.
23 Ibid.
24 Humphreys, *The Best of Friends* (London: Hodder & Stoughton, 1978), p. 332.
    Further references to this novel in this section will be included in the text.

[25] Emyr Humphreys, *Open Secrets*, p. 52.
[26] Jacqueline Rose, *Why War? – Psychoanalysis, Politics, and the Return to Melanie Klein* (Oxford: Blackwell, 1993), p. 19.

Notes to Chapter 5

[1] Judith Butler, *Gender Trouble* (Lonodn and New York: Routledge, 1990), pp. 24–5.
[2] Emyr Humphreys, *A Man's Estate* (London: Eyre & Spottiswoode, 1955), p. 170. Further references to this novel in this section will be included in the text.
[3] Catherine Belsey, *Desire: Love Stories in Western Culture* (Oxford: Blackwell, 1994), p. 91.
[4] Ibid., p. 90.
[5] Ibid., p. 33.
[6] Ibid., p. 34.
[7] Sarah Gamble (ed.), *The Routledge Companion to Feminism and Postfeminism* (London and New York: Routledge, 2001), p. 310.
[8] Emyr Humphreys, *The Taliesin Tradition* (Bridgend: Seren, 1983), p. 4.
[9] Stephen Knight, *A Hundred Years of Fiction* (Cardiff: University of Wales Press, 2004), p. 147.
[10] Emyr Humphreys, *The Best of Friends*, p. 258.
[11] Ibid., p. 316.
[12] Stephen Knight, *A Hundred Years of Fiction*, p. 148.
[13] Ibid., p. 151.
[14] Ibid.
[15] Ibid., p. 150.
[16] Elizabeth Meehan, 'British feminism from the 1960s to the 1980s', in Harold L. Smith (ed.), *British Feminism in the Twentieth Century* (Amherst: University of Massachusetts Press, 1990), p. 189.
[17] Gamble (ed.), *The Routledge Companion to Feminism and Postfeminism*, p. 230.
[18] Martin Pugh, 'Domesticity and the decline of feminism', in Smith (ed.), *British Feminism in the Twentieth Century*, pp. 146 and 147.
[19] Emyr Humphreys, *The Best of Friends*, p. 213. Further references to this novel in this section will be included in the text.
[20] Judith Butler, *Excitable Speech: A Politics of the Performative* (London and New York: Routledge, 1997), p. 91.
[21] Kirsti Bohata, *Postcolonialism Revisited* (Cardiff: University of Wales Press, 2004), pp. 60–1.
[22] Ibid., p. 60.
[23] Benjamin A. Brabon and Stéphanie Genz (eds), *Postfeminist Gothic* (London: Palgrave Macmillan, 2007), pp. 1–2, Introduction.
[24] Ibid., p. 298.

[25] Stéphanie Genz and Benjamin A. Brabon, *Postfeminism: Cultural Texts and Theories* (Edinburgh: Edinburgh University Press, 2009,) p. 28.

[26] Ibid.

[27] Ibid., p. 29.

[28] Belsey, *Desire*, p. 73.

Notes to Chapter 6

[1] Linden Peach, 'The Woolf at Faulkner's door: modernism and the body in Emyr Humphreys's 1950s fiction', Tony Brown (ed.), *Welsh Writing in English: A Yearbook of Critical Essays*, 6 (Cardiff: University of Wales Press, 2000), p. 146.

[2] Papurau Emyr Humphreys, B11/13/12.

[3] M. Wynn Thomas (ed.), *Emyr Humphreys: Conversations and Reflections* (Cardiff: University of Wales Press, 2002), p. 66.

[4] Humphreys, *A Man's Estate* (London: Eyre & Spottiswoode, 1955), p. 182. Further references to this novel in this chapter will be included in the text.

[5] Kathy Dow Magnus, 'The unaccountable subject: Judith Butler and the social conditions of intersubjective agency', *Hypatia*, 21, 3, 2 (spring 2006), 83.

[6] 'The rich man in his castle,/ The poor man at his gate,/ God made them high and lowly/ And ordered their estate'. See Diane Green, 'Narrative patterning in the novels of Emyr Humphreys' (Ph.D. thesis, University of Wales Swansea, 2000), 12.

[7] Alison Findlay, *Illegitimate Power: Bastards in Renaissance Drama* (Manchester and New York: Manchester University Press, 1994), p. 214.

[8] Magnus, 'The unaccountable subject', 83.

[9] Ibid.

[10] Judith Butler, *Gender Trouble* (London and New York: Routledge, 1990), p. 147.

[11] Papurau Emyr Humphreys, B/11/13/1.

[12] Ibid., B11/13/6.

[13] Ibid.

[14] Ibid., B11/13/1.

[15] Ibid., B/11/13/12.

[16] Findlay, *Illegiimate Power*, p. 214.

[17] Antonio Gramsci, 'Notes on Italian history' , *Selections from the Prison Notebooks*, trans. Quintin Hoare and Geoffrey Nowell-Smith (London: Lawrence and Wishart, 1971), p. 55.

[18] Colin Graham, 'Subalternity and gender: problems of postcolonial Irishness', in Claire Connolly (ed.), *Theorizing Ireland* (Basingstoke: Palgrave Macmillan: 2003), pp. 151–2.

[19] Ibid., p. 156.

[20] Ioan Williams, *Emyr Humphreys* (Cardiff: University of Wales Press, 1980), p. 43.

Notes to Chapter 7

1   Emyr Humphreys, *A Toy Epic*, p.17.
2   Emyr Humphreys, *A Toy Epic*, ed. M. Wynn Thomas (Bridgend: Seren Books, 1989), p. 122, Afterword.
3   A differently inflected reading is offered in Diane Green, 'Narrative patterning in the novels of Emyr Humphreys' (Ph.D. thesis, University of Wales Swansea, 2000), 87–8, and in Linden Peach, 'The Woolf at Faulkner's door: modernism and the body in Emyr Humphreys's 1950s fiction', in Tony Brown (ed.), *Welsh Writing in English: A Yearbook of Critical Essays*, 6 (Cardiff: University of Wales Press, 2000), pp. 144–62.
4   BBC/ Wales North East/Local History: *http://www.bbc.co.uk/wales/northeast/ sites/denbighshire/pages/rhy2.shtml*.
5   Jaqueline Rose, *Why War? – Psychoanalysis, Politics, and the Return to Melanie Klein* (Oxford: Blackwell, 1993), p. 17.
6   M. M. Bakhtin, *The Dialogic Imagination: Four Essays*, ed. Michael Holquist, trans. Caryl Emerson and Michael Holquist (Austin: 1981), p. 230.
7   Rose, *Why War?*, p. 16.
8   Ibid., p. 22.
9   Ibid.
10 Ibid., p. 24.

Notes to Chapter 8

1   Emyr Humphreys, 'Under the yoke', Papurau Emyr Humphreys, DIII/40/II, 2.
2   Ibid., 6.
3   Jacques Derrida, *Of Grammatology*, trans. Gayatri Chakravorty Spivak (Baltimore and London: John Hopkins University Press, 1976), p. 85.
4   Wynn Thomas points out that 'the final title of the novel emerged quite late in the day'. Much of it was written under 'the working title of "Of the event", and among other ideas entertained were "Where is now?" and "A Welsh dream"'. M. Wynn Thomas, '*Outside the House of Baal*: the evolution of a major novel', in Sam Adams (ed.), *Seeing Wales Whole* (Cardiff: University of Wales Press, 1998), p. 129.
5   Ibid., p. 125.
6   Ibid., pp. 125–6.
7   Henri Bergson, *Time and Free Will: Essay on on the Immediate Data of Consciousness*, trans. F. L. Pogson (London: George Allen and Unwin, 1910 [1887]).
8   Thomas, '*Outside the House of Baal*: the evolution of a major novel', p. 130.
9   Emyr Humphreys, *Outside the House of Baal*, p. 5. Further references to this novel in this chapter will be included in the text.
10 Thomas, '*Outside the House of Baal*: the evolution of a major novel', p. 137.

11 Ioan Williams, *Emyr Humphreys* (Cardiff: University of Wales Press, 1980), p. 57.
12 Jacqueline Rose, *Why War? – Psychoanalysis, Politics, and the Return to Melanie Klein* (Oxford: Blackwell, 1993), p. 19.
13 Jacques Derrida, *Specters of Marx: the State of the Debt, the Work of Mourning and the New International*, trans. Peggy Kamuf (London and New York: Routledge, 1994), p. 99.
14 Robert Pope, *Building Jerusalem: Nonconformity, Labour and the Social Question in Wales, 1906–1939* (Cardiff: University of Wales Press, 1998), p. 84.
15 Ibid., p. 94.
16 Ibid.
17 Ibid., p. 107.
18 Ibid., pp. 77–8.
19 M. Wynn Thomas, 'Emyr Humphreys: regional novelist?', in K. D. M. Snell (ed.), *The Regional Novel in Britain and Ireland 1800–1990* (Cambridge: Cambridge University Press, 1998), p. 209.
20 Pope, *Building Jerusalem*, p. 78.

Notes to Chapter 9

1   Emyr Humphreys, '*Land of the Living*', *http://www.uwp.co.uk/book_desc/Land.html*.
2   Papurau Emyr Humphreys, B1/3/9.
3   Humphreys, '*Land of the Living*'.
4   Bertolt Brecht, *Brecht on Theatre: The Development of an Aesthetic*, ed. and trans. John Willett (London: Methuen, 1964), p. 23.
5   Ioan Williams, *Emyr Humphreys* (Cardiff: University of Wales Press, 1980), pp. 69–70.
6   *Brecht on Theatre*, p. 23.
7   Emyr Humphreys, *Salt of the Earth*, p. 28.
8   Ibid.
9   Ibid.
10 Williams, *Emyr Humphreys*, pp. 69–70.
11 *Brecht on Theatre*, p. 39.
12 Ibid., p. 23.
13 Ibid.
14 Humphreys, '*Land of the Living*'.
15 Stephen Knight, *A Hundred Years of Fiction* (Cardiff: University of Wales Press, 2004), pp. 146, 145.
16 Ibid., p. 144.
17 Ibid., pp. 144–5.
18 Humphreys, '*Land of the Living*'.
19 Emyr Humphreys, *The Best of Friends*, p. 90.
20 Williams, *Emyr Humphreys*, p. 78.
21 Ibid., p. 79.

22 Ibid., p. 83.
23 *Brecht on Theatre*, p. 23.
24 Homi K. Bhabha, *The Location of Culture* (London and New York: Routledge, 1994), p. 10.
25 Humphreys, *The Best of Friends*, p. 26.
26 Ibid., p. 25.
27 Emyr Humphreys, *Salt of the Earth*, p. 28.
28 Humphreys, *The Best of Friends*, p. 35.
29 Ibid., p. 112.
30 Ibid., p. 113.
31 Ibid., p. 27.
32 Ibid., p. 25.
33 Rose, *Why War? – Psychoanalysis, Politics, and the Return to Melanie Klein* (Oxford: Blackwell, 1993), p. 64.
34 Ibid.
35 Humphreys, *Salt of the Earth*, p. 68.
36 Ibid., p. 183.
37 Ibid., p. 182.
38 Ibid., p. 102.
39 Ibid.
40 Humphreys, *The Best of Friends*, p. 1.
41 Ibid., p. 137.
42 Ibid., p. 37.
43 Ibid., p. 113.
44 Humphreys, *Salt of the Earth*, p. 100.
45 Emyr Humphreys, *Open Secrets*, p. 67.
46 Ibid., p. 63.
47 Ibid., p. 23.
48 Rose, *Why War?*, p. 66.
49 Knight, *A Hundred Years of Fiction*, p. 149.
50 Ibid., p. 148.
51 Humphreys, *Open Secrets*, p. 63.
52 Ibid., p. 3.
53 Knight, *A Hundred Years of Fiction*, p. 147.
54 Humphreys, *Open Secrets*, p. 6.
55 Ibid.
56 Humphreys, *Salt of the Earth*, p. 1.
57 Ibid., p. 6.
58 Ibid.
59 Ibid., p. 9.
60 Humphreys, *The Best of Friends*, p. 17.
61 Humphreys, *Salt of the Earth*, p. 7.
62 Ibid.
63 Gerry Smyth, *The Novel and the Nation: Studies in the New Irish Fiction* (London: Pluto Press, 1997), p. 52.
64 Humphreys, *The Best of Friends*, p. 103.

65   Ibid., p. 136.
66   Ibid.
67   Bhabha, *The Location of Culture*, p. 164.
68   Ibid.
69   Humphreys, *Open Secrets*, p. 81.
70   Humphreys, *Salt of the Earth*, p. 79.
71   Humphreys, *The Best of Friends*, p. 158.
72   Ibid.
73   Humphreys, *Salt of the Earth*, p. 98.
74   Ibid., p. 214.
75   Humphreys, *Open Secrets*, p. 49.
76   Knight, *A Hundred Years of Fiction*, p. 146.
77   Humphreys, *Open Secrets*, p. 41.
78   Ibid., p. 22.
79   Ibid.
80   Ibid.
81   Ibid., p. 3.
82   Ibid.
83   Ibid., p. 4.
84   Ibid., p. 106.
85   Ibid., p. 89.
86   Ibid., p. 139.
87   Ibid., p. 27.
88   Ibid., p. 25.
89   Ibid., p. 26.
90   Ibid.
91   Humphreys, *The Best of Friends*, p. 52.
92   Knight, *A Hundred Years of Fiction*, p. 145.
93   Diane Green, 'Narrative patterning in the novels of Emyr Humphreys' (Ph.D. thesis, University of Wales Swansea, 2000), 134–5.

Notes to Chapter 10

1   Diane Green, 'Narrative patterning in the novels of Emyr Humphreys', (Ph.D. Thesis, University of Wales Swansea, 2000), 20–1.
2   Emyr Humphreys, *Unconditional Surrender*, p. 117. Further references to this novel in this section will be included in the text.
3   Jacqueline Rose, *Why War? – Psychoanalysis, Politics, and the Return to Melanie Klein* (Oxford: Blackwell, 1993), p. 20.
4   Emyr Humphreys, *The Gift of a Daughter*, p. 112. Further references to this novel in this section will be included in the text.
5   Humphreys, *Unconditional Surrender*, p. 109. Further references to this novel in this section will be included in the text.
6   Rose, *Why War?*, p. 17.
7   Humphreys, *The Gift of a Daughter*, p. 86.

Notes to Chapter 11

1   M. Wynn Thomas (ed.), *Emyr Humphreys: Conversations and Reflections* (Cardiff: University of Wales Press, 2002), p. 181.
2   Ann Charters, 'A brief history of the short story', in Ann Charters (ed.), *The Story and Its Writer: An Introduction to Short Fiction* (New York: St Martin's Press, 1987), p. 1359.
3   Thomas (ed.), *Emyr Humphreys: Conversations and Reflections*, p. 189.
4   Ibid.
5   Ibid.
6   Stephen Slemon, 'The scramble for post-colonialism', in Chris Tiffin and Alan Lawson (eds), *De-scribing Empire: Post-colonialism and Textuality* (London and New York: Routledge, 1994), pp. 17 and 18.
7   Emyr Humphreys, *Natives*, p. 33. Further references to this collection in this section will be included in the text.
8   Thomas (ed.), *Emyr Humphreys: Conversations and Reflections*, p. 185.
9   Rose, *Why War? – Psychoanalysis, Politics, and the Return to Melanie Klein* (Oxford: Blackwell, 1993), p. 19.
10 Ruth Parkin-Gounelas, *Literature and Psychoanlaysis: Intertextual Readings* (Harmondsworth: Penguin, 2001), pp. 124–5.
11 Ibid., p. 118.
12 Ibid., p. 119.
13 Ibid., p. 118.
14 Emyr Humphreys, *Ghosts and Strangers*, pp. 62, 75. Further references to this collection in this section will be included in the text.
15 Emyr Humphreys, *Old People are a Problem*, p. 9. Further references to this collection in this section will be included in the text.
16 Rose, *Why War?*, p. 205.
17 Ibid.
18 Ibid., p. 202.

Notes to Chapter 12

1   Jacqueline Rose, *Why War? – Psychoanalysis, Politics, and the Return to Melanie Klein* (Oxford: Blackwell, 1993), p. 19.
2   Ruth Parkin-Gounelas, *Literature and Psychoanalysis: Intertextual Readings* (Harmondsworth: Penguin, 2001), pp. 124–5.
3   Emyr Humphreys, *The Shop*, p. 28. Further references to this novel in this chapter will be included in the text.
4   Sarah Gamble, 'Growing up single: the feminist novel', *Studies in the Literary Imagination* 39, 2 (fall 2006), 61.
5   Ibid.
6   Ibid.
7   Ibid., 62–3.

8   Ibid., 63.
9   Ibid., 71.
10 Susan Sontag, *On Photography* (Harmondsworth: Penguin, 1977), p. 155.
11 Ibid., pp. 22–3.
12 Jacques Derrida, *Of Grammatology*, trans. Gayatri Chakravorty Spivak (Baltimore and London: John Hopkins University Press, 1976), p. 85.
13 Ibid., p. 23.
14 Ibid.
15 Ibid., p. 24.
16 Ibid., p. 23.
17 Jacques Derrida, *Specters of Marx: the State of the Debt, the Work of Mourning and the New International*, trans. Peggy Kamuf (London and New York: Routledge, 1994), p. 10.
18 Sontag, *On Photography*, pp. 111–12.
19 Murray Watts, 'The dissident condition: Emyr Humphreys interviewed', Planet, 71 (October/November 1988), 29.
20 Francis Fukuyama, 'The end of history', *National Interest*, 16 (1984), 3–4.

Notes to Chapter 13

1   Emyr Humphreys, *The Woman at the Window*, p. 95. Further references to this collection in this chapter will be included in the text.
2   M. Wynn Thomas, '*Outside the House of Baal*: the evolution of a major novel', in Sam Adams (ed.), *Seeing Wales Whole* (Cardiff: University of Wales Press, 1998), pp. 125–6.
3   James Donald, 'How English is it? Popular literature and national culture', in Erica Carter, James Donald and Judith Squires (eds), *Space and Place: Theories of Identity and Location* (London: Lawrence and Wishart, 1993), p. 167.
4   Emyr Humphreys, *The Taliesin Tradition: A Quest for the Welsh Identity* (1983; Bridgend: Seren, 1989), p. 234.
5   M. Wynn Thomas, (ed),, *Emyr Humphreys: Conversations and Reflections* (Cardiff: University of Wales Press, 2002), p. 62.

Select Bibliography

Novels
The Little Kingdom (London: Eyre & Spottiswoode,1946).
The Voice of a Stranger (London: Eyre & Spottiswoode, 1949).
A Change of Heart: A Comedy (London: Eyre & Spottiswoode, 1951).
Hear and Forgive (London: Gollancz, 1952).
A Man's Estate (London: Eyre & Spottiswoode,1955).
The Italian Wife (London: Eyre & Spottiswoode, 1957).
A Toy Epic (London: Eyre & Spottiswoode, 1958).
The Gift (London: Eyre & Spottiswoode, 1963).
Outside the House of Baal (London: Eyre & Spottiswoode, 1965).
National Winner (London: Macdonald & Co., 1971).
Flesh and Blood (London: Hodder & Staughton, 1978).
The Best of Friends (London: Hodder & Staughton,1978).
The Anchor Tree (London: Hodder & Staughton, 1980).
Jones: A Novel (London: J. M. Dent & Sons, 1984).
Salt of the Earth (London: J. M. Dent & Sons, 1985).
An Absolute Hero (London: J. M. Dent & Sons,1986).
Open Secrets (London: J. M. Dent & Sons, 1988).
Bonds of Attachment (London: Macdonald & Co., 1991).
Unconditional Surrender (Bridgend: Seren, 1996).
The Gift of a Daughter (Bridgend: Seren, 1998).
Ghosts and Strangers (Bridgend: Seren, 2001).
The Shop (Bridgend: Seren, 2005).

Short stories
Natives (London: Secker & Warburg, 1968).
Old People are a Problem (Bridgend: Seren, 2003).
The Rigours of Inspection: Poems and Stories (Carreg Gwalch, 2005).
The Woman at the Window (Bridgend: Seren, 2009).

Other prose works
'The road to Rhyl', *Planet*, 52 (1985).
The Taliesin Tradition (1983;Bridgend: Seren, 1989).

Interviews with Emyr Humphreys
Thomas, M. Wynn (ed.), *Emyr Humphreys: Conversations and Reflections* (Cardiff: University of Wales Press, 2002).
Watts, M., 'The dissident condition: Emyr Humphreys interviewed', *Planet*, 71 (1988).

Criticism: Fiction of Emyr Humphreys
Gramich, K., 'Both in and out of the game: Welsh writers and the British dimension', in M. WynnThomas (ed.), *Welsh Writing in English* (Cardiff: University of Wales Press, 2003).
Green, D., *Emyr Humphreys: A Postcolonial Novelist* (Cardiff: University of Wales Press, 2009).
Knight, S., *A Hundred Years of Fiction* (Cardiff: University of Wales Press, 2004).
Peach, L., 'The Woolf at Faulkner's door: modernism and the body in Emyr Humphreys's 1950s fiction', *Welsh Writing in English: A Yearbook of Critical Essays*, 6 (2000).
Thomas, M. Wynn (ed.), *Welsh Writing in English* (Cardiff: University of Wales Press, 2003).
Thomas, M. Wynn, *Corresponding Cultures: The Two Literatures of Wales* (Cardiff: University of Wales Press, 1999).
Thomas, M. Wynn, 'Emyr Humphreys: regional novelist?', in K. D. M. Snell (ed.), *The Regional Novel in Britain and Ireland 1800–1990* (Cambridge: Cambridge University Press, 1998).
Thomas, M. Wynn, '*Outside the House of Baal*: the evolution of a major novel', in Sam Adams (ed.), *Seeing Wales Whole* (Cardiff: University of Wales Press, 1998).
Thomas, M. Wynn, *Internal Difference: Twentieth-century Writing in Wales* (Cardiff: University of Wales Press, 1992).
Thomas, M. Wynn, 'Emyr Humphreys: mythic realist', in J. J. Simon and Alain Giuev (eds), *English Studies 111* (Centre Universitate de Luxembourg, 1991).
Wiliams, G., 'Options and allegiances', *Planet*, 7 (1988).
Williams, I., *Emyr Humphreys* (Cardiff: University of Wales Press, 1980).

Other works of criticism
Bakhtin, M. M., 'Forms of time and of the chronotope in the novel: notes towards a historical poetics', in Michael Holquist (ed.), *The Dialogic Imagination: Four Essays*, trans. Caryl Emerson and Michael Holquist (Austin: University of Texas Press, 1981).

Belsey, C., *Desire: Love Stories in Western Culture* (Oxford: Blackwell, 1994).
Bhabha, H. K., *The Location of Culture* (London and New York: Routledge, 1994).
Bohata, K., *Postcolonialism Revisited* (Cardiff: University of Wales Press, 2004).
Brabon, B. A. and S. Genz (eds), *Postfeminist Gothic* (London: Palgrave Macmillan, 2007).
Butler, J., *Excitable Speech: A Politics of the Performative* (London and New York: Routledge, 1997).
Butler , J., *Gender Trouble* (London and New York: Routledge, 1990).
Carter, E., J. Donald and J. Squires (eds), *Space and Place: Theories of Identity and Location* (London: Lawrence and Wishart, 1993).
de Certeau, M., *The Practice of Everyday Life*, trans. Steven Rendall (Berkeley: University of California Press, 1984).
Derrida, J., *Specters of Marx: The State of the Debt, the Work of Mourning and the New International*, trans. Peggy Kamuf (London and New York: Routledge, 1994).
Derrida,J., *Of Grammatology*, trans. Gayatri Chakravorty Spivak (Baltimore and London: John Hopkins University Press, 1976).
Gamble, S., 'Growing up single: the feminist novel', *Studies in the Literary Imagination*, 39, 2, fall (2006), 61.
Gamble, S. (ed.), *The Routledge Companion to Feminism and Postfeminism* (London and New York: Routledge, 2001).
Genz, S. and B. A. Brabon, *Postfeminism: Cultural Texts and Theories* (Edinburgh: Edinburgh University Press, 2009).
Giddens, A., *The Transformation of Intimacy: Sexuality, Love and Eroticism in Modern Societies* (Stanford, California: Stanford University Press, 1992).
Gramich, K. and A. Hiscock (eds), *Dangerous Diversities: The Changing Faces of Wales* (Cardiff: University of Wales Press, 1998).
Gramsci, A., *Selections from the Prison Notebooks*, trans. Quintin Hoare and Geoffrey Nowell-Smith (London: Lawrence and Wishart, 1971).
Meehan, E., 'British feminism from the 1960s to the 1980s', in Harold L. Smith (ed.), *British Feminism in the Twentieth Century* (Amherst: University of Massachusetts Press, 1990).
Morrison, J., *Contemporary Fiction* (London: Routledge, 2003).
Mutnick, D., 'Time and space in composition studies: "Through the Gates of the Chronotope"', *Rhetoric Review*, 25, 1, (2006).
Parkin-Gounelas, R., *Literature and Psychoanlaysis: Intertextual Readings* (Harmondsworth: Penquin, 2001).
Pope, R., *Building Jerusalem: Nonconformity, Labour and the Social Question in Wales, 1906–1939* (Cardiff: University of Wales Press, 1998).
Rose, J., *Why War? – Psychoanalysis, Politics, and the Return to Melanie Klein* (Oxford: Blackwell, 1993).

Sontag, S., *On Photography* (Harmondsworth: Penguin, 1977).
Vice, S. (ed.), *Psychoanalytic Criticism: A Reader* (London: Polity Press, 1996).
Willet, J. (ed. and trans.), *Brecht on Theatre: The Development of an Aesthetic* (London: Methuen, 1964).

Index